Praise for "The Business Style Handbook"

"The Business Style Handbook" is a very useful reference for my international business students who have been taught British English and are unfamiliar with American English in the U.S. workplace. The book also provides helpful explanations and examples for its alphabetized entries in addition to basic American writing guidelines. It's a wonderfully concise and easy-to-use book!

> **– Wendy Vierow, Ph.D., State University of New York, New Paltz**

I use this book in my basic business writing classes because it is so user friendly. It has an A-to-Z guide, so you don't have to know the categories you're looking for. My participants give it rave reviews, and lots of them give it to their high-school and college-aged kids to help them too.

> **– Nancy Hatch Woodward, business writer/editor/teacher**

As a dining service company with clients in business, the arts, academia and the public sector, we pride ourselves on the meticulous attention we pay to the quality of our food and service. It's essential to project that same image in our written communications. Many of the professionals throughout all of our departments consider "The Business Style Handbook" an indispensable tool in their daily activities – from proposals, presentations and press releases to marketing materials, menus, our social media platforms and trade show presence. This book is a great tool to help our people meet our high standards for all forms of professional communication.

> **– Thomas Eich, president & COO, CulinArt, Inc.**

Cunningham and Greene cover the most critical components of writing (business or otherwise) clearly and succinctly. "The Business Style Handbook" is an effective learning tool and a must-have reference for business professionals.

– Kerry Fina, M.A., Doane College, adviser and adjunct faculty

As a professor and business consultant, I find "The Business Style Handbook" to be an excellent reference. The book is well organized and easy to use for both students and professionals. It contains invaluable tips to help you thrive in today's business world.

– Holly G. Green, The Human Factor, Inc., managing director

The Business Style

HANDBOOK

An A-to-Z Guide for Effective Writing on the Job

Revised & Fully Updated Second Edition

HELEN CUNNINGHAM · BRENDA GREENE

•

TO OUR FAMILIES

•

CONTENTS

ACKNOWLEDGMENTS

To UPDATE THE SECOND EDITION, we again surveyed Fortune 500 communications professionals (from Fortune magazine's 2010 list). Their expertise greatly enhanced the second edition. We are indebted to **Aetna,** Scot Roskelley, communications director – mid-America region; **Aflac,** Glenn E. Wells, editorial consultant; **Bemis Company, Inc.,** Kristine Pavletich, public relations specialist; **Dana Holding Corporation,** Jeff Cole, director of marketing communication; **Franklin Templeton Investments,** Cynthia Hanson, senior copy editor; **Masco Corporation,** Kathleen Vokes, director of corporate communications; **Owens & Minor,** Duriechee Friend, director of communications; **Progress Energy,** Linda Wootton, proofreader; **Southern Company,** Marc Rice, corporate communication account executive – environment; **Union Pacific,** Tom Lange, director of corporate communications. Seven other individuals from Fortune 500 companies also participated this time around but asked us not to list their names or companies. Glenn Wells, Jeff Cole and Marc Rice also participated in our 2001 survey.

In addition, we thank the 50 communications professionals from the Fortune 500 (1999 list) who participated in our 2001 survey. So much of the information they provided in 2001 is still relevant today, so we kept much of the material they provided.

The 2001 survey consisted of 33 questions for corporate communications departments at the Fortune 500. Professionals at 50 companies participated in the survey, providing information on their standards, the standards within their departments and the writing style of their employees in general. At that time, those 50 companies all combined represented more than 3.6 million employees.

As time has passed, some of the companies have merged, been acquired or no longer rank among the Fortune 500. Some individuals, meanwhile, have moved to other companies or have been promoted. Our list, for the most part, reflects the status of companies and individuals at the time we received responses to both surveys.

Again, we extend our appreciation to the following professionals for their time and thoughtful responses for the 2001 survey: **Aflac,** Glenn Wells, editorial services; **Ameritech Corporation,** Diane L. Calvert, manager, communications quality; **AT&T Corp.,** Jean Hurt, editor; **Bell Atlantic Corporation** (now **Verizon**), Ken Terrell, executive director, employee communication; **Cigna Corporation,** Tony Branco, director, corporate media relations; **Circuit City Stores, Inc.,** Ann Collier, vice president, financial and public relations; **Coca-Cola Company,** Robert E. Byrd, senior manager, executive communications; **CompUSA Inc.,** Suzanne Shelton, director, public relations; **Conseco, Inc.,** James Rosensteele, director, communications; **Cooper Industries, Inc.,** Victoria Guennewig, vice president, public affairs; **Dana Corporation,** Jeff Cole, manager, marketing communication; **Detroit Edison,** Dan Vecchioni, principal communications specialist, employee communications; **Dominion Resources, Inc.,** James Evans, executive writer; **Eli Lilly and Company,** Gail Sax, associate communications consultant; **FedEx Express,** Anne L. Swearingen, senior communication specialist; **Georgia-Pacific Corporation,** Greg Guest, senior manager, corporate communications; **GTE Corporation** (now **Verizon**), Peter Thonis, senior vice president, external communications; **Home Depot, Inc.,** Beth Aleridge, director, internal communication; **Ingersoll-Rand Company,** Paul Dickard, director, public relations; **Intel Corporation,** Jeanne Forbis, manager, media relations; **International Paper Co.,** Vicki Tyler, manager of publications, corporate communications/publications; **Kmart Corporation,** Mary Lorencz, director, corporate media relations; **Lockheed Martin Corp.,** Raymond V. Bartlett, director, communications; **McKesson HBOC, Inc.,** Clara Degen, manager and editor, employee communications; **The Mead Corporation,** Doug Draper, vice president, corporate communications; **Monsanto Company,** Sue Courtney, manager, strategic communications; **Nabisco, Inc.,** John Barrows, senior manager, marketing communications; **Newell Rubbermaid Inc.,** Dean L. Werner, director, corporate communications; **Nike, Inc.,** Scott Reames, senior communications manager; **Pharmacia & UpJohn Inc.,** Maury Ewalt, director, corporate internal communications; **PPG Industries, Inc.,** John Ruch, manager, corporate public information; **Praxair, Inc.,** Susan Szita-Gore, associate director, communications; **The Prudential Insurance Company of America,** Marie Pavlick, director, communications; **Quantum Corporation,** Kevin Heney, creative director; **R.R. Donnelley & Sons Company,** Vera C. Panchak, director, corporate communication; **Safeway Inc.,** Tom Conway, vice president, communications; **SCI Systems, Inc.,** Alma Kiss, newsletter editor, publications department; **Sempra Energy,** Ed Struble, manager, publications; **Southern Company,** Marc Rice, communication specialist, corporate communication; **Sprint National Consumer Organization,** Russ Robinson, director, global business markets public relations; **The St. Paul Companies, Inc.,** William Tamlyn, manager, communications; **Unicom Corp.,** Mark Mandernach, manager, corporate internal communications; **UnitedHealth Group Corporation,** Barbara J. Gustafson, manager, corporate communications; **United Technologies Corp.,** David Mackey, manager, publications; **USAA,** Thomas D. Honeycutt, specialist, public affairs; **U S West** (now **CenturyLink**), Mike Fernandez, vice president; **Viacom Inc.,** William Bartlett, manager, editorial services; **Wal-Mart Stores, Inc.,** Thomas Williams, senior manager, public relations; **WellPoint Health Networks Inc.,** Lisa Mee-Stephenson, senior consultant, corporate communications; **Williams Communications Group,** Lynne S. Butterworth, senior manager, corporate communications.

In addition to our survey participants, others contributed to the book. They are the people who took the time to painstakingly review our manuscript to make sure it was comprehensive, current, relevant and accurate. We greatly appreciate their input.

We want to thank Jacqueline Flynn, our agent at Joelle Delbourgo Associates, and Joelle Delbourgo, who represents us now as well as when this book came out in its first edition in 2002. At McGraw-Hill, we extend our thanks to Tania Loghmani, Janice Race, Judy Duguid and the rest of the team for their efforts in publishing the second edition.

We also thank our family members and other loved ones for their support and encouragement.

INTRODUCTION

IN TODAY'S BUSINESS WORLD, everyone writes for a living. "The Business Style Handbook" is a resource to help people do so more effectively.

Because it's valuable to know best practices at leading corporations, we conducted a survey of corporate communications professionals at 50 Fortune 500 companies for the first edition of "The Business Style Handbook." For this second edition, we checked in again with the Fortune 500 to update and supplement the original findings. The results of both surveys, consolidated in Chapter 1, give an overview of the state of writing at some of the world's largest companies.

Writing: a core competency

Whether you write emails, memos, proposals, letters, presentations, marketing materials or reports; whether you write on a computer or mobile device; whether you are IMing or texting, it all constitutes writing. Your writing skills are on display as never before and, in the workplace, it's important to get it right.

You need to write clearly, concisely and without errors. You must gather information, synthesize it and put it into a reader-friendly form – fast. Your reputation and success in the business world are increasingly dependent on these skills.

"Countless careers rise or fall on the ability or the inability of employees to state a set of facts, summarize a meeting or present an idea coherently," said William Zinsser in the book "On Writing Well." And if you think you are a project manager, not a writer, that kind of thinking is dated. Today the ability to communicate effectively is a requisite. It also gives you a competitive advantage.

Communication skills are increasingly cited as a primary hiring consideration at major corporations. The CEO of Delta Airlines, Richard Anderson, was asked whether there had been a change over the past decade in the qualities he looks for when hiring. His answer was yes. The ability to communicate is "getting more and more important," he said in a 2009 interview with the New York Times under the headline "He Wants Subjects, Verbs and Objects."

Good writing drives results. The way you write also reflects on you. It projects an image of you to people across your company as well as externally. And your external communications present an image of your organization to the outside world. So the stakes are high. In a competitive job market and work environment, no one can afford to send communications that are sloppy and full of errors.

In the Financial Times, management columnist Lucy Kellaway observed a trend toward better writing in a 2009 column. "Just as recession encourages people to put on ties, it also makes them look more kindly on the capital letter and semicolon. When people are losing their jobs, correct dress and correct usage of words seem like a good insurance policy."

How to meet the standard

Writing effectively on the job is not a straightforward challenge. The primary goal is to communicate what your audience needs to know; writing it properly helps you achieve that goal.

The writing part starts with knowing the basics of grammar, spelling and punctuation. It entails organizing your messages effectively and being concise.

It includes being up to speed on the language of business, which in today's global interconnected economy is more dynamic than ever.

People at work continually confront questions about writing, many of which are specific to the corporate world. Do you capitalize job titles? Is *website* one word or two? Are *euro, yen* and *renminbi* capitalized? When do you hyphenate *end to end?* Is *setup* hyphenated? How do you write academic degrees? Do you write *e.g.* or *i.e.?*

While online resources make it easy to research writing issues, search-engine results are not always reliable and require making judgments.

In striving to achieve all these on-the-job writing objectives, you rarely have the luxury of time. "The Business Style Handbook" can help you meet the challenge. It is business-focused, authoritative and user-friendly. It will help you resolve questions, quickly.

Here's how "The Business Style Handbook" can help you:

- It includes a single A-to-Z format, with more than 1,500 alphabetical entries selected for their relevance to a business environment.

- It incorporates research on writing best practices at Fortune 500 corporations.

- It is written in plain English.

- It contains chapters on how to write effectively on the job, why style matters and what the best practices are for email, including a section on the integration of office email systems with mobile devices.

We hope "The Business Writing Handbook" will become a well-worn resource that earns a place by your side wherever and whenever you need to write.

1

FORTUNE 500
SURVEY RESULTS

"The Business Style Handbook" is a writing guide for the workplace. It is tailored to the person who writes on the job, which today is everyone who uses a computer and/or mobile device for work.

Professional writers in corporations have lots of stylebooks, resources and expertise at their disposal. The same is not generally true for the rest of the employee population, which is why we wrote "The Business Style Handbook." Different from most stylebooks, this one has a business focus. It is also written specifically for people in the business world who don't think of themselves as writers, even though they write throughout the day. This revised edition reflects the many changes that have taken place in business and technology over the past decade.

We tested the market for the first edition of "The Business Style Handbook" by surveying 50 communications executives at the Fortune 500 in 2001. At that time, survey results confirmed our assumption that, although most employees were required to write on the job, the majority had no reference guide for style, punctuation and grammar. The executives we polled saw the need for a business style guide, saying their employees would benefit from a resource that was easy to use, spoke specifically to business issues and made sense of conflicting information about usage and style.

"The Business Style Handbook" met that need in 2002. Today, it is frequently cited as a recommended book for business writing courses in corporations and at universities. It is on the recommended reading list for Microsoft Education Written Competencies and for the U.S. State Department's Foreign Service Institute's Leadership and Management Training Continuum. It has been cited as a valuable resource in discussions on LinkedIn. It is recommended on business writing websites and on job sites, such as Monster.com, which includes it among its Top Resources for Business Writing. And it has been published in the world's two most populous nations: China (in translation) and India.

After the book had been in the market for a decade, we decided it was time to write a second edition. Ten years is a long time in the world of business, communications and technology, and this edition both reflects and addresses the new environment.

We again checked in with Fortune 500 executives to supplement and update our initial research. The new responses reveal some shifts in business writing practices, and also confirm the fact that the basics of good writing on the job don't change dramatically over time.

A decade on, the words that define good business writing remain the same: clear, concise, accurate, consistent. What's more, brevity, always welcome in the business world, has gotten a big boost thanks to the widespread use of new communications tools, such as smartphones, IM and texting.

It matters

Good writing matters in the workplace – and it makes a difference in career advancement. That was the consensus among the Fortune 500 survey respondents in 2012 and in 2001. A comment in the 2012 survey sums it up succinctly: "No matter the level of employee, clearly communicating ideas is critical to the success of initiatives."

In 2012, a new theme surfaced to underscore the importance of good writing: the role of regulation in business. "We are often communicating things that have policy/legal implications, making the ability to write clearly and concisely all the more important," said Scot Roskelley, Aetna's communications director – mid-America region.

The topic of generational writing styles yielded a positive finding. Most of the Fortune 500 executives surveyed in 2012 said they did not generally encounter sloppy writing among their younger employees. They attributed this fact to good hiring practices and to training programs and coaching sessions with younger employees to help them understand what constitutes appropriate business communications.

Guidelines, with caveats

Many companies have corporate-wide writing guidelines for employees. The ability to post these guidelines on corporate intranets has contributed to the broader distribution of them, which marks an advance for writing over the past decade. In the 2001 survey, only eight companies had company-wide guidelines. For the remainder, guidelines were used primarily in communications, media and marketing departments and in some other areas of the company.

The ability to make guidelines easily available to all employees online is an example of technology advancing the cause. One survey respondent noted that her company's guidelines are posted on the internal employee website and occasionally highlighted in a weekly push email. Aflac's Glenn Wells explained his company's approach, which is even more extensive given the need to maintain consistency in the branding of corporate publications: "We provide online references and guidelines for style and for formatting manuals, letters, brochures and training materials," and "We also conduct classes on writing for new employees."

Some companies have multiple guidelines depending on the area of the company. "Corporate writing is spread over a few different functional areas that write for varying audiences that require different writing styles," said Owens & Minor's Duriechee Friend, a director of communications. "Hence, one set of guidelines would not serve us well." Another executive said her company has no corporate-wide guidelines, although she has created an in-house stylebook that has limited distribution.

Globalization creates another issue. Franklin Templeton's Cynthia Hanson said, "We have a U.S. editorial style guide but not an equivalent for our many overseas offices."

The extensiveness of guidelines varies from industry to industry. While pharmaceutical companies tend to have voluminous guidelines, manufacturing companies may be more minimalist.

In 2012, the major difference in the discussion of guidelines is the increase in writing platforms and tools. People regularly write content for print and online vehicles, and they are writing on computers (using word processing, email and IM), smartphones and netbooks. This trend has created the need to define where standards are applied and, in some cases, to develop new standards.

The content explosion

The proliferation of writing outlets has raised the question of where to apply style standards.

When queried on this point in 2012, the executives surveyed indicated that formal corporate content, especially material for external audiences, generally adheres to standards. Corporate publications, press releases, marketing materials and the corporate website topped the list.

"Formal communication on behalf of the company goes through a review process where style standards are applied," said Jeff Cole, director of marketing communication, Dana Holding Corp. A similar point was made by another respondent. "If it is an official publication or 'voice' of the company, we apply standards," he said. "Email would not fall under this standard unless we were communicating with certain individuals (media, for example) outside the company."

"Executive" communications, both internal and external, are also on the list of materials to which standards are applied, including messages from the CEO and other senior executives, annual reports and personnel announcements.

Today, most corporate content is distributed in print and/or digital formats, a reality that does not seem to be a major factor in deciding when to use standards, according to the 2012 survey results. "Much of our content is used in both media," explained Aflac's Wells. Other typical comments: "One standard fits all." "We have one style and use it consistently both internally and externally."

However, some survey respondents offered a different perspective. They noted that their corporations adapt style standards, depending on the medium; some companies are developing digital standards.

Internal communications, such as email, IM and social media, are not generally subject to standards. "Business correspondence from an individual – both internal and external – is exempt from style standards, as it reflects the personal voice of the author," Cole noted. "That is not to say style standards are necessarily ignored, but they are not applied as rigorously."

Another executive made a similar comment. "We apply standards to anything representing a communication from the company," said Tom Lange, director, corporate communications, Union Pacific. "Employee-to-employee communications, such as email or instant messages, do not fall into this category."

This approach to internal communications tracks results from the 2001 survey, with the distinction that a decade ago, the discussion was limited to email. In that survey a senior vice president of external communications at GTE (now Verizon) noted that email guidelines were unnecessary because email is intended to be fast and informal. Then, like now, some executives advocated the broad use of standards. For example, Praxair's associate director of communications said writing standards should be standard regardless of the medium. Eli Lilly's associate communications consultant agreed, noting that writing standards for email regarding grammar, punctuation and spelling should be the same as for other written documents.

What other factors play into decisions about where to apply standards? "It depends on the audience and the distribution," said Glenn E. Wells, editorial consultant at Aflac. "Internal, informal and short-lived materials can be more relaxed. Advertising and communications to customers are more strictly edited, particularly where extensive legal and regulatory considerations apply."

Influence of technology

Keeping up with new technologies – and how to write for them – is an uphill battle. "It is challenging because the style rules for many of the new platforms are not yet firmly established," said Marc Rice, Southern Company's corporate communication account executive – environment.

Much has been written about how texting, IM and social media are contributing to the decline of good writing. "The multiple tools and platforms used for communicating today have further eroded workplace writing," said Union Pacific's Lange. "I recently questioned someone about antecedent agreement and was asked whether there is an app for that."

Other Fortune 500 executives held a similar view in 2001, but at that time, the discussion was narrower: no mention of smartphones back then. When asked whether the general business population was writing better because of computers, the response was 3-to-1 in favor of no. The comments about computers were in the same vein as those now made about smartphones. WellPoint's senior consultant for corporate communications noted in 2001 that employees were writing more but not necessarily better. Quantum's creative director noted that technology gave publishing power to poor writers but did not necessarily improve grammar and spelling. St. Paul's manager of communications said that, on the positive side, people were writing more because of the technology, but on the negative side, they often became careless because of the need to write and respond quickly.

Regardless of your view on this topic, it's undeniable that brevity has been a big beneficiary of the new environment. "Social media requires a more fluid style of writing than do other forms of formal communications, to promote brevity and readability," said Owens & Minor's Friend. Real time and digital time are melding in the business world – and getting the message out quickly matters more than ever. No one is interested in long-winded treatises. Kathleen Vokes, a director of corporate communications at Masco Corporation, commented: "Executives tend to be very direct in their communications." Another survey respondent said articles are shorter at her corporation, with more bulleted items to make skimming easier.

A shift in the tone of business writing, particularly for internal communications, is also attributed partly to the new technologies. *More casual, more relaxed, informal* and *less structured* were some of the words used to describe how technology has impacted writing in the workplace.

How employees are writing

Both the 2012 and 2001 surveys indicate that many employees struggle with their writing, but in 2012 brevity topped the list of issues that confound writers in the workplace. That is a shift from 2001, when brevity was not cited as a concern. At that time, the top two problem areas were clarity and consistency. The heightened focus on brevity no doubt reflects the explosion of content along with the new technologies and platforms, for which verbosity is the bane.

Other writing issues were consistent across both surveys: grammar/ punctuation, style, clarity, acronym overkill and excessive jargon. In 2012, survey respondents also cited lack of focus on the audience, insufficient context, hyphenation, overly long quotes, incorrect use of trademarks, excessive use of the passive voice, poor structure, their/they're/there confusion. Over-capitalization is another common corporate phenomenon. "Everybody seems to want their title, department, group, etc. uppercased," said Marc Rice of Southern Company.

In both surveys, the good news was that spelling is not a major concern.

Seniority continues to make a difference when it comes to good writing, confirming it is a competency that contributes to career growth. When asked to rate the writing skills of their senior executives in the 2012 survey, 64% gave an excellent/very good rating and 29% a good rating. Ten years ago, the numbers were similar.

When you need a stylebook

The issues that send professional communicators in search of a stylebook vary widely. When asked in 2012 the reason for most recently consulting a style manual, Marc Rice answered, "I use a stylebook almost daily for writing and editing." That response mirrors one from the 2001 survey. "I use it too often to remember, but it probably involved hyphenation."

Here are some of the other reasons people resorted to stylebooks in 2012: whether to capitalize *the* in *The Netherlands* and *S* in *Southeast Asia;* whether to spell out numerals that refer to units of measure; whether to hyphenate *setup;* which cities don't take state abbreviations; whether to omit the periods in *U.S.* and similar abbreviations; how to format dates in British English; how to use *compare with* versus *compare to;* how to spell *checkup;* how and when to use parentheses, commas and titles; how to punctuate a bulleted list; when to use *that* versus *which;* how to handle academic titles and degrees.

Here are some of the reasons professional communicators consulted stylebooks in 2001: how to use the word *comprise;* when to use *altogether* versus *all together;* what word to use for people from the Philippines (*Filipinos*); how to abbreviate a state; what kind of capitalization and punctuation to use for bullets; whether to upper- or lowercase *web;* whether to capitalize *commonwealth* when writing *commonwealth of Kentucky;* how to use quotation marks; when to use commas; how to treat large numbers; what makes a word a collective noun; how to handle capitalization.

Stylebooks used by companies' professional writers

Every one of the corporate communications professionals surveyed in both surveys uses a stylebook. And in 2012, everyone is using a combination of print and digital editions.

The most frequently used guide is "The Associated Press Stylebook," whose 2011 edition is titled "The Associated Press Stylebook and Briefing on Media Law."

Some respondents noted other sources, such as "The Chicago Manual of Style," "The Elements of Style," "The Business Style Handbook," "Words into Type," "The Gregg Reference Manual," "Franklin Covey Style Guide," "The Careful Writer," "The New York Public Library Writer's Guide to Style," "Wired Style" and "The Elements of Internet Style."

If the business is highly technical, other books – such as the "American Medical Association Manual of Style" – are also used. On this point, one 2012 survey respondent, Union Pacific's Tom Lange, said, "We developed a company-specific stylebook to address industry terminology."

Of the stylebooks cited by the professionals surveyed – as both primary and secondary sources – "The Business Style Handbook" is the only one that specifically targets people who write on the job. As a rule, stylebooks continue to be written primarily for journalists and academics, rather than business writers.

The popularity of "The Associated Press Stylebook" can be attributed to several factors, including its widespread usage and acceptance as authoritative; its alphabetical format and accessibility; the frequency with which it is updated; and the fact that it is now available electronically.

In addition, many corporate communications professionals have journalistic backgrounds. In explaining why her department uses "The Associated Press Stylebook," one 2012 survey respondent said that the majority of the communications employees at her company have previous academic/professional experience with this stylebook.

Coping with lag time

The language of business and its usage are constantly racing ahead of most stylebooks, creating uncertainty for people who write on the job. Examples of style questions that could arise in 2012 include whether to hyphenate *clickthrough* and *right-click;* whether to use *yuan* or *renminbi;* how to write *IM* in the past tense; whether to spell out *LGBT;* when *login* is one word versus two; whether to use a singular or plural verb with *ergonomics;* when to use *and* versus *&;* whether to use a singular or plural verb with *human resources;* when *buyback* is one word versus two; how to alphabetize Spanish surnames; and whether *access* is a verb. The list goes on.

At the same time, new words, phrases and usage rules constantly enter the workplace. When the 2012 survey asked respondents to name a new word or phrase that has become mainstream, answers included *onboarding, emailable,*

Occupy (Wall Street) and *Arab Spring, Quick Response (QR) barcode, mobile platform, smartphone, must-win battle, BlackBerry(s), game-changer, tweet, screenshot, podcast, mouseover, friend* (as a verb), *emoji, G3* and *G4*.

To illustrate the passage of time in business English, here are some of the answers given by 2001 survey respondents when asked to name a new word or phrase that had become mainstream: *online, go-live, bricks and mortar, clicks and mortar, Y2K, impact* (as a verb), *cyberspace, proactive, value-added, going forward, FedEx it, best practices, synergies, e-tail, globalize* and *dot-com*. At that time, all but four respondents said their companies wrote *email* with a hyphen.

When asked how they establish standards for words and phrases that have not yet made their way into stylebooks and dictionaries, respondents indicated a range of resources. Most people go online for answers. Several respondents to the 2012 survey explained their process, which includes researching common practices online, having a discussion among the editors, establishing a rule and then sticking to it. One company writes all new entries into a spreadsheet that is maintained online and available to anyone in the company.

Other companies see how a word or phrase is used elsewhere, trying to find examples that are similar in context, and then determine what seems to be the prevailing standard.

The practice of looking to authoritative third parties in establishing standards for new words and phrases was also prevalent in the 2001 survey results. Many companies indicated that they relied on usage in large newspapers. Three respondents, Georgia-Pacific's senior manager of corporate communications, Nike's senior communications manager and Safeway's vice president of communications, went to the New York Times when a new word or phrase cropped up. Dana's manager of marketing communications turned to the Wall Street Journal if an answer wasn't in "The Associated Press Stylebook." UnitedHealth Group's manager of corporate communications also used the Wall Street Journal. An editor at AT&T relied on both the New York Times and the Wall Street Journal. Home Depot's internal communication director turned to USA Today.

The creative director at Quantum checked with the International Association of Business Communicators. Viacom's manager of editorial services used his own judgment, while Intel's media relations manager sought the opinion of the legal department. USAA's specialist for public affairs noted that "corporate consensus" determined standards for new words, while Mead's vice president of corporate communications said "group consensus" carried the day.

"Wired Style" was the source used for new technology terms by R.R. Donnelley's director of corporate communication, as well as United Technologies' manager of publications. Ameritech's manager of communications quality cited various sources, including the Federal Communications Commission website. CompUSA's director of public relations cited the trade press as one of her sources.

In 2001, most stylebooks were updated every 10 years or so, leaving a huge gap for authoritative direction on style. Nowadays most publishers of stylebooks have concluded that 10 years is an eternity as far as language is concerned.

Strong views on buzzwords

In both the 2012 and 2001 surveys, buzzwords were a hot-button issue for communications executives. In each of the surveys, this issue brought out the exclamation points.

Here are some comments from the 2012 survey: "Avoid buzzwords at all costs!" "Don't like them. Now more than ever. Today's buzzword is tomorrow's cliche." "Trite buzzwords should be avoided." "Keep them to a minimum." "I think they're becoming a crutch for many people and are a hindrance to clear communications."

About half the communications professionals surveyed in 2001 indicated they did not like buzzwords. Some emphatically stated that they disliked, detested, hated or tried to avoid buzzwords. Aflac's manager of editorial services noted that he hated buzzwords, including the word "buzzword."

A new point pertaining to buzzwords that surfaced in the 2012 survey was the globalization of the workforce. Several respondents noted that buzzwords do not translate well. One person stated that his company translates most of its company-wide internal communications and finds translating buzzwords difficult to manage. Another person concurred, adding that her company has given employees training that discourages the use of buzzwords for this reason.

The 2012 survey indicated that some respondents take a more relaxed approach to buzzwords in internal communications as opposed to external communications. "I prefer plain English whenever possible, but on occasion we use them internally. They're essentially verboten for external usage," said one executive. "In limited circumstances when corresponding via email with a familiar colleague, buzzwords would be OK to use," said Kristine Pavletich, public relations specialist, Bemis Company. Another executive said that buzzwords are acceptable in internal communications where the audience will be familiar with them.

Preferred dictionaries

Most companies surveyed have a standard dictionary, two of which stood out across the 2012 and 2001 surveys: "Merriam-Webster's Collegiate Dictionary" (not the same as "Webster's New World College Dictionary") and "The American Heritage Dictionary." Companies are also are using "Webster's New World College Dictionary" because it is the dictionary of choice for both "The Associated Press Stylebook" and "Gregg." And in 2012, everybody is using a combination of print and digital editions (with our favorite being www.m-w.com). Another online dictionary cited by Fortune 500 survey participants is Dictionary.com.

Other dictionaries used by survey respondents include "The Oxford English Dictionary" (various editions), "Black's Law Dictionary," "Webster's Third International Dictionary" and "Stedman's Medical Dictionary."

How it all adds up

When creating the original questionnaire for "The Business Style Handbook" in 2001, our goal was to obtain an overall idea of large organizations' priorities and preferences for effective communication as well as the kind of standards they adhere to. We had no preconceived notions about corporate America's style practices. In the 2012 survey, our goal was to check in and assess what had changed over the previous decade, so that we could update the book.

The combined survey results are consistent in overwhelmingly confirming the fact that good writing matters at large organizations. What's more, even though a growing number of corporations make writing guidelines and training available to their employees, writing well remains a challenge.

We hope the new edition of "The Business Style Handbook" will help employees meet this challenge.

- *For information on the 2012 and 2001 surveys, see Acknowledgments.*
- *The respondents' participation in this survey does not necessarily indicate an endorsement of this stylebook.*
- *Note that percentages cited from the surveys are based on the number of respondents who answered that particular question.*

2

WHY STYLE MATTERS

YOU MAY WONDER WHAT ALL THE DETAILS of style covered in this book have to do with communicating well. You are, after all, a businessperson – not a grammarian. Your customers are going to buy the new equipment or contract your services regardless of where you place your commas or whether you lowercase all your words. So why should you take the extra time to improve your writing skills when you could be researching new prospects and making more sales?

The answer is simple: credibility.

To get your message across to readers – whether they are customers, employees, vendors, regulators or colleagues – you need credibility. When inaccuracy, error, inconsistency, jargon and carelessness riddle a print or online communication, you put your credibility on the line. Business relationships thrive on trust, of which credibility is a key factor. Communication that is unfocused and unreliable sends a message about your organization that could result in lost opportunities.

You may also question the value of good writing in today's fast-moving economy, where so much business transacts online. In a BBC news article about online sales, Charles Duncombe, a British businessman, makes an astute observation about the intersection of internet companies and business writing. "Often these cutting-edge companies depend upon old-fashioned skills," he says. The title of the article is telling: "Spelling Mistakes 'Cost Millions' in Lost Online Sales."

In referring to "Good to Great," by Jim Collins, Fortune magazine notes the "culture of discipline" that separates "so-so companies" from "great" companies. These "inner-directed" companies build cumulatively instead of reacting to the whims of the next big thing. Good communication skills are part of the discipline of the corporate culture of "great" companies. When these organizations place a premium on communication skills, it can make all the difference. When they don't, companies pay the price.

Good communication skills are increasingly viewed as a core competency in the corporate world. "More and more, the ability to speak well and write is important," said Richard Anderson, CEO of Delta Airlines, in the New York Times. "Writing is not something that is taught as strongly as it should be in the educational curriculum. . . . People really have to be able to handle the written and spoken word. And when I say written word, I don't mean PowerPoints."

William Zinsser, in his classic book, "On Writing Well," makes the same point. "Any organization that won't take the trouble to be both clear and personal in its writing will lose friends, customers and money," Zinsser says. "Let me put it another way for business executives: a shortfall will be experienced in anticipated profitability."

Using clear and simple language while paying attention to even the smallest details is more challenging than it sounds. All our Fortune 500 communications professionals know how difficult it can be to turn the jargon of an IT developer into readable prose. The initiative to improve communication must come from the top and work its way down to the entry level. Tools that encourage clarity, consistency and accuracy in communication are a first step.

Language is dynamic

To reach your reader, which is the primary aim of written communication, you need to adhere to certain conventions of style. These conventions are part of the discipline of language. They exist to promote understanding, not to thwart your creative energies. A simple paragraph, however, may contain enough style questions to stump even a seasoned writer.

That's why stylebooks were created. They reinforce principles of grammar and punctuation. They keep the vernacular current and fresh. They clear away the discrepancies of conflicting information. Overall, good stylebooks keep you alert and thoughtful, helping you to think more clearly about the best way to communicate effectively.

They also simplify your life, because writing style is multilayered. According to "The Oxford Essential Guide to Writing," there is grammar, usage (how you are supposed to write as a member of a certain community), mechanics (how certain conventions make writing consistent and clear) and approach (how you convey the message to readers). All these layers can conspire to slow the writing process. In fact, they can be real hurdles. Not only can you get tangled up in the mechanics of a complex sentence, but you may also struggle with the tone or approach your document should take.

To make matters more difficult, language is dynamic. It evolves continually to reflect the environment from which it springs. Keeping up with all the change can be daunting. The Global Language Monitor, which adds new words to the lexicon once they have been cited at least 25,000 times, claims the English language has more than a million words – more than any other language. In our fast-moving, interconnected world, new words pop up every day – and writers must make decisions about how to use them. People who write on the job may be *IMing* with colleagues all day long but have doubts about how to cast that word in a sentence.

And not only do people who write on the job have to think about whether *website* is one word or two or whether to hyphenate *email* or close it up, they also have to consider the communication platforms they are using. Websites, smartphones, texting and social media have pushed business writers out into the wide world – exposing both their strengths and deficiencies in communication. Never before has writing been more public.

That is why you cannot assume you have all the skills you need to communicate well. You have to take into account that language is dynamic and your objectives will change from one project to the next. Writing habits developed in high school and college may not be appropriate for your current job. You need to continually assess the way you use language and make sure you achieve your aim, which, in the world of business, is to reach your readers – whether they are colleagues, supervisors, customers, regulators, potential new hires or the media.

Writing that gets the job done

People fall into corp-speak at work because it is easy and familiar, and because no one is steering them away. And the rationale for such language exists.

Your business is so complicated, so dense, so incomprehensible to the average mind that only you and a select few are privy to its secrets and mysterious beauty. That is why you need to write in a language no one understands.

This approach can be counterproductive. Imagine going on a sales call with rumpled hair and in your weekend attire. What's the likelihood of making a sale? Ignoring the way you present material to the reader is like dressing inappropriately. It undermines you, sends the wrong message about your company and defeats your purpose. It suggests you may be as careless in your business as you are in communication. Back to Zinsser: "Ultimately the product that any writer has to sell is not the subject being written about, but who he or she is." Writing is part of your brand.

At its best, writing is a balancing act between you and your readers. It is tempting to fall into the jargon of your business, but you should always ask yourself if your writing gets the job done. This doesn't mean technical language isn't useful. We use a lot of terms in this book that would make a strict grammarian wince, but these terms are useful in business, so you may as well know how to use them. The span of business covers everything from nuts and bolts to meta-worlds and packet-switching. It is a complicated world, but it is your job to make it comprehensible.

So aim for simplicity, and realize time is not on your side. Readers are bombarded with information from multiple sources. Attention spans are shrinking. Twitter has made people accustomed to communicating in 140 characters. Your words are competing for attention with photos circulated in near-real-time and videos from YouTube. If you cannot catch the interest of the members of your target audience quickly, chances are you will lose them. Your mother may be patient with you, but readers are not.

While there is no guarantee that you will grab each reader every time, you can improve your chances immensely if you aim for writing that is clear, concise and accurate. Remember, it is impossible to influence people if your thinking is fuzzy, your objectives are camouflaged and your language confounds.

That's why it's important to develop a style that is accessible, functional and simple. Ultimately, your writing style tells your readers what you think of them. When you take the time to write clear sentences – with the proper punctuation, correct grammar and spelling, and consistent organization – you make your readers' lives easier, you tell them you value them and you demonstrate that you are capable.

Flannery O'Connor, the renowned short story writer, once said, "The writer is only free when he can tell the reader to go jump in the lake." This notion may appeal to students and fiction readers, but it will not serve you well when you write a business proposal for the new initiatives committee. Business writing style is more craft than art. Your primary objective is to influence readers – and you cannot do this if you overburden, belittle or confuse them. A simple, clear, concise style is a courtesy to the reader and serves your best interest. And like most courtesies in business, it is a requirement.

Take charge

You are not trying to win a Pulitzer Prize for writing, but you can improve the skills you already have. All you need is willingness and guidance.

Writing is a process. Each communication starts with a first draft and ends with the final review. As you work through this process, you need to be willing to be simple rather than complex, clear rather than fuzzy, accurate rather than sloppy and brief rather than long-winded.

In your everyday life you probably write as you speak. You will say and write *I like hot chocolate after shoveling snow because it warms my bones.* You write this way because it seems natural and appropriate. But the minute you walk into the office, your tone changes. You write instead *It is beneficial to consume 8 ounces of hot chocolate after removing frozen precipitation from the earth's surface because it raises body temperature to an agreeable level.*

You distance your readers almost unconsciously by choosing unsuitable words to get your message across. It is unnecessary but inescapable – unless you pay attention to how your style works for or against you. If you want to get the job done, your best bet is a direct, simple, clear style.

Pulling it together

You also have to adhere to the grammar, usage and mechanics that will promote clear writing. Clarity, consistency and accuracy are essential for writing to be authoritative and persuasive. If your communications are full of errors and inconsistencies, your readers will lose patience and fail to take you and your message seriously. It also can hurt the bottom line.

Exact figures on how much inaccuracies and errors cost companies are impossible to tally, but the prevalence of mistakes in business communication is well documented. A BBC article about how spelling mistakes diminish online sales addresses this topic. "Poor spelling is a serious problem for the online economy," says British businessman Duncombe, who conducted an analysis of website figures that indicated a single spelling mistake can cut online sales in half. In his assessment, when you sell or communicate on the internet, 99% of the time it is done by the written word.

To further complicate matters, on any given day a writer may be challenged by the placement of a comma, the correct punctuation of quotations or the intricacies of the semicolon. Who cares? If meaning is not jeopardized, what's the big deal if you forget to put in a comma or spell *website* as one word or two? Why get tangled up in minutiae, especially when the deadline is an hour away?

The fact is that attention to detail is not up for grabs in business. Good form, accuracy and consistency are the hallmarks of authoritative writing. A careless style – or even an idiosyncratic style – can undermine a project. The details matter.

Without a doubt, errors are costly. And too often people who write on the job can get hung up on a comma and forget to double-check to make sure the numbers are adding up. But, besides the enormous expense of mistakes, errors also impact credibility. When Victoria's Secret came out with a new Michigan State T-shirt with rival University of Michigan's slogan of "Hail to the Victors" emblazoned on the front, the U of M Wolverines weren't the only ones having a chuckle. And when an Interstate 71 sign to Cleveland read "Norht to Cleveland," the Ohio Department of Transportation took as much flak for the blunder as the contractor for wasting taxpayer dollars. The British businessman Duncombe also emphasizes the importance of spelling to a website's credibility in a world where people are concerned about the security of their data. "When there are underlying concerns about fraud and safety, then getting the basics right is essential," he says.

Lack of attention to detail takes its toll inside the company as well as outside. It was reported that the founder of J. Crew once stormed out of a meeting because someone wrote "SPR 94" on a report instead of "SP 94," which was how he wanted to see the word "spring" abbreviated. This illustrates not only how a boss's expectations can be rigorous, but also that many style decisions are subjective. Some style choices are merely preferences, but, for the sake of coherence and consistency, you need to adhere to them. A growing number of organizations expect employees to be on the same page when it comes to style and usage.

Content is paramount in communication, but writers cannot afford to downplay style, either. In this age of information, writing skills are on full display. The expectation at most companies is that writing be clear, concise, simple and direct. In a New York Times interview, Nell Minow, cofounder of the Corporate Library, bluntly stated, "I won't hire anybody who can't write. . . . It's just tremendously important, their precision, their vocabulary, their sense of appropriateness in communication."

Language is dynamic, not neat and tidy. To harness this unruly process, people who write on the job need guidance. Without becoming rigid or pedantic, this stylebook should help to provide the direction you need.

3

THE CASE FOR STANDARDS

COMPANIES, LARGE AND SMALL, increasingly recognize the importance of investing in their employees as a source of competitive advantage. In this environment, strengthening writing skills is an obvious contender for investment, particularly now that the digital age has made everyone a writer. In fact, writing is a competency that is more important than ever in today's business world.

Joyce E.A. Russell, the director of the Executive Coaching and Leadership Development Program at the University of Maryland's Robert H. Smith School of Business, wrote a 2011 article in the Washington Post titled "Are Writing Skills Necessary Anymore?" Here's an excerpt. "I recently posed this question to a number of executives, consultants and business leaders from various disciplines. I thought that some of them, especially the younger ones, might actually agree that writing is overrated. On the contrary, all of them emphasized the criticality of good writing skills and said that writing is even more important than in previous years. Professionals spend more time each day writing and are inundated with written communications (emails, reports, memos and such), so it is imperative that employees be able to write succinctly and write well."

Even though writing is critical, many people struggle when writing on the job. One of our Fortune 500 participants from the insurance industry said, "What I notice from people who take my business writing class is the inability to write a clear, cogent letter that sounds like it is spoken. Too many employees use archaic language and want to write a letter that sounds formal. I always question my students as to why people write like that. This fall, one of my students, a recent college graduate, said he thinks it's because he never had to write a business letter in college. If it's not taught, how do we expect people to write clearly and concisely?"

Stanley Fish, a professor of humanities and law at Florida International University, was concerned about the papers written for a literature graduate course: "They [the students] could manage for about six words and then, almost invariably, the syntax (and everything else) fell apart." He decided to take a look at the lesson plans of composition classes and found that out of the 104 sections on composition at the school, only four actually focused on the "craft of writing."

A growing number of universities recognize the problem and are doing something about it. "At employers' urging, many schools are taking steps to improve their students' writing. The Wharton School at the University of Pennsylvania plans to double its communication coursework to 12 courses starting in 2012," wrote Diana Middleton on WSJ.com. The title of her article: "Students Struggle for Words; Business Schools Put More Emphasis on Writing amid Employer Complaints."

So writing is getting more attention at business schools, which will benefit the next generation of executives. At the same time, to address the needs of the current workforce, more corporations offer writing courses and make company-wide writing guidelines available to their employees on corporate intranets. It is a considerable service to employees who are required to write. In addition, standards give all employees the support that corporate communications professionals, who always use one or more stylebooks, have always relied on. At long last, companies are giving their nonwriters the same writing tools the organizations' writers can't do without!

Time for companies to invest in the users

If schools are not teaching basic business writing that emphasizes clarity and accuracy, is it the company's responsibility to pick up the slack? Many companies are willing. The College Board's National Commission on Writing estimated in 2005 that private companies spent more than $3 billion each year to teach employees how to write.

As computers became ubiquitous in the workplace in the last century, companies focused on upgrading the computer workstation (which, according to Jeremy Rifkin in "The Age of Access," has a life span of less than 24 months). Now companies are also investing in employees' know-how – including their writing skills. This includes creating standards, which help an organization to:

- **Improve the quality of communication.** Ultimately the goal of standards is to promote clear, concise writing, which is what everyone in business wants to read. When an organization puts all employees – from the programmers to the engineers to the accountants – on the same page for writing style and usage, it raises the bar on written communication and it sends a message that good writing matters.
- **Increase competitiveness.** Good communication skills have never been as important as they are today. Employees who communicate effectively will give companies a competitive edge in the 21st century. It is fundamental to good business. Successful companies not only recruit the best people; they also develop them.
- **Empower employees.** Standards give employees a tool to improve their writing skills. It's one thing to tell people they should write better; it's another to give them guidelines to get there. CEOs may be able to rely on the corporate communications department to write, edit and proof their memos, but most employees don't have the same luxury. A reference guide that reinforces the fundamentals of grammar, punctuation and style empowers employees.
- **Increase efficiency.** Standards make life easier for the writer – which translates into efficiency. When writing and editing documents, employees don't need to waste time deciding how to write, punctuate or abbreviate a word. Instead they can spend their time on content and the challenge of writing quickly and effectively.

• **Ensure consistency.** Standards introduce consistency across all the organization's materials and audiences. Take the example of two employees at a pharmaceutical company. Laura Kelly in corporate communications refers to a stylebook to write the client newsletter, while Vincent Uibel in human resources relies on instinct to write about an employee benefits package. Kelly writes *healthcare,* while Uibel writes *health care.* Who's right? They both are, but within one company everybody should write it the same way.

Create a standard

More and more companies recognize the benefits of writing guidelines. And instituting a standard need not be complicated. The first step is to raise awareness that the quality of written communication is important. This may involve a memo from a senior executive or an entry in the company handbook. At a bare minimum, employees can be actively encouraged to run their documents through spellcheck and to do a global search on words that can be written more than one way to make sure they are used consistently.

Taking the concept to the next level entails giving all employees a reference guide for grammar, usage and spelling. Although all professional communicators use such guides, the notion may remain unfamiliar to most employees who have not worked in communications fields. The relevant department (e.g., corporate communications, media, training) can choose a stylebook that addresses the company's needs or spearhead the creation of in-house guidelines. An alternative is the hybrid approach that more companies are adopting, which selects a stylebook and then supplements it with additional guidelines that are particular to the company and industry.

Win employee buy-in

Convincing employees that standards are in their best interest may take some work. Initially they may react by wondering how they can be expected to spend time honing writing skills when they already eat lunch at their desks every day.

That's precisely the point. Standards free everyone from the time-consuming preoccupation of deciding what's standard and what's not. Even though the highest standards are not foolproof, they still can liberate the busy employee from making decisions about the hundreds of details that trip up even the seasoned writer. Rather than impose on employees, standards provide a service to them.

Another issue is that old habits are hard to break. When we asked colleagues to review our manuscript, one questioned writing *website* as one word and lowercased. We made that decision because language is dynamic. While *website* is written several ways in 2012, we believe there's a good chance the one-word form will eventually become the standard because it is ultimately the simplest form. Ten years ago, many corporations wrote *e-mail,* whereas today *email* is far more prevalent. Stylebooks, which typically were revised about every 10 years, are now updated more frequently to address the ever-changing standards and influx of new words generated by the new technology.

Language is a powerful tool. And employees should use it to the maximum advantage. Their careers depend on it. Aflac's Glenn Wells told us in the most recent survey, "Aflac is selective in hiring, strongly emphasizing training and education, and makes communication skills a key requirement for promotion."

William Zinsser, in "On Writing Well," takes that thought a step further: "Good English is your passport to wherever you need to go in your writing, your work and your life."

Applying standards to the way language is used at the workplace has never made better sense.

4

WRITE WITH PURPOSE

To communicate effectively in the business world, you need to convey your message in language that is clear, direct and simple. You need to do it fast and make it as concise as possible. Everyone is busy today, operating under information overload.

Don't waste people's time by making them struggle to decipher your message. Have a strategy when you write. Approach writing as a process and break this process into steps.

A key consideration in today's workplace is the platforms on which you'll be writing and distributing your communication. This chapter is devoted primarily to formal communications that will not be contained in emails. See Chapter 5, "Email: Before You Hit Send," for a discussion of email communications.

Have a goal

Think it through. Ask yourself why you are writing and what you expect to achieve. Are you writing to inform, to make a request, to make a recommendation, to solicit feedback, to initiate discussion, to convince, to complain? According to a senior manager of corporate communications at Williams Communications, writers should determine what they want the audience to do and then write in a way that persuades them.

Be clear about your subject matter. In business, the subject of your communication is often predetermined. You are writing a business plan for next year and need management's sign-off. You want to increase your department's budget for software. That's the purpose of your memo. Think critically about your subject. Gather the facts and ask yourself if they warrant your effort and your readers' attention. If senior management has asked all departments to cut expenses by 5%, this is probably not the time to ask for a budget increase.

Anticipate questions to ensure you achieve the desired outcome. If you are mapping out a product-launch strategy, provide a timetable. If you are requesting a response, give a deadline. If you are lobbying for a budget allocation, put a number on it. If you are asking someone to call you, be sure the person has your direct telephone number. If you are referencing a website or material from online sources, include links.

Know your audience

Communications professionals at the Fortune 500 emphasized over and over again how essential it is to write with your readers in mind.

Understand what your readers know about the subject and the level of detail they will want. The vice chairman may ask for a memo on how foreign exchange rates are affecting profitability, but chances are he does not want details about currency fluctuations in every market. Customers want to know how a new online service will help them, not how the technology operates. The mailroom needs to know when the annual report will be sent out, not that the mailing list is being updated. If a prospective client asks for information on your firm's experience in healthcare mergers and acquisitions, it's overkill to include your accomplishments in entertainment M&A as well.

Write and think at the same time

Often the hardest part of writing is sitting down in front of a blank screen. A director of public relations at CompUSA observed that writers should just get started, rather than worry about getting it right on the first try.

Also remember that as you write, the thought process continues to evolve. "Writing is thinking on paper. Anyone who thinks clearly can write clearly, about anything at all," according to William Zinsser, author of "On Writing Well." The many decisions you make as you write will shape your message and influence your audience's response.

Use the right language

Choose words that convey your meaning in the simplest terms. "Employers and writing coaches say business-school graduates tend to ramble, use pretentious language or pen too-casual emails," said Diana Middleton in an article on WSJ.com.

Avoid the temptation to write in the idiom of your business or specialty. It may be familiar, save you time and send the signal that you are an insider. But is it appropriate? Again, be guided by your audience. For an email to an IT group versed in technology and systems, technical language works. If you are sending the same email to the entire organization, write in plain English so that everyone understands.

Likewise, avoid using language better suited for texting or IM in more formal communications. Nell Minow, cofounder of the Corporate Library, said in a New York Times article that she won't hire people who can't write. "If they're using texting language in a memo, that's a bad sign," she said.

A good guideline is to write as you speak. Readers are confused, not impressed, by legalistic or esoteric vocabularies. Write simply because simplicity is a product of careful thought and choice. Your audience will appreciate it.

Make clarity a priority when selecting words. Shoot for the specific and concrete, not the ambiguous and abstract. "If you do not choose words wisely, words will, in effect, choose you, saying things about the topic you do not intend and affecting readers in ways you do not want," said Thomas S. Kane in "The Oxford Essential Guide to Writing."

Keep it short . . . most of the time

The senior manager of marketing communications at Nabisco offered some concise advice to those who write on the job: Be brief. Write short sentences and paragraphs and put the most important information up front.

Use strong, well-chosen words to make an impact: *The consumer foods division increased revenues by a record 22% in the third quarter.* Don't dilute the message and take up more space with wordy, roundabout sentences, such as *During the third quarter of the year, revenues in the consumer foods division were up by 22%, which is the highest quarterly increase ever in the company's history.* Direct sentences start with a noun and follow closely with the verb. Don't tax the reader with sentences that are loaded down with adjectives and adverbs.

Does that mean a short sentence is always preferable to a long one? Not necessarily. A paragraph of short sentences can sound choppy. And a long sentence can be well written and concise, provided every word counts. To create balance, mix up sentence length, but always remember that space is at a premium, more than ever if your message will be read on a mobile device.

Make longer documents user-friendly

Fortune magazine reported on a good model set forth by one corporation: "Procter & Gamble is, of course, famous for insisting upon one-page memos to ensure crisp, rigorous and focused analyses. Two-page memos don't get read."

If the communication must be lengthy, lead with an executive summary. "The executive summary, all one page of it, is the most important part of a business plan," said Guy Kawasaki, author and cofounder of Alltop.com and former chief evangelist of Apple. "You should spend 80% of your effort on writing a great executive summary and 20% on the rest of the plan."

Also include a table of contents for longer communications. Good organization promotes economy and emphasis in your writing, and your documents will be easier to read as a result.

For material that is more than one page, write headings that succinctly state what each section discusses. This helps you focus during the writing process and also guides readers, telling them what the document covers. In addition, it allows your audience to read selectively and find what they're looking for easily.

Write headings that say something and can stand on their own. For example, the heading *Longer Documents* is vague, whereas *Make Longer Documents User-Friendly* is a recommendation and also tells the reader what to expect in this section.

Bullets are another way to make documents readable and more concise, which in turn makes your message clearer. You could write *Fortune 500 companies are strong candidates to buy this product. U.S. government organizations are also potential customers, as are multilateral institutions and universities*, but it's more effective to write:

The market for this product is broad and includes:

- Fortune 500 companies
- U.S. government organizations
- Multilateral institutions
- Universities

Another advantage of bullet points is their flexibility. You can write them as single words or phrases (as in the preceding example); with a concise introductory phrase, followed by an explanation (see the next section); or as a complete thought, as in the following example:

The three action steps are:

- Research the competition for the proposed service.
- Propose a three-year budget.

- Conduct a thorough ROI analysis.
- Make a recommendation to the board by June 15.

Be consistent in how you start each bullet point. This will be determined by the lead-in sentence, which unifies the entire section. In the preceding examples, notice how in the first example each bullet has no verb or period, while in the second, each bullet is a complete sentence and ends with a period. If the lead-in sentence to the bulleted material ends with a colon, treat the bulleted points as part of that sentence with the proper punctuation (see the following examples).

Get right to the point

Start with your conclusion – it's possible your entire communication will not be read – and then make your case in order of importance. Take the same approach with each paragraph, putting the main point in the first sentence.

For many communications it is useful to begin by synthesizing key points into a bulleted phrase, followed by a brief summary of the point. Whenever possible, use concrete numbers, examples and reliable sources to persuade. The following three examples illustrate this approach.

1. I recommend we open a Brazil office next year. Reasons include:

   - **Cost savings.** It will cut our cost of doing business in the Brazilian market by 15% over the next three years.

   - **Higher regional sales.** Demand for our products is growing 10% p.a. in Latin America. We can use our Brazilian operation to source other Latin markets and to further increase brand awareness throughout the region.

2. You should switch to our service for the following reasons:

   - **24/7 customer service.** Someone will be available whenever you have a question.

   - **A strong global network.** We have offices in more than 80 cities around the world, so you can contact us even when you travel.

3. I am pleased to announce Andrei Savin will join us as CFO, effective June 22. His credentials include:

   - **Outstanding experience.** Andrei has worked in global finance for more than 25 years at three multinational companies. FYI, here is a link to his LinkedIn profile. [Insert link.]

   - **Excellent references.** The CFOs at Andrei's former employers uniformly commend his talent and dedication.

If you need to develop each point in more detail, do so later in the communication. If you need to include extensive background information, do so with links or an attachment.

Take the credit

Use language to convey that your department, your company or you are in control. For example, *The Asian division grew market share in Vietnam to 40% last year* credits the division with growing share – it didn't just happen. It is much stronger than *Market share in Vietnam grew to 40% last year.* (This suggests that market share grew itself without any effort from the Asian division.)

In general, write in the active, not passive, voice. It is stronger and puts the subject in command. *The company delivered the new product on schedule* emphasizes that the company met its commitment. The active voice is more direct than this construction: *The new product was delivered on schedule.* (This leaves the company out of the picture entirely, which is usually not what you want to do.)

Writing in the active voice does not always come naturally. You may need to go back and rework some sentences. Look for *is/was/are/were* followed by a past-participle verb (*is delivered/was written/are produced/were positioned*). For example, change *The memo was written by Roopa* to *Roopa wrote the memo.* Remember that the most vital word in every sentence is the verb, so use it to full advantage.

Shift the emphasis

For all its merits the active voice is not always the best choice. When you need to be tactful or to emphasize what is happening to the object rather than the subject, the passive voice is more effective. In "Plain Style: Techniques for Simple, Concise, Emphatic Business Writing," Richard Lauchman says, "The passive is often necessary and writers who believe it is 'bad' or 'weak' will often emphasize the wrong idea."

Say you want to be imprecise about who is responsible for an action to avoid allocating blame. In this case the passive voice works: *The white paper was not completed on schedule.* (It's unclear who missed the deadline.) Compare that with *The investor relations department did not complete the white paper on schedule.* (In this sentence the responsibility lies squarely with investor relations.)

Here is another example of the passive: *The quarterly earnings projections were missed.* The numbers were off, but the phrasing is vague about who's at fault. Compare that with *The software division missed its quarterly earnings projections.* (Here the software division is accountable.)

In a sentence about a study and its authors, a passive construction allows you to emphasize the study (the object), as in *A groundbreaking study on the treatment of migraines was written by researchers in Sweden.* Compare that with the active construction, which gives the authors top billing: *Researchers in Sweden wrote a groundbreaking study on the treatment of migraines.* Choose which construction to use depending on where you want to place your emphasis.

Take a stand

Sometimes you need to state a position. It is often best to do so with conviction. Strip out phrases that weaken your thought. Use language that conveys confidence: *I recommend we end the joint-venture talks immediately.* Compare that with *In my opinion, it would be worth considering whether or not we should contemplate putting an end to the joint-venture talks as soon as possible.* The preceding sentence is full of hedges.

Take out words that sound soft. *I believe we can correct this problem by Tuesday.* If it is something you really believe, write *We will correct this problem by Tuesday* or *I am confident we will correct this problem by Tuesday.* Note that in writing about the future, *will* is stronger than *can.*

Other words that weaken your position include *feel* and *think. We feel we need to issue a memo about the compensation study.* If you're committing it to writing, presumably it is what you feel, so it is better to write *We will issue a memo about the compensation study.*

Remember, *can* is more decisive than *could,* and *will* is more decisive than *would.*

Think about point of view

Be deliberate about your choice of *I, we* and *you* (pronouns). These words change your relationship to the reader, making a difference in tone as well as results. At the same time, maintaining a consistent point of view unifies and strengthens a communication.

A memo to the head of HR could read: *I will ask all employees to submit ideas for the new intranet.* This suggests it is your initiative. Alternatively you could write *We will ask all employees to submit ideas for the new intranet.* The *we* indicates that your group or division is asking. It is usually advisable to use *we* in business writing when more than one person is involved in a decision or initiative, which is generally the case.

We can also be used to speak on behalf of the organization. A letter to clients might read *We appreciate the opportunity to serve you.* This is friendlier than *The company appreciates the opportunity to serve you,* although you'll probably need to switch between the two in most communications of that sort.

Many business writers avoid writing *I* or *we,* but remember that these words can be effective when your identity and opinion count.

The use of *you* speaks directly to your readers: *We invite you to complete the attached questionnaire.* Compare that with *The company invites all employees to complete the attached questionnaire.* The *we/you* sentence is personal, direct and cordial. It pulls readers into the initiative.

When the facts have to speak for themselves, use the third person: *The company is accepting applications for the risk management department.* This is the voice of just the facts, please. It is also the preferred form in scientific, legal and academic writing, in which the writer remains transparent because objectivity takes precedence. But avoid taking the third person to the extreme. For example, *The writer believes* instead of *I* sounds awkward and potentially pretentious. The same is true for *one*. In business writing try to avoid sentences such as *One will benefit from buying the complete insurance package.* Instead write *You will benefit* or *Customers will benefit.* Whatever your choice of pronoun, select one that will dominate.

Keep a tight timeframe

Pay attention to the verb tense you use and try to be as consistent as possible throughout the communication. Avoid switching back and forth among past, present and future, even though you may need more than one tense to deal with time factors.

Unify your writing by tense to ensure clarity. For instance, the time sequence is confusing in the following two sentences: *The timetable was unrealistic. Quality assurance is at risk, and our schedule was already tight.* Compare that with the use of *is* throughout: *The timetable is unrealistic. Quality assurance is at risk, and our schedule is already tight.*

Confusing and inconsistent verb tenses make the reader work too hard, which is not what you want your communication to do. Whenever possible, write in the simple present or past tense, unless you are trying to convey a specific time sequence.

Also minimize use of the *-ing* form of verbs (called the perfect tense). It is more decisive and cleaner to write *The company plans to roll out the new product in March* than *The company is planning to roll out the new product in March.* Another example: *The CEO will discuss the fourth-quarter financials* *at the meeting* is stronger than *The CEO will be discussing the fourth-quarter financials at the meeting.*

Strengthen your professional brand

Your skills as a writer, now more than ever, are on display, so make sure everything you write cultivates an image of you that enhances your prospects and sends out a strong, cohesive message. Identify the activities at work that engage you fully and allow you to make a solid and unique contribution. Whatever makes you stand out at your company – makes you a go-to person – that's the capability you want to build on and leverage. Write a brief mission statement about your strengths and make that your personal brand at the workplace. Build a reputation around these skills and strengths.

Nowadays, you can express yourself in writing on many platforms – email, the intranet, forums, blogs, Facebook, LinkedIn, Twitter, to name a few. Examine everything you write on the job (and off) and ask yourself – before committing it to print – how it reflects on you. Make sure your contributions are always well written and productive, even if it means you have to do some self-censoring. Have a message and communicate with your audience by creating content that adds value.

Review everything

After you finalize a communication, spellcheck it; and if it's important, review it on hard copy for content and clarity. Allocate enough time for this part of the process and follow the advice of a communications specialist at Southern Company: Put yourself in the reader's place. If time permits, also ask a colleague to read it over for you.

Be sure your communication covers all your points and is clear. Check that it flows logically and has smooth transitions. Then review it again, looking for ways to cut it, to make it more concise. Take out words, phrases or paragraphs that are repetitive or add no value. Tighter language conveys focus and is more likely to be read attentively. A shorter communication also saves the reader time.

Go back and verify all the facts. Check to make sure that numbers and calculations are correct, quotes are exact and sources cited are accurate. If you're including a link, click it to make sure it will take the reader to the right site. Verify the spelling of all proper names, including people, organizations and places. Check that titles are correct. Also make sure names and titles are correct on distribution lists.

Next put your communication through a rigorous review for grammar, spelling, punctuation and style. Errors and inconsistencies are distractions that compromise your message and subtly undermine your credibility, "the written equivalent of a misbuttoned shirt," said Michael Sinsky, senior deputy prosecuting attorney for King County in the state of Washington. Once you've gone through the trouble of composing a well-written communication, don't undermine yourself with mistakes of this nature.

Finally, if you're sending an email, be sure the right person or persons are in the To and cc lines. If you're sending a letter or using a courier service, double-check addresses and phone numbers on the letter and on the envelope; if it's a fax, double-check fax numbers.

Make it look good

Don't underestimate the power of visual elements; review the communication for its look. Even if it's not on a conscious level, readers notice the overall design of a communication, and a busy or haphazard layout will discourage them from continuing.

Bold type is one way to make communications user-friendly, but don't overuse it; otherwise it loses its impact and communications start to look busy. Also be aware that when applied to more than a few words, bold renders text more difficult to read. Make sure the punctuation following bold type is in the same font.

Put headings and subheadings in bold to make them stand out. It reinforces the written break in the text with a visual differentiation. Also use bold to emphasize words in text that provide critical information, as in **January 12 is the deadline.** But, in general, minimize the use of bold within the body of your text. Try to convey the emphasis in your writing instead.

For bulleted information, it is sometimes effective to set off introductory words in bold to guide the reader. But don't go overboard and bold the entire thought; then you lose the emphasis and weaken the communication visually. See the following example:

The quality initiative will encourage a culture of learning, in which employees learn from:

- **Customers,** by actively seeking their feedback to understand their needs, issues and points of view.
- **Each other,** by sharing information across the entire company to build knowledge.
- **The marketplace,** by benchmarking against similar organizations and the competition and by adopting best practices.
- **The experts,** by attending seminars and by staying abreast of developments in the field.

Compare that with the following example, in which the whole point of bolding is lost:

The quality initiative will institute a culture of learning, in which employees learn from:

- **Customers, by actively seeking their feedback to understand their needs, issues and points of view.**
- **Each other, by sharing information across the entire company to build knowledge.**
- **The marketplace, by benchmarking against similar organizations and the competition and by adopting best practices.**
- **The experts, by attending training seminars and by staying abreast of developments in the field.**

A few more guidelines for fonts:

- Use italics when you want to differentiate text but with a less pronounced visual impact than bold. Italics are often a better choice within blocks of text, but remember that italics do not always transmit to portable devices.

- Don't use bold and italics together for more than a few words; it's difficult to read and redundant.

- Avoid underlining to emphasize text; it makes a communication look less polished, and many people find it difficult to read.

- Use different font sizes sparingly; otherwise your communication begins to look chaotic. For example, in long communications a larger type size can be useful to create title and section breaks. But, in general, keep the alternate type sizes fairly close in size to the rest of the text. It's excessive, for example, to create 36-point section headings for a communication written in 12-point type. A better choice for the heading would be 14-point type, which is clearly distinguishable without being overwhelming.

  If using different font sizes, be consistent. If a communication contains titles and you put the first title in 14-point type, make sure each subsequent title is also in 14-point type.

- Avoid mixing fonts within a communication. If you start out with Times New Roman, use it throughout. Don't switch to Bookman midstream.

Budget your time

Finally, give yourself enough time to put all the pieces together. Omitting the last page of your report is as serious as having incorrect numbers. To create accurate and professional communications, budget your time so that you can complete the task and be confident in its quality.

5

EMAIL:
BEFORE YOU HIT SEND

EMAIL REMAINS THE PRIMARY TOOL for business communication, despite the proliferation of other platforms such as texting, IMing and social networking. Among the Fortune 500 companies surveyed for the second edition of this book, email remains the most frequently used communications tool by far, with 87% of respondents saying they use it all the time (the remaining 13% use it frequently).

That said, a major shift has occurred in email usage over the past decade. Now, corporate email systems are integrated with mobile devices, so that business emails are sent, received and read on BlackBerrys, Android phones and iPhones, as well as tablets and laptops. This trend has impacted business email in several ways.

In addition, the ubiquity of smartphones, IM and texting has brought a more casual style of writing to the workplace. "Emails are looking and sounding more like text messages, and the overall tone in our retail division has become less formal," said Cynthia Hanson, senior copy editor, Franklin Templeton Investments.

So what's the bottom line for business email? The tone may be more flexible thanks to the new communication tools, but the basics of good writing remain unchanged. In deciding how to write an email, be guided by who's receiving it, what the culture is like at that person's organization, whether you're sending it to one individual or a group and what the correspondence is about. If a more casual style is suitable, use it. For formal business communications, make that your tone.

Always remember that any communication sent out under your name reflects on you – and you never know who else will see it. Here's how a Fortune 500 communication professional sums it up. "We must be accountable for our communication, regardless of the platform," said Marc Rice, Southern Company's corporate communication account executive – environment.

Review your message for content, clarity, grammar, spelling and tone. Then before hitting Send, see if you can shorten it because brevity is also a priority. Be sure you use email to its best advantage.

Write smartphone-friendly emails

The integration of portable devices with office email systems has led to some shifts in email conventions, while reinforcing the importance of good writing.

The widespread usage of smartphones makes it more important than ever to write concise, clear, accurate emails. Put yourself in the shoes of a recipient who is probably not at a desk and is in a rush, scrolling through your message on a small screen. Space has joined time as a consideration for communicating with busy people. Think carefully about what you are writing and make sure every word is necessary (just as you would if you were leaving a voicemail), especially when writing to senior executives or other critical constituents.

Readability is also key. How will an email sent from your computer appear on a smartphone? If you're writing to an executive who will read your message on a BlackBerry, a crisply written, easy-to-access email increases the odds that your entire message will be read and responded to, if that is your objective.

Say you are sending a draft memo to an executive, with the assumption that she will give it a quick initial review on a smartphone. Write a clear, concise subject line and a brief cover note and attach the memo. Then paste the full contents of the memo into the body of the email beneath your note and check the formatting to be sure it hasn't shifted. This smartphone-friendly email will allow the executive to see the content of your document without having to open your attachment, which is extremely helpful for someone on the go. It saves time and battery life and obviates the need to download documents, which may not even be accessible, depending on the person's location.

Later, the executive can open the document when she is back at a computer. "Reading your email on a wireless device is just to catch up," said Ida Lowe, an IT executive and project manager who has worked at international corporations and taught courses on email at the City University of New York. "Serious email-related work is done on the device that has the applications needed to read and review attachments."

Also be mindful of the emails you send from your portable device. Remember that even if you are dashing off a quick reply on your Android phone from a meeting, some recipients will probably read your message on their office computers. So any mistakes you make will be visible on a full-sized screen, which tends to magnify them. Have you ever received a short, sloppy email from someone on your desktop and wondered how he could have sent such a poorly written email? Then, you realize it was probably sent in a hurry from a smartphone, but the initial impression lingers. Admittedly, many wireless devices do not have the spell- and grammar checks that PCs have, so mistakes are more likely. That is why many people include a tagline in their wireless device signature stating that the message was sent from that device.

Still, no matter where you send it from or what disclaimers you use, that email ultimately reflects on you, so make it count. Don't get into the habit of falling back on the excuse that the error-laden message everyone received was sent from your iPhone at midnight. Smartphones don't give you license to write sloppy communications. Better to take the extra few minutes to be sure your messages are error-free.

Good writing is a habit. Initially, it may take some effort to transfer that habit to your mobile device, but it's worth it. Think about it as a reflection of your work and professionalism. Make it part of your professional brand.

Choose the right style

As with all business correspondence, the style you use in email depends on whom you're writing to and what you're communicating. If you're sending a message to the general counsel, make sure your grammar, spelling, punctuation and capitalization are in order. He may not notice that your email is well written, but he will surely notice if you make mistakes. If you're writing to a prospective client, also make it error-free and treat it as formal correspondence. It makes a good first impression.

If you're sending a message to a peer to request her input for a report you are writing, you can relax your approach. "Writing styles for internal, employee-to-employee communications have become less formal and structured," said Kathleen Vokes, director of corporate communications at Masco Corporation. Still, always be sure to observe the boundaries of what is appropriate in the workplace, and remember that you never know who else will see your email.

Also be guided by the emails you receive. If you're dealing with a client company in which everyone takes an informal approach, follow that lead. While conducting research for the first edition of "The Business Style Handbook," we sent Jeff Bezos, Amazon.com's CEO, an email to ask his preference for writing *Amazon* since it appears as both *amazon* and *Amazon* in the company's own materials. The response was a good indication of Amazon's corporate style. "Feel free to capitalize or to not capitalize our name. I've seen it done both ways as well. Since we're an internet company, we're not too caught up in convention and formal procedures," replied Ryan Kipple, who answered for Bezos.

In 2012, we wrote again to Bezos. Here is the reply. "Hi Helen and Brenda – Jeff forwarded me your email. The approach that Ryan outlines below still works today. Thanks for checking." It came from Craig Berman, Amazon's vice president, global communications.

The messages from both Berman and Kipple suggest a relaxed style, and mirroring it could actually advance your cause with companies that have an informal style. But remember that relaxed doesn't mean grammatical and spelling mistakes are all right. It's more about tone. (Note that the emails from Amazon were informal but also error-free.)

If, on the other hand, you are dealing with a company where tradition and a buttoned-down style prevail, conduct your correspondence with an eye toward the "convention and formal procedures" that Amazon shrugs off.

And, as always in business, no matter who the recipient is, it's a good idea to spellcheck and proofread emails before sending them.

Be cautious with content

To state the obvious, there is no such thing as privacy in email.

Always remember that your emails can be forwarded to anyone and everyone. All it takes is a few keystrokes for an email to go viral. For some reason, this immutable fact is overlooked time and again in the business world, even though it has caused resignations and embarrassment right up to the level of CEOs and top government officials. How would you feel if an email you wrote to one person ends up being parsed by your entire company or circulated out there in the global blogosphere? If this thought makes you uncomfortable, do you really want to send it?

Exercise judgment with every email you send. Always err on the side of caution regarding content. Don't put anything into an email that could offend others, embarrass you or come back to haunt you. Refrain from using your office system to send nonbusiness files, to forward chain emails or to push political, social, fundraising or other causes.

Be aware that every time you send and receive emails, copies are made on servers, where they can be retrieved by someone at your company or a hacker. Many organizations monitor email and have policies clearly stating that all email sent through the office system is the property of the company. You risk being fired for using the system to send or forward messages that are sexist, racist, pornographic, homophobic or otherwise inappropriate. And remember that lawyers regularly subpoena email for court cases.

"You must be very clear that every time you use office email, you are representing the corporation," said Lowe. "The content is owned by the company; they can read it and they are liable for it."

In general, corporations delete emails from their systems within a set period of time, such as 120 days, after which they cannot be retrieved, according to Lowe. "However, some companies retain email longer for legal, regulatory or contractual obligations," she added. So be sure to become acquainted with the policy at your company. For example, under the Sarbanes-Oxley Act of 2002, publicly traded U.S. companies must retain certain records, including email, for seven years.

So protect your reputation, and use email as an opportunity to enhance it rather than jeopardize it.

Other reasons for caution with email include:

- **You don't control distribution.** Once you hit Send, you never know who will end up receiving your message – inside and outside the organization. An email you write to human resources about a personnel problem in your department could end up being forwarded FYI to your boss. A confidential email you forward to an acquaintance about an internal investigation could end up making the rounds and being forwarded to a reporter, landing your company in the news – and it wouldn't take your information security office long to track the email trail back to you. Always remember that the Forward function makes it incredibly easy to disseminate information quickly, widely and indiscriminately.
- **All or part of your message can be forwarded.** Emails can be revised and then forwarded. Words taken out of context can be misconstrued.
- **You can inadvertently send messages to the wrong person.** If your company has two people named Price, for example, they probably get email for each other on a regular basis. Also, if you're replying to an email message, you could inadvertently reply to everyone on the cc distribution, when you intended to respond only to the original sender.
- **With the bcc feature, you never know who's included in correspondence.**

- **Many organizations monitor email.** This includes both business and personal messages, incoming and outgoing. In fact, many companies use programs that automatically read your email to ensure laws and regulations are not broken, according to Lowe, who added that the programs will also pick up private information like Social Security numbers. So always remember that someone in your organization may be reading your correspondence.

When to use email, and when not to

Email is used for virtually every type of communication in the workplace. Today, short communications, such as memos, minutes of a meeting and action items, are sent as email messages rather than attached documents. What's more, using links to send information in emails has become a standard business practice.

"Sending links instead of actual documents is highly recommended for managing email and particularly email storage," said Lowe. "Usually the document is stored in a limited-access SharePoint site, which provides additional protection from non-authorized readers." Links also save space by limiting the size of the messages.

Documents, photographs, pdfs, videos can also be sent through email. Anyone who prefers hard copies of emailable files will print them from the email. In addition to being extremely efficient, email has the advantage of creating a record for all parties. You can track when you sent a file, and the recipient can track when it was received (as can your auditing and legal departments).

Email is essential, without a doubt. But keep in mind another fact of business life. "Email is being overused," said Lowe. "We are all getting way too much email."

As convenient as it is, email is not always the best option for communicating on the job. "Too many people are using email for problem-solving, troubleshooting and conversations," said Lowe. "A long-winded email chain with dozens of recipients asking and answering questions is neither efficient nor effective," she said. "Sometimes to solve a problem you need a conference call – get on the phone, it is still the fastest way to resolve issues and problems quickly."

At the other end of the spectrum, if you just need a quick piece of information or want to see if someone is available for a phone call, IM is a better way to go for internal communication, in Lowe's assessment. "It's more informal; just remember that the same corporate rules apply to IM as to email."

Finally, remember that email may not be the best option for writing a condolence message. A personal note generally remains more appropriate.

Use cc, bcc and Reply to All appropriately

The cc function is useful. It allows people other than the primary recipient to see an email and/or links, and it allows everyone on the routing to know who else received it. It is also overused.

Blind copying (bcc) allows the sender to share information with the bcc recipient, unbeknown to the other people on the routing.

Bcc is useful for preventing unwanted Reply to All responses. "The bcc should be used every time you send a widely distributed message for which you do not want responses to go to everyone in the thread," said Lowe. "And most people will know bcc is being used because there are no recipients in the To field."

Another use of bcc is to send a distribution in which everyone gets a blind copy in order to protect the privacy of individuals and their email addresses.

As a sender, remember that the bcc is exclusionary and, if detected, it can alienate some people. For example, if the person you bcc'd hits Reply to All, then everyone will know you used bcc, which might not reflect well on you. As a recipient, remember that with bcc you can never be sure who else received an email.

The cc/bcc functions have led to a great deal of unnecessary email traffic, clogging people's inboxes as well as corporate email systems. Each situation and work environment differs, but, in general, don't copy bosses on all emails. It's better to obtain an understanding of what they want to be copied on than to err through overinclusion.

Here's a concise piece of advice from IT executive Lowe: "Stop cc'ing everyone on email; include only those necessary." Moreover, if a message or an attachment is really important for someone to see, send it directly rather than via a cc.

The overuse of Reply to All is also problematic. "It generates hundreds of unnecessary emails that no one wants to receive," Lowe said. Particularly annoying is the gratuitous Reply to All thanks. "A thank you sent to hundreds of people is overkill," she said. "It may be appropriate in a verbal conversation, but the office email is not intended for conversational exchanges."

Use Reply to All sparingly. Just because the sender copied 25 people on an email doesn't mean the same 25 people need to see your reply. In some cases they will, but think it through before you automatically hit Reply to All.

Likewise, refrain from sending Reply to Sender emails that merely say thank you or OK, even though you would normally make such a comment verbally. You will save busy people the trouble – perhaps annoyance – of opening another email. (If you are concerned that an individual might find the absence of a thank you to be brusque, then send it, but limit your message to that person.)

Make it easy on your reader

Make your email easy to read and file.

- **Use the Subject line.** Tell recipients what your email is about in the Subject line. Keep it informative, clear and concise. If the content is urgent or sensitive, say so in the Subject line. Capital letters are an option. *URGENT: Washington Post media inquiry* or *ACTION*

REQUIRED: Washington Post media inquiry or *CONFIDENTIAL: draft memo on new chairman.* (It's one of the few times that all caps are OK in email.)

A concise, clearly written Subject line makes it easier for the person on the other end to prioritize, find the email quickly and save it to a folder, if necessary.

If you're forwarding an email and the existing Subject line is unclear or no longer appropriate, then write a new Subject line for your recipient.

- **Think about the To line.** Put people who need to know the content of your email, and anyone you want to respond, in the To line.

- **Think about the cc line.** Put people who need to know the content of your email, but don't need to respond, in the cc line. Refrain from overusing cc.

- **Think about the bcc line.** Use bcc for preventing unwanted Reply to All responses on widely distributed messages. Most recipients will know bcc is being used when they see the To line has no recipients.

- **Keep it short.** Brevity is a priority.

- **Make it readable.** Use bullets if that will help. Break paragraphs with a line of space. Avoid long messages, especially if they will be read on mobile devices.

- **Put important information in bold.** It takes a bit longer to add bold, but if it will make your message easier to read and understand, it's worth the effort.

- **Be careful with pasting.** If you are pasting content into email from a document or website, remember that the formatting from the original content may not carry through to email. After you paste anything, scroll through the entire email to check for formatting and readability before you send it.

- **Avoid attachments when possible.** For short messages, place the text directly into your email. This is faster and easier for the reader than opening an attachment after opening your email. For example, if you are sending a three-sentence notice to employees that the office will close early Friday, just write it in the body of your email.

- **Include/check links.** Use links to supplement your message, give recipients easy access to any material you reference and protect the security of documents. Always click them after pasting to be sure they will take the reader to the right place.
- **Attach formatted documents.** If links are not an option, use attachments when material is specially formatted because otherwise formatting may be lost or garbled. This includes tables, charts, graphs, etc.
- **Label attachments.** If you're sending attachments, label them clearly, particularly if you're attaching more than one file per email. This will enable the recipient to distinguish among the files.
- **Manage replies that include previous messages.** Don't automatically send back an entire message with your reply. Do so only if it's necessary for your answer to be understood clearly, if you want to keep an email trail, if you are adding new parties to the routing or if you want to respond to specific points without rewriting those points yourself.
- **Clean up messages before forwarding.** If you're forwarding a message or string of messages, delete any miscellaneous material that your recipient doesn't need to see. This makes your message cleaner and easier to read.
- **Use abbreviations judiciously.** Be sure readers will recognize any abbreviations you use. In many organizations this will reflect the corporate culture. Some standard business abbreviations include *FYI, ASAP, cob (close of business)*. Abbreviations that are typical in IM and texting (like *BTW, LOL*) are informal, so use them sparingly in email.
- **Use emoticons sparingly.** These symbols, such as ;-), which means wink, or :-o, which means shocked, are informal and best reserved for one-to-one messages. They are often used in a friendly manner to clarify an intention or soften a statement when something was misstated or misunderstood.
- **Use the Out of Office notification.** Notify people who send you email that you are out of the office, and include in the notification the date you'll return. If necessary, specify the person to contact in your absence, including a full name, email address and/or telephone number.

Be formal in formal email

If you are using email for formal correspondence, both within and outside your organization, apply the same standards you would to memos, reports, publications, marketing materials, press releases or web content. Remember that your email may be printed on the other end.

If your formal correspondence is in an attachment or link, reference the attachment/link in your message, using the same greeting, closing and degree of formality you use in the attachment/link. See the following example:

Dear Mr. Kelleher:

Attached please find a letter outlining the pricing information you requested. I look forward to hearing from you.

Sincerely,

Dinesh Agarwal
Director of Internet Business Solutions
Telephone: 415.000.0000

Be appropriate with greetings

Err on the side of formality if you're uncertain. The greeting will depend on how well you know the person and the situation.

For external correspondence, use *Dear Mr. Kazmi:* or *Dear Ms. Kalil:* (which is always safe). Avoid *Mr. Kazmi:* (without the *Dear*); it's a bit abrupt. If you're on a first-name basis, either *Dear Bassam:* or *Bassam:* is appropriate. Note that business correspondence generally takes a colon (:) rather than a comma after the name, although the use of a comma (,) is increasingly common. This stylebook suggests the colon; whichever you choose, use it consistently.

In general, avoid the *Hi Bassam* or *Hello Bassam* greeting in business unless you have a personal relationship with the recipient. It conveys a level of informality that some people may consider overly familiar.

Avoid starting business emails without a greeting, even though the recipient's name is in the To line; it could be construed as impolite. If you don't know the recipient's name, go with a time-tested letter greeting, such as *To Whom It May Concern:*.

For correspondence within an organization, drop the *Dear* and just write the person's first name or *Mr./Ms.* with the last name, followed by a colon. If the corporate culture has different norms, follow them.

Sign off

Even though email systems include the sender's name, sign off with your name in business correspondence. Also include a closing, which should mirror your greeting in tone. Formal closings include *Sincerely, Yours truly, Best regards, Best, Regards, Cordially*.

Be sure your sign-off gives recipients the information they need about you. The fastest and easiest way to convey this information is to create an email signature that includes the name of your organization and a link to its website, along with your full name, title, email address and telephone number (and regular address if necessary). Many companies have a template for signatures that you must follow. If you use an automated signature, don't repeat your name by also typing it at the end of your message. (Nowadays most large organizations include legal disclaimer language at the end of emails, adding to their length.)

For correspondence within organizations, closings are optional and can be informal, as in *Feel free to contact me with questions, Thanks, Talk to you later*. If you don't use the signature feature, include your name at the end. Just write your first name or your initials (first and last).

Avoid ending emails and other business correspondence with a *PS*. It's preferable just to include that thought in the email.

Be smart about email

Treat email as an opportunity to put your best foot forward. Your boss could forward your memo to a senior executive, giving you unexpected visibility. A client in one division of a company could forward your email to a different division that is considering hiring you for a project. Your note of thanks to a colleague, copied to her boss, could end up with the head of human resources, saying as much about you as it does about the colleague.

Here's the view of one Fortune 500 executive. "The trend toward communicating through smartphones, social media, etc. has led to more casual, less formal communications in general," said Scot Roskelley, Aetna's communications director, mid-America region. "Nonetheless, we apply the same standards for this type of writing as to print communications."

Take these extra steps to be sure your correspondence works for and not against you:

- **Spellcheck.** Use spellcheck, but remember you can't rely on it to catch all errors. For example, if you typed *you* instead of *your,* the spellcheck will miss it because both are words.
- **Proof it.** If the email is sufficiently important, in addition to spellchecking it, take the time to proof it carefully – printing it out if necessary.
- **Avoid emotional emails.** The speed of email can sometimes backfire on you. Messages written in anger and haste often convey a harsh tone that is rarely well received and can exacerbate a tense situation. When time permits, draft difficult emails and review them again several hours later or the next day.
- **Don't shout.** Writing in all capitals is considered shouting in email.
- **Use receipt notification judiciously.** Email systems can notify you when your email has been successfully sent and opened. These tools are useful, especially when you're waiting for replies. Just remember that depending on recipients' preference settings, they may be getting an email every time you ask for notification.
- **Respond promptly.** As with all business communication, respond as quickly as possible, especially when senders indicate they are on a deadline. And remember, if someone requests information from you via email, he or she has a record of when the request was made. If the request will take some time, then respond immediately to acknowledge it and specify when you will get back to the person.

- **Refrain from using the exclamation point in formal business communications.** It can add a friendly touch to an email to a peer, but it is probably not appropriate for someone who is senior to you. Save the exclamations for peers, friends and family.

THE A-TO-Z ENTRIES

H.L. Mencken said, "A living language is like a man suffering incessantly from small hemorrhages, and what it needs above all else is constant transactions of new blood from other tongues. The day the gates go up, that day it begins to die."

Many entries in "The Business Style Handbook" reflect the "new blood" in the language of business. Our intent is to promote consistency and clarity in all written materials while taking into account how language is used in the workplace. In addition, while some writing conventions are inflexible, many of the choices made in this book are a matter of preference. "The Business Style Handbook" strives to make distinctions between the hard-and-fast rules and these individual preferences.

The following key defines terminology and also spells out the thinking that informs many of the style choices in "The Business Style Handbook."

- **First reference:** When a term is introduced for the first time in text, it is called a *first reference.* The usual practice in a first reference is to write the complete name (with an explanation if necessary). Then in the subsequent references, the shortened form or abbreviation is sufficient. For example: *The Federal Reserve Board lowered interest rates. The Fed meets again in two weeks.*

- **The language of grammar:** In general, "The Business Style Handbook" avoids grammatical terms that may be unfamiliar to nonprofessional writers.

- **Books:** Put *book titles* in quotation marks, not in italic font, as in "The Business Style Handbook," "First Break All the Rules," "Good to Great," "America's Girl." The italic font does not transmit well via new technologies. The same guideline applies to movies and television shows.

- **Examples:** In the entries, examples are in italics to differentiate them from the explanations (not because the words should be in italics).

- **Keystroke guideline:** In our high-speed world, the fewer keystrokes it takes to form a word, the better. "The Business Style Handbook" adopts this approach whenever possible as long as it does not jeopardize comprehension. We also advocate what "The Chicago Manual of Style" calls "down style." Use capital letters sparingly and lowercase terms whenever possible: *website, french fries, the cloud, marketing department, chairman.*

  We have minimized punctuation so that abbreviations without periods are preferred, though there will always be exceptions. Writing *FYI* (for *for your information), IPO* (for *initial public offering)* or *OK* (for *okay)* without periods is not confusing. But *cod* (for *c.o.d.)* and *am* (for *a.m.)* may not work as well, so in these and some other instances, this book recommends using periods.

- **Consistency:** In business writing, consistency is a priority. Writing *website* three different ways in a single communication makes it look unprofessional. It's not that one version is right and the other is wrong; it's a question of consistency. "The Business Style Handbook" suggests *website.*

- **Capitalization:** The instruction to capitalize a word or phrase means to capitalize just the first letter of the word or main words, not the entire word or all words.

- **Numbers:** Entries that begin with numbers, such as *24/7* or *360-degree review,* are listed before letter entries, so that both *24/7* and *360-degree review* appear at the beginning of the T section.

- **Alphabetization:** Alphanumeric entries and abbreviations with figures come after entries that are all numbers, so that *3D* comes after *24/7*. Alphanumeric entries, such as *401(k)*, *3D*, *50–50*, come before words that are all letters. They are alphabetized as though the numbers were spelled out: *401(k)* (four), *3D* (three), *50–50* (fifty).

  Phrases formed from two or more words are alphabetized as though they were a single word, so that *today* comes before *to-do; serviceable* comes before *service mark; minuscule* comes before *minus sign; question mark* comes before *questionnaire; real-time* comes after *really; y-axis* comes after *yard.* This applies for phrases with and without hyphens.

  Entries that are acronyms or abbreviations are alphabetized by the letters in the abbreviated form, so that *FYI* is alphabetized using *Y* as the second letter. This means *FYI* appears after the entry *FY* rather than after the entry *forward.*

- **Newspapers/Periodicals:** When mentioning newspapers or periodicals in text, do not capitalize the *the,* even if it is part of the official newspaper name, such as *Myra read* the *New York Times article to her sister* or *Have you seen the piece about shortages in* the *Atlantic Monthly?* (This stylebook favors dropping italics and quotation marks for newspapers and periodicals; italics are used here only to illustrate examples.)

- **Formal versus informal:** Audience determines whether the writing is formal or informal. Formal writing is expected in an annual report; informal writing is the norm for emails among colleagues.

- **Accents:** "The Business Style Handbook" has changed its stance from the first edition on accents because they create problems in transmission, so write *resume,* not *résumé.* While most word processing programs have symbol inserts for diacritical marks, such as the acute accent (*é*), grave accent (*è*), umlaut (*ü*), circumflex (*ê*), tilde (*ã*), cedilla (*ç*), these marks often end up garbled on the recipient's end. We have also removed accents from foreign phrases for the same reason.

- **Nonstandard usage:** Because this stylebook focuses on business writing, we favor the use of some words and phrases that may be considered nonstandard (such as *trolling* as a verb) because of their obvious usefulness. Strict grammarians may disagree.

- **Ephemeral words:** Most of the entries cover style issues that have plagued writers for a long time; however, we may have included some ephemeral words (words that will never make it into the dictionary because they will be superseded by other words). Language is dynamic, but it still is helpful to know how to deal with ephemeral words (such as *value-add*) during their life span.

The rest of the material in the entries should need no further explanation. Language is inherently logical. As long as you strive for consistency, value brevity and aim for clarity, most sentences will fall neatly into place. "The Business Style Handbook" is a tool to help you achieve these goals.

· A ·

a, an Use *a* before consonant sounds: *a briefcase, a historic day* (unlike British English, American English pronounces the *h* in *historic), a letter, a one-time deal* (the *o* sounds like *w), a United Way campaign* (the *u* sounds like *y). Use *an* before vowel sounds: *an even match, an hour, an NYU graduate* (the *n* sounds like *en), an MRI* (the *M* sounds like *em).

abbreviations Use abbreviations only if they will not confuse your readers. Always keep your audience in mind when writing. Also remember that a communication top-heavy in abbreviations may cause drowsiness. Abbreviations are acceptable in tabular material.

- To check if a company uses abbreviations in its full name, visit the company's website, check its marketing or other branded materials (such as advertising, business cards) or use "Standard & Poor's Register of Corporations, Directors and Executives." Hoover's Online is another reliable source (www.hoovers.com). According to communications executives at the Fortune 500, a particular company's style (in punctuation, abbreviations) should be followed. Use the full name of the company in an address. Also use the full name in the first reference to the company in a communication, as in *I recommend we buy the*

63

products from Intel Corporation. Intel has the best technology for our needs.
Always check the spelling, capitalization, punctuation and abbreviations
in company names. See **company names** entry.

- Abbreviate the following titles when used before a full name: *Mr., Ms.,*
  Mrs., Dr.
- For medical doctors, write *Dr. Heidi Waldorf* or *Heidi Waldorf, M.D.*
  (with a comma). Do not write *Dr. Heidi Waldorf, M.D.*
- For dentists, write *Dr. Nancy Coughlin* or *Nancy Coughlin, D.D.S.* (with
  a comma). Do not write *Dr. Nancy Coughlin, D.D.S.*
- For nonmedical doctors, write *Raymond Murray, Ph.D.* (with a comma)
  or *Dr. Raymond Murray.* Do not write *Dr. Raymond Murray, Ph.D.*
- For the esquire title used by lawyers, write *Clara Marshall, Esq.* (with a
  comma). Do not write *Ms. Clara Marshall, Esq.*
- Abbreviate and capitalize *junior* or *senior* after an individual's name:
  Michael Brown, Jr. (with a comma).
- For the abbreviations of states, use standard state abbreviations in text as
  long as the town or city is included: *We will be going to Ponte Vedra, Fla.,*
  to see John about the contract. Do not abbreviate state names when they
  stand alone in text: *John lives in Florida.* Use the two-letter Postal Service
  abbreviations with full addresses, including ZIP codes. For a list of the
  state abbreviations, see **state abbreviations** entry.
- Do not abbreviate (or capitalize) job descriptions (which are different
  from titles), even if they precede the name, as in *technologist Robin*
  Smith.
- Use abbreviations in tabular material, slide shows and bibliographies.
- Do not abbreviate the days of the week, unless they appear in tabular
  material or slide shows. See **days of the week** entry.
- For months, abbreviate *Jan., Feb., Mar., Apr., Aug., Sept., Oct., Nov.,*
  Dec. in text as long as they are followed by numerals: *Dec. 27, Jan. 29,*
  Sept. 7. Do not abbreviate *May, June* or *July,* even if followed by a figure:
  July 12. Always spell out the month if it appears alone or with just the
  year: *December, October 1984* (no comma is needed between the month
  and the year).

- With the word *number*, abbreviate to *No.* (a capital *N*) only with figures: *Mr. Friedman will stay in room No. 23. The company is Spain's No. 1 internet service provider.*
- When lowercased phrases are abbreviated, such as *a.k.a.*, which stands for *also known as*, use periods if the abbreviation would look like an error or create confusion (for instance, *a.m.* could be mistaken for the word *am*).
- In text, spell out *Avenue, Boulevard, Street* when figures are not present: *Corporate offices are on Maple Avenue.* Use the abbreviated form when the number is present in the address: *Corporate offices are at 1200 Maple Ave.* (No comma is used in the number *1200* because it is an address.) Style has changed for the plural construction, as in *The office is between Maple and Elm Avenues,* so it is no longer necessary to lowercase *Avenues.*
- For compass points, abbreviate and capitalize when they appear after street names, as in *The doctor's office is at 100 Boyer Ave. E.* Spell out and capitalize when they come before street names: *The doctor's office is at 100 East Boyer Ave.*
- When using abbreviations, replace *and* with *&*, so that *research and development* becomes *R&D*, *profit and loss* becomes *P&L*. (Do not use an ampersand in place of the word *and* in text. Write *Tim and Edward will handle the request,* not *Tim & Edward will handle the request.*)

ABCs No apostrophe needed.

about, approximately Use *about* instead of *approximately*, unless the writing is scientific.

above Avoid using the word *above* to refer to preceding material, except where it is certain the reference will appear on the same page: *The prices above are in effect until Dec. 31.* (The same guideline applies to the word *below*.) Usually the word *previously* or *following* can be substituted, respectively, for *above* or *below*.

academic degrees When referring to credentials in text, write *Julia has a master's in science,* not *Julia has an M.S.* For resumes, when listing credentials, either spell out the degree and capitalize, *Bachelor of Arts, Master of Science, Master of Business Administration,* or use the abbreviations, *B.A., M.S, M.B.A.* When an abbreviated credential is used after a full name, such as *Isabel Smith, Ph.D., joined the company in June,* put commas before and after it.

academic designations Do not capitalize *freshman, sophomore, junior* or *senior.* Also lowercase *alma mater.*

accents Do not use accents, as in *His resume is posted on LinkedIn* (not *résumé*). Accent marks do not transmit well.

accept, except Because these words sound alike and are near-homonyms, they are occasionally misused, but there's a big difference in meaning, so double-check if you are unsure.

access Using *access* as a verb is standard in business writing. *You can access the white paper from the company's website.*

accommodate Often misspelled. Remember two *c*'s and two *m*'s.

accounting, bookkeeping There is a difference between these two terms. *Accounting* requires judgment when recording debits and credits – and in the preparation of statements concerning the assets, liabilities and operating results of a business. *Bookkeeping* is the uncritical recording of the accounts and transactions of a business.

Achilles' heel Write with an apostrophe because it is a possessive. Note that for the possessive, classical names often follow a different form from other names, so it is not written *Achilles's heel.* An *Achilles' heel* is a seemingly insignificant weakness that can lead to a downfall.

acknowledgment This is the preferred spelling (not *acknowledgement*).

acronym An *acronym* is a word formed from the first letter or letters of a series of words. Acronyms are pronounced as single words, as in *NASA, NATO, NOW.* If the acronym is longer than four letters, capitalize the first letter and lowercase the remaining letters, as in *Nasdaq, Unctad.* Follow a company's style. Most acronyms do not require periods. When acronyms cross over and become generic terms, lowercase them, as in *radar, captcha, modem, abend (abnormal end of task).* If you are unsure about an organization's name, go to the website.

Initialisms do not form words and are pronounced by letter, as in *IRS* (for *Internal Revenue Service* and pronounced *I-R-S)* or *CBOE* (for *Chicago Board Options Exchange* and pronounced *C-B-O-E).* Most initialisms are capitalized without periods, as in *UPS.*

To write acronyms or initialisms, follow this guideline: Spell out the entire phrase in the first reference; use just the acronym/initialism afterward. *John Andrews is employed by the Brotherhood of Locomotive Engineers and Trainmen. He works at BLET headquarters in Cleveland.* If an acronym or initialism is widely recognizable, however, it's not necessary to spell out in first reference, as in *Nasdaq.*

active voice Write in the active voice whenever possible rather than the passive voice. In the active voice, the subject acts. *The sales manager corrected the account executive.* In the passive voice, the action is done to the subject, as in *The account executive was corrected by the sales manager.* The emphasis changes. The active voice is stronger and more direct.

While the active voice is preferred in most business writing, there are instances where the passive voice is necessary. See Chapter 4 for more information on active and passive voice.

AD, BC *AD* stands for *anno Domini:* in the year of our Lord. *BC* indicates a calendar year *before Christ.* Use abbreviations in all references. The year goes after *AD,* as in *AD 76.* Do not write *the second century AD.* It is redundant. The *second century* is sufficient. For *BC,* the year goes before: *1445 BC.*

addresses Follow these guidelines:

- In text, spell out *Avenue, Boulevard, Street* when figures are not present: *Corporate offices are on Maple Avenue.* Use the abbreviated form when the number is present in the address: *Corporate offices are at 1200 Maple Ave.* (No comma is used in the number *1200* because it is an address.) Style has changed for the plural construction, as in *The offices are between Maple and Elm Avenues,* so it is no longer necessary to lowercase *Avenues.*

- When compass points are in an address, abbreviate and capitalize when they appear after street names, as in *The CEO's office is at 100 Boyer Ave. E.* Spell out and capitalize when they come before street names: *The CEO's office is at 100 East Boyer Ave.*

- Use the two-letter Postal Service abbreviations (e.g., *CO, TX)* for states with full addresses, including ZIP code. No comma is needed between the state abbreviation and the ZIP code. The Postal Service requests that the two-letter state abbreviations be used on all mail. Note that the four-digit add-on ZIP codes take a hyphen, as in *80452-2511.* When writing a letter, the inside address should duplicate the address on the envelope. See **state abbreviations** entry.

- For state names in text, use the standard state abbreviations instead of the two-letter state abbreviations (e.g., *Calif.* instead of *CA)* when the name of a city is included. If the state name stands alone, spell it out. See **state abbreviations** entry.

ad hoc Italics are not needed for this familiar Latin phrase, which means for a specific purpose or situation at hand. *The ad hoc committee disbanded when the project ended.*

adjective It is a word that describes or limits (modifies) the meaning of a noun or pronoun: *strategic plan, demanding boss.* When two or more words before a noun act together to form an adjective (called a compound modifier), the words are usually hyphenated, as in *two-year plan, full-time job, low-hanging* *fruit, billion-dollar-a-year software maker, cubicle-to-office ratio, 2-for-1 stock split*. See **hyphen** entry.

adverb It is a word that describes or limits a verb, an adjective or another adverb. It answers the question where, how or how much, or when: *walk slowly, very short, do it now, run up*. Do not hyphenate phrases containing adverbs when they precede a noun, as in *fully vested employee, completely renovated office, highly complex contract*. See **hyphen** entry.

adverb placement The stylebook of the New York Times states: "In fluid writing, an adverb used with a compound verb should normally be placed between parts of the verb: *He will usually take the opposing side*. A similar rule applies when a verb, such as *is*, links a noun to its modifier: *Refundable fares are often expensive* (not *often are expensive*)."

adviser This is the preferred spelling (not *advisor*, the British spelling).

affect, effect *Affect* as a verb means to influence: *How will interest rates affect the economy?* Usually *affect* is a verb. *Affect* as a noun refers to various psychological states and the corresponding emotional responses (such as interest-excitement, enjoyment-joy, surprise-startle, fear-terror, distress-anguish, anger-rage). Most business writers will not have many opportunities to use *affect* as a noun.

Effect as a noun means result: *The delay had a negative effect on the production schedule*. Usually *effect* is a noun. *Effect* as a verb means to cause or bring about a specific result: *The new head of finance will effect major change in that department*.

African-American Use a hyphen and capitalize both *A*'s. The term *African-American* is preferred to *black* in business writing.

after- Most *after-* words are one word, as in *aftertax, afterhours, aftershock, aftermath, afterthought*.

after all Write as two words.

afterward This form is preferable to *afterwards.*

Age Capitalize an age with specific time periods: *Stone Age, Jazz Age, Bronze Age, Age of Reason, Gilded Age, Dark Ages.* When the time period does not have a fixed time, lowercase *age: space age, digital age, nuclear age.*

age Always express with figures: *The 21-year-old student did not participate in the internship. The exchange delisted the 1-year-old company's stock.* Note that the rule to spell out numbers under 10 does not apply to age. See **numbers** entry.

agreement A common mistake in writing is a mishap in subject/verb/pronoun agreement. The best way to avoid this is to identify the subject of the sentence; then check the verb and pronouns to make sure they agree. If the subject is singular, it must take a singular verb and singular pronouns; if the subject is plural, it must take a plural verb and plural pronouns. *The two departments, which* have *a healthy rivalry, were comparing* their *sales figures for August. The department, which* is *responsible for sales, was reviewing* its *figures for August.* Agreement can get tricky when a phrase comes between the subject and verb. In these instances, the subject agrees with the verb (not the nouns or pronouns of the phrase), as in *One of the supervisors, as well as his employees,* is *attending the company picnic* or *Neither of the two copy machines* is *working.*

With fractions, percentages, amounts and distances, use a singular verb, as in *Three hundred orders* is *the average monthly quota* or *It's a fact that 1 in 10 Americans* takes *antidepressants.* If fractions, percentages, amounts and distances are followed by an *of* phrase, the verb agrees with the noun closest to the verb. *A quarter of the books* were *water damaged by Hurricane Irene* or *Almost 10% of the workers* are *unemployed.*

Remember that collective nouns take a singular verb and pronoun, even though they refer to more than one person or thing.

CORRECT: *A flood at the company shut down **its** business for a day.*

INCORRECT: *A flood at the company shut down **their** business for a day.*

CORRECT: *Members of the sales team meet each Friday to discuss **their** progress.* (The subject is *members*, not *team.*)

CORRECT: *The sales team meets each Friday to discuss **its** progress.* (The subject is *team.*)

aid, aide Often confused. The first, as a verb, means to give assistance. *Aid* is also a noun, meaning assistance or a person who assists. An *aide*, according to "Merriam-Webster's Collegiate Dictionary," is "a person who acts as an assistant; specifically: a military officer who acts as an assistant to a superior officer." Do not use *aide* as a verb.

a.k.a. Use *a.k.a.* with periods in all references. It stands for *also known as.*

Alaska Do not abbreviate in text, but use *AK* with full addresses, including ZIP code. *AK* is the two-letter Postal Service abbreviation. Seven other states are not abbreviated in text: *Hawaii, Idaho, Iowa, Maine, Ohio, Texas, Utah.* See **state abbreviations** entry.

all ready, already *All ready* means everybody and everything ready: *They were all ready to board the plane. Already* means previously: *They have already arrived at the convention.*

all right Two words (not *alright*).

all-time Use a hyphen, as in *The U.S. dollar hit an all-time high against the yen.*

all together, altogether *All together* means everybody and/or everything together, a group. *The administrative assistants sat all together at the luncheon. Altogether* means completely or utterly: *She gave up the project altogether. Altogether* also means all told or all counted: *Altogether 12 people attended the meeting.*

a lot The only acceptable form for *a lot* is two words (not *alot).*

alpha Lowercase *alpha* in this construction: *The company is alpha-testing the new customer-relationship software.* Software often goes through two stages of release testing: *alpha* (in-house) and *beta* (outgoing).

alphabetization Follow these guidelines:

- For phrases formed from two or more words, alphabetize as though they were a single word, so that *today* comes before *to-do; serviceable* comes before *service mark; minuscule* comes before *minus sign; question mark* comes before *questionnaire; real-time* comes after *really; y-axis* comes after *yard.* Note that this applies for phrases with and without hyphens.
- When alphabetizing words beginning with *Mac/Mc,* do so as though all letters were lowercased: *MacDougal, Mackey, McDonald.*
- If alphabetizing by last names, put *Jr., Sr.* or a Roman numeral (e.g., *III)* last, as in *Bond, Michael, Jr.* (not *Bond, Jr., Michael).*
- When alphabetizing Spanish last names in which both the mother and father's family names are used, such as *Pablo Beltran Gabarra* (*Beltran* is the father's name and *Gabarra* is the mother's name), always put the father's surname first, as in *Beltran Gabarra, Pablo* (not *Gabarra, Pablo Beltran).*
- Alphabetize acronyms or abbreviations by the letters in the abbreviated form, so that *FYI* is alphabetized using *Y* as the second letter rather than alphabetizing it where *for your information* would go.
- For numbers that form words or phrases, such as *20/20* and *24/7,* alphabetize before letter entries, so that both *20/20* and *24/7* appear before all *T* words. When a slash is used, alphabetize as though the number before the slash were spelled out, so that *20/20* (twenty) comes before *24/7* (twenty-four).
- For alphanumeric words or abbreviations with figures, such as *401(k), 360-degree review, 3D,* alphabetize after numbers and before words that are all letters. Alphabetize as though the numbers were spelled out: *401(k)* (four), *3D* (three).

- For titles of works of art, books, publications, etc., alphabetize by the first principal word so that *"The Canterbury Tales"* is listed under *C* (not *T*).

alumna, alumnae, alumnus, alumni *Alumna* refers to a woman who graduated from the school; *alumnae* is plural for women. *Alumnus* refers to a man who graduated from the school; *alumni* is plural for men. *Alumni* is the plural for the men and women who graduated from the school.

AM/FM Capitalize and use a slash.

a.m., p.m. Lowercase with periods. Use figures, as in *We will meet at 9 a.m. in the conference room* (not *nine a.m.*). Note the space between the number and *a.m.* If the time is on the hour, it is not necessary to include a colon and two zeros. Just write *9 a.m.* Use the colon for fractions of hours, as in *9:15 a.m.* It is better to specify *a.m.* or *p.m.* instead of using the *o'clock* form. If the *o'clock* form is used, spell out the number (*one* through *nine*), as in *nine o'clock,* not *9 o'clock.*

Amazon.com The company logo lowercases *amazon,* but on the website, in press releases and other corporate materials, it is written with a capital *A.* When we contacted the company about its preference, the reply was: "Feel free to capitalize or to not capitalize our name. . . . Since we're an internet company, we're not too caught up in convention or formal procedures." So use the capital *A* all the time.

American English Many differences exist between American English and British English, especially in spelling and punctuation. In the U.S., American English takes precedence over British forms. For instance, write *theater* instead of *theatre* (unless *Theatre* is part of the proper name).

amid Preferred to *amidst.*

among *Among* is preferred to *amongst.* Use *among* with more than two persons or things: *She divided the tasks among the four departments. Between* is used with two persons or things: *She divided the tasks between the finance and marketing departments. Between you and me, there is not a lot of room for flexibility at this organization.* (Note it is *between you and me,* not *between you and I.*)

amount, number Use *amount* for things that cannot be counted one by one, as in *The amount of time spent on the reports varies each quarter.* Use *number* for things that can be counted one by one, as in *The number of days spent on the reports varies each quarter* or *She put a number of coins on the counter.*

ampersand (&) Use the *ampersand* in an organization's formal name if that is what the organization uses, as in *Barnes & Noble* (do not write *Barnes and Noble*). But do not use the *&* in place of *and* in text. Write *Trinidad and Tobago,* not *Trinidad & Tobago.* If, however, you are using abbreviations, replace *and* with *&,* so that *research and development* becomes *R&D, profit and loss* becomes *P&L.*

analog Note the spelling. The opposite of *analog* is *digital.*

and Do not replace the word *and* with an ampersand *(&).* Write *Trinidad and Tobago,* not *Trinidad & Tobago.* But if an organization uses an ampersand in its name, as in *Procter & Gamble,* do not write *Procter and Gamble.* When using abbreviations, replace *and* with *&,* so that *research and development* becomes *R&D, profit and loss* becomes *P&L.*

And, But It is acceptable to begin sentences with either of these words.

angry, mad These two words are not interchangeable. Use *angry* when the meaning is irritation. Use *mad* when the meaning is insane.

annual Do not write *first annual event.* It does not become an annual (yearly) event until it is held for two consecutive years.

anti No hyphen is needed for most words following *anti,* unless they begin with an *i,* as in *anti-inflationary.* However, if the absence of a hyphen could cause confusion, then use it. For instance, write *anti-hero* rather than *antihero*, which is difficult to read.

anticompetitive One word in all references. *The regulators questioned the company's anticompetitive practices. The regulators questioned whether the company's practices were anticompetitive.*

antitrust One word.

anxious It means worried, full of anxiety: *He was anxious about the product launch.* Do not use *anxious* in place of *eager,* which means desirous: *She was eager to complete her degree.*

anybody, anyone, any one The one-word forms are used to mean any person. *Anybody who speaks Spanish can take the call. Anyone* and *anybody* always take a singular verb. Use two words when singling out someone within a group: *Any one of the managers can go to the meeting.*

anymore Use the one-word form in all references.

apostrophe Follow these guidelines for the apostrophe:

- Use it to indicate possession. The singular possessive is formed by adding an *'s: the manager's chair, the managing director's parking space.* The plural possessive is formed by adding just an apostrophe: *the vice presidents' budgets, businesses' operations.* For a plural that does not end in *s,* form the possessive with an *'s: the children's nursery, women's rights, the men's room.*
- A difference of opinion exists about whether nouns ending in *s* require a second *s* as well as the apostrophe to form the possessive: *the hostess's dinner party, Myles's umbrella.* Most stylebooks, including "The Business Style Handbook," advocate using the second *s.* But if the next word begins with *s,* drop the *s* after the apostrophe, as in *the hostess' salad, for goodness' sake.*

- Classical names often do not take the second *s* to form the possessive, as in *Achilles' heel, Moses' commandments* (not *Achilles's heel, Moses's commandments*).

- Joint possession is formed by placing an *'s* on the last element of a series: *Smith and Johnson's proposal* or *Andrea and Bart's apartment.*

- Use an apostrophe in a contraction. Place the apostrophe where the letter is omitted: *have not* = *haven't, let us* = *let's, we are* = *we're, do not* = *don't.* One of the most common mistakes in print is to confuse the possessive pronoun *its* (belongs to it) with the contraction *it's* (it is). *The department always meets its deadlines* but *It's a deadline that must be met.*

- For *decades,* use this style: *1990s* or *'90s* (whichever form you choose, use it consistently).

- Use an apostrophe to indicate missing letters, as in *ne'er do well.* (The apostrophe stands in for the letter *v.*)

app Use this shortened form of *application* in all references, as in Apple's trademarked tagline, *There's an app for that.*

appraise, apprise Do not confuse these terms. *Appraise* means evaluate, as in *Mary Ward will appraise the recently acquired art before we buy insurance. Apprise* means inform, as in *I will apprise Coleen of all developments.*

Arab Spring Capitalize the *s* in *Spring.*

Argentine, Argentinian Both terms are correct; this stylebook prefers *Argentine. The Argentine government announced new measures to promote exports. The Argentinian government announced new measures to promote exports.* Be consistent.

ASAP This is informal for *as soon as possible.* Use all capitals for business correspondence. Spell out the entire phrase in formal communications.

ASCII This is a simple text format; it stands for *American Standard Code for Information Interchange.* Pronounced *askee,* documents saved as *ASCII* can be used across all platforms. Many resume banks require resumes to be submitted in this format (plain text) – minus all the formatting.

Asian-American Capitalize both words and use a hyphen.

as per It is preferable to use *according to.* And less is more when using the phrase *as per your request,* so write *as requested* instead. Also avoid *as to whether;* just use *whether.*

asterisk A star-like figure (*) used in writing to indicate either an omission or a reference to a footnote.

at Avoid *at* unless it contributes to the meaning: *Where is it?* Do not write *Where is it at?* Also avoid *We will meet at about 9 a.m.* Instead write *We will meet about 9 a.m.*

at sign Use the symbol @ in email addresses and for URLs, but in text write it as the *at sign.*

attorneys general Add an *s* to the first word to form the plural of most compound nouns. Another example is *sisters-in-law.*

attribution Attribute all material, with the exception of general knowledge, to the appropriate individual or source. Most readers want to know, "Who says so?" and telling them gives the statement more credibility. *Ergonomics reduces repetitive stress injuries* is an assertion that needs backing up. When the writer states that *OSHA's study claims ergonomics reduces repetitive stress injuries,* the assertion has more authority.

audio conference Two words.

autumn Lowercase *autumn,* which is interchangeable with *fall.* Lowercase all seasons.

avatar Note the spelling of this word for a graphic character that represents an online user.

average Do not confuse *average* with *ordinary,* which means usual, without distinction. It is better to write *It was an ordinary day on the floor of the exchange* than to write *It was an average day on the floor of the exchange. Average of* takes a plural verb in a construction such as this: *An average of 1,000 jobs were lost when gas prices rose to a new high.* The verb agrees with *jobs* (jobs were lost), not *average.*

awhile, a while When written as one word, *awhile* is an adverb: *She will stay with him awhile.* The two-word form is preceded by a preposition: *She plans to stay for a while.*

· B ·

"Style rules for many of the new platforms are not yet firmly established; however, we still try to emphasize clarity, consistency and accuracy. We must be accountable for our communication, regardless of the platform."
— Marc Rice, corporate communication account executive – environment
Southern Company

B.A., B.S. See **bachelor of arts, bachelor of science** entry.

baby boom, baby boomers These phrases refer to the population surge after WWII and the people born during that period (1946–64). Do not capitalize. The shortened form is *boomers*.

bachelor of arts, bachelor of science It is also correct, but less specific, to write *a bachelor's degree* (which applies to both the *B.A.* and the *B.S.*). If spelled out in text, lowercase *bachelor of arts* and *bachelor of science*. Also lowercase terms designating academic years: *freshman, sophomore, junior, senior.* It is common practice to uppercase *Bachelor of Arts, Bachelor of Science* when listing degrees in a resume. When using the short forms, capitalize and write with periods: *B.A., B.S.*

back-and-forth Write with hyphens, as in *After some back-and-forth, we decided to expand the distribution list.*

backslash One word.

back-to-back Write with hyphens. *I have back-to-back meetings all day Friday.*

back up, backup Write as two words when used as a verb, as in *She will back up the files at the end of the day.* Write as one word when used as an adjective or noun. *The backup files are on the servers in Korea* and *Marie is the backup for Jane.*

backward Use *backward* in all cases. Even though *backward* and *backwards* are interchangeable in some instances, only *backward* works as an adjective: *The misprint in the advertisement was a backward letter.*

bad, badly *Bad* is an adjective (describing what someone or something is like); *badly* is an adverb (how something is done). Confusion on which word to use occurs with some verbs. Use *bad* when the verb explains how someone or something feels, smells, tastes or looks: *Marie feels bad because she did not submit the proposal on time. Marie feels badly* suggests that Marie's sense of touch is poor.

barcode One word.

bare bones, bare-bones No hyphen when used as a noun. *The service is bare bones, but the company plans to expand its functionality next year.* Write with a hyphen when used to modify the noun. *The bare-bones service will not attract many customers.*

BC, AD *BC* indicates a calendar year *before Christ.* Note the year goes before *BC,* as in *1445 BC. AD* stands for *anno Domini:* in the year of our Lord. The year goes after *AD,* as in *AD 76.* Do not write *the second century AD.* It is redundant. *The second century* is sufficient. Use abbreviations in all references.

bcc, blind carbon copy Use *bcc* in all references. But if the abbreviation creates confusion, write *blind copy* instead (you don't need the *carbon*). Changing *blind copy* or *bcc* into a verb is common practice. *Jim blind-copied his boss on the memo* (note the hyphen in the verb form) or *Jim bcc'd his boss on the memo.* When referring to the bcc function on email, lowercase, as in *Be sure to bcc Tracy on your email.* (The *bcc* and *cc* are exceptions to the guideline that computer and email functions should be capitalized, as in the *Send button.*)

bear, bare Use this word for the phrase *bear with me* (not *bare*).

bear, bull Both *bear* and *bull* are lowercased and can be used to describe people. A *bear* feels generally cautious about the financial market or is *bearish*. A *bull* feels generally positive about the market or is *bullish*. *The bulls on Wall Street predict the market can only get better, while the bears caution that the bubble is about to burst.* A *bear market* exists when stock prices are declining or when stock prices are expected to decline. A *bull market* exists when stock prices are rising.

behemoth Lowercase this word when referring to a large organization and meaning something enormous in size or power. In the Old Testament of the Bible, a Behemoth was a large and powerful animal. *The fly gobbled up the mighty behemoth when Shutterfly bought Kodak's online photo service.*

bellwether Use the term *bellwether* to indicate a trend. *Absenteeism is a bellwether for employee morale.* Note the spelling of *bellwether.*

below Avoid using the word *below* to refer to material that follows, except where it is certain the reference will appear on the same page: *The prices below are in effect until Dec. 31.* (The same guideline applies to the word *above.*) Usually the word *following* or *previously* can be substituted, respectively, for *below* or *above.*

belt-tightening Use a hyphen, as in *The COO wrote a memo on the need for belt-tightening* or *The COO announced a series of belt-tightening measures.*

beside, besides Use *beside* when the meaning is next to: *Lenny's desk is beside the window.* Use *besides* when the meaning is *in addition to* or *except for: Who besides Lenny sits in this area?*

best case, best-case Write with a hyphen when the two words are used to modify the noun, as in *best-case scenario* (or *worst-case scenario).* No hyphen in this example, as in *That proposal is the best case of clear writing I have seen in a long time.*

best seller Do not hyphenate this term. *The biography of Cleopatra was a best seller* or *The biography of Cleopatra rose to the top of the best seller list.* Even though *best seller* acts as an adjective in the second sentence, no hyphen is needed because the meaning is clear. If the meaning of a phrase is clear without the hyphen (*best seller list, real estate agent, income tax form, word processing program),* don't use one.

beta Lowercase *beta* in this construction: *The company is beta-testing the new customer-relationship software.* Software often goes through two stages of release testing: *alpha* (in house) and *beta* (outgoing).

better, well *Better* means still in the process of recovering. *Well* means completely recovered. *Mary Ann is feeling better. The doctor expects her to be well after she takes the antibiotic for 10 days.*

between, among *Between* is used with two persons or things. *She divided the tasks between the finance and marketing departments. Between you and me, there is not a lot of room for flexibility at this organization.* (Note it is *between you and me,* not *between you and I.)*

Use *among* with more than two persons or things. *She divided the tasks among the four departments. Among* is preferred to *amongst.*

biannual, biennial *Biannual* means twice a year. *Biennial* means once every two years. *Bimonthly* means every other month, while *semimonthly* means twice a month. Using these terms occasionally confuses readers. In most cases it is better to write *twice a month, every two months. The report is published every other month.* The same applies to *biweekly* and *semiweekly.*

bibliography Some business writing needs to include a bibliography, which is an alphabetical list of the sources used, whether footnotes are included in the text or not. The list, which appears at the end of the work, can also be called *Works Cited* or *References.* If a bibliography is extensive, many thorny issues can arise. A good source for a bibliography, especially for formal or academic writing, is "The Chicago Manual of Style." If the citation is simple and straightforward, follow this style: author, title, place of publication, publisher, date.

Use these examples as guidelines:

For a book by a single author:
Rifkin, Jeremy. "The Age of Access." New York: The Putnam Publishing Group, 2001.

For multiple authors:
Varney, Charles Edward, and Abdullah F. Akbar. "The Jewel Carriers." Balboa Island, Calif.: Creative Ink, 1999.

For a book by editors:
Hairston, Maxine, and John J. Ruszkiewicz, eds. "The Scott, Foresman Handbook for Writers." Glenview, Ill: Scott, Foresman and Company, 1988.

For a book with an edition number:
"American Heritage Dictionary." 5th ed. Boston/New York: Houghton Mifflin Company, 2011.
(Note that the reference to the edition uses the ordinal number and has a lowercased *ed.)*

For an article from a periodical:
Bryant, Adam. "Think 'We' for Best Results." New York Times, Apr. 19, 2009.

(An online periodical should include a URL, which should be cited after the date. See "For the internet.")

For a corporation, institution or association:

American Medical Association. "The American Medical Association Encyclopedia of Medicine." New York: Random House, 1989.

For a paper:

Horton, Sabina. "Preventing Workplace Injuries." Paper presented at the Annual Meeting of the International Society of Wellness Professionals, Hilton Head Island, S.C.: April 2012.

For the internet:

"Dow Closes Above 13,000; First Time Since 2008," New York Times, Feb. 28, 2012, www.nytimes.com/2012/02/29/business/daily-stock-market-activity.html?_r=1&ref=business.

"The nutrition puzzle," Economist, Feb. 18, 2012, www.economist.com/node/21547771.

(Electronic books should include author, title, edition, etc. It is also important to include a URL. Access dates for URLs are no longer necessary.)

For the sciences:

Sagar, A. 2001. J2EE design patterns: The next frontier. Java Developer's Journal, Aug.: 10+.

(The sciences use a different style for bibliographies. Check relevant stylebooks.)

Big Board Spell out *New York Stock Exchange* in first reference; use *Big Board* (capitalize both *B*'s), *NYSE* or *the exchange* afterward. The parent company of the New York Stock Exchange is NYSE Euronext.

Big Brother Capitalize both *B*'s in this term, which comes from the book "1984" by George Orwell. The term often refers to the invasive aspect of telecommunications and data gathering, where issues of privacy are at stake. If the term *big brother* refers to an older sibling, lowercase it.

big data, big money Lowercase these expressions.

Big Three automakers General Motors, Ford, Chrysler. Note that *Big Three* is capitalized, but *automakers* is not.

billion, million Use the word *billion* or *million* instead of writing out the zeros. A billion is equal to a thousand million. (FYI: A billion in Britain, Canada and Germany is equal to a million million [what U.S. English calls a *trillion*].)

biodiversity No hyphen needed.

biofuel No hyphen needed.

biotech, biotechnology Use these interchangeably.

Bing Capitalize the name of Microsoft's search engine.

birth date Write as two words, unlike *birthday*.

black Lowercase racial descriptions that are derived from skin color. *African-American,* with a hyphen, is the preferred term when talking about U.S. citizens.

black and white, black-and-white This takes no hyphens when used as a noun. *The issue of where to build the backup center is not black and white.* Write with two hyphens when used as an adjective. *He printed a black-and-white version of the report.*

BlackBerry(s) Capitalize both *B*'s; write the plural with an *s*. Use *BB* for short.

bloc, block A *bloc* is a grouping of countries, people or interest groups with a shared purpose or goal, as in *Divergent economic policies hampered efforts to form a regional trade bloc.* Write *block* with a *k* for other references.

blog This word is a noun, as in *The CEO writes a customer blog;* an adjective, as in *The company offers blog services;* and a verb, as in *The CFO blogs twice a week.* Other variations include *blogger, blogging, blogged* and *blogosphere* (one *g).*

Bluetooth One word.

Blu-ray Hyphenate this term for an optical disc format; no *e* in *Blu.*

board of directors Lowercase and spell out in the first reference. Shorten to *the board* afterward. Use the abbreviation *BoD* in informal writing. Note the verb. *The board of directors meets Thursday.* It agrees with *board* (the board *meets),* not with *directors* (the directors *meet). Boards of directors* is the plural.

boldface Reserve the use of boldface for headlines, headings, subheads, etc. When emphasis is needed, use boldface sparingly in text; otherwise it can look muddy. Put the punctuation following a font in the same font. For example, if you have a bold word followed by a colon, then put the colon in bold also. **Update:** *The meeting will take place Friday at noon.* (Note the bold colon.)

bondholders One word.

books Put book titles in quotation marks ("America's Girl"). The first edition of this stylebook recommended italics for book titles. Because of the new technologies, we now recommend quotation marks instead of the italic font for book titles.

bottom line, bottom-line Two words when used as a noun, as in *How will the price increases impact the bottom line?* Write with a hyphen when used as an adjective: *It is too soon to assess the bottom-line impact of the price increases.*

boundaryless One word, no hyphen. *The annual report described the company's strategy for a boundaryless world.*

brackets Do not use brackets *[ ]* and parentheses *( )* interchangeably. Use brackets:

- When it is necessary to use parentheses within parentheses. *The actuary table was not included in the monthly report (the statistics, however, are included in the new annual report [due to be published in March]).*
- To insert comments or explanations into direct quotations. *Newman said, "Charlie Sommers [director of marketing] will be promoted to vice president this year."*
- To acknowledge errors originating in quoted material: *Mark Smith said, "The moral [sic] of the company is at an all-time low."* The *[sic]* tells your reader that the word *moral,* which should be *morale,* is not an error on the writer's part but is actually faithful to the original material.

brainstorm One word.

brand name *Brand name* is a nonlegal term for a service mark or trademark. When *brand names* are used, capitalize them. *Marie needed to Xerox 100 copies.* Some words, originally brand names, have become generic terms and are no longer capitalized, as in *petri dish, zeppelin.*

Brazilian names See **Portuguese names** entry.

breadcrumb One word. This term refers to the navigation trail on websites.

breakup Write as one word when used as a noun, as in *The Justice Department ruling will force a breakup of the company.*

bricks and mortar This term is used to refer to businesses that have physical structures as opposed to online companies. *Clicks and mortar* refers to companies that have integrated a website with existing fulfillment, logistics and marketing. Both phrases often are used as adjectives (in which case hyphens are used and the *s* is dropped), as in *The company is making the transition from successful brick-and-mortar retailing to a click-and-mortar business.*

bring, take *Bring* means to carry toward the speaker. *Take* means to carry away from the speaker. *Bring me the file on the cabinet. Take this file and put it away.*

Britain See **Great Britain** entry.

broadband One word, no hyphen.

broadcast As the past tense of the verb, write *broadcast* (not *broadcasted*): *CBS broadcast the news bulletin this morning.* As an adjective: *The CEO sent a broadcast email about the acquisition.* As a noun: *Millions viewed the live broadcast.*

broker/dealer This can be written with a slash (/) or with a hyphen (-). Slash is the preference in this stylebook. The plural is *broker/dealers.*

brothers-in-law Make the plural by adding an *s* to *brothers,* not *law.* Same goes for *holes-in-one* and *runners-up.*

building Do not abbreviate if it is a part of the proper name. *The Empire State Building was lit up in green for St. Patrick's Day.* Note that *Building* is capitalized because it is part of the formal name. When *building* is not part of a formal name, lowercase it.

bullet Use bullets to make communications more readable. Business writers generally prefer bullets to outline style (with numbers and letters), but don't overuse bullets. When punctuating bulleted material, if the text following a bullet is a complete sentence, use a period. If the text following a bullet is not a complete sentence, do not use a period.

- Use a period here. (The subject is implied, so it's a complete sentence.)
- No period here

If the lead-in sentence to the bulleted material has a colon, then consider the bulleted item as part of that sentence (making it a complete sentence ending with a period), as in,

I recommend we open a Brazil office next year. Reasons include:

- **Cost savings.** It will cut our cost of doing business in the Brazilian market by 15% over the next three years.
- **Higher regional sales.** Demand for our products is growing 10% p.a. in Latin America. We can use our Brazilian operation to source other Latin markets and to further increase brand awareness throughout the region.

This stylebook favors using *bullet* as a verb, even though it may be considered nonstandard. *He bulleted the year's accomplishments in the executive summary.*

bulletproof One word. *Margaret assured management the new systems had bulletproof security and reliability.*

bureau Capitalize when it is part of the formal name of an organization or agency; lowercase when used alone or to designate a corporate subdivision: *The Bureau of Labor Statistics reported the unemployment rate dropped to 3% in the last quarter. The newspaper is expanding its Paris bureau.*

bureaucratese What you want to avoid when writing. Keep your writing simple and remove unnecessary words. Instead of writing *as per your request,* write *as requested.* Instead of writing *Due to the fact that,* write *Because.*

burn out, burnout Use two words when it is a verb, as in *The project leader warned management that the programmers would burn out if they continued working 24/7.* Write as one word when used as a noun, as in *The project leader warned management that burnout among the programmers was a concern.*

business casual Lowercase this term for less formal business attire. *Our dress code is business casual every day.*

businesses This is the plural of *business.* Form the plural possessive by adding just an apostrophe, as in *businesses' operations.*

businesslike One word.

businesspeople One word.

businessperson One word. If it sounds stilted, rewrite the sentence. *A group of businesspersons will accompany the senator to Vietnam* can be changed to *A group of business executives will accompany . . .* or *A group of businesspeople will accompany. . . .*

business school Spell out in the first reference; use *B-school* afterward.

business-to-business Spell out in the first reference; use *B2B* afterward. *The head of the company's business-to-business division announced three new B2B initiatives.* This refers to communications and transactions conducted between businesses as opposed to between businesses and consumers.

busywork One word. *The intern spent most of the summer doing busywork.*

But It is acceptable to begin sentences with *But* (and *And*). Do not use *but* after the expression *cannot help*. Write *The purchasing manager cannot help seeing the difference in quality* (rather than *The purchasing manager cannot help but see the difference in quality*).

buy back, buyback This is two words when used as a verb. *The company will buy back up to $2 billion of its stock.* Write as one word when used as a noun, as in *The buyback is set for the third quarter.*

buzzword The Fortune 500 communications professionals surveyed for this stylebook are split when it comes to the use of buzzwords in business writing. About half disdain buzzwords of any kind, while the other half think some buzzwords are effective (for instance, *bottom line, globalize, incentivize, leverage, paradigm shift, proactive, robust, synergy* and *value-add*). As a general rule, use buzzwords judiciously, always keeping the readers in mind.

byline A byline is a notation at the beginning or end of an article carrying the writer's name. For internal and external publications, establish a style for bylines and use that style consistently throughout the publication, as in *by Karen Rester, By Karen Rester, BY KAREN RESTER* or just – *Karen Rester.* It is also useful to establish a policy on which material gets a byline. Generally all front-page material and feature articles get bylines. Short news items generally do not (although initials preceded by a dash [–] are sometimes given as a courtesy to the writer).

byproduct One word.

· C ·

"Never assume. Check everything."
– Clara Degen, manager and editor, employee communications
McKesson HBOC, Inc.

callback When used as an adjective or a noun, use the one-word form: *The company receives thousands of callback requests each week.* Use two words for the verb: *call back.*

can, may These two words are not interchangeable. *Can* means able: *Rob can write the memo. May* means permission is implied: *Lori may leave work early to attend her daughter's basketball game.*

cancel, canceled, canceling, cancellation These are the preferred spellings.

can hardly Do not use *can't hardly;* it is a double negative. Instead write *After working the night shift, the manager can hardly keep her eyes open.*

cannot One word – always.

capital, capitol *Capital* is the term for a town or city that serves as a seat of government. *Capital* also means money or wealth. A *capital letter* is an uppercase letter. *Capitol* is a term for the building in which a legislative assembly meets.

capitalization Always think twice about capitalizing a word. Many business writers use capitals where they are not necessary. Some general rules follow. Consult a dictionary for specific questions.

- Capitalize all proper nouns: *Jeremy Lin, Carnegie Hall.*
- Capitalize the names of companies, organizations and schools following their style in the first reference. In subsequent references substitute the full name with a shortened form (e.g., *Nike, FedEx, the Fed, Rutgers)* or a lowercased shortened form *(company, corporation, commission, university). Verizon Communications changed its privacy policy. Verizon announced the decision last week. The company also introduced new consumer services.*
- Capitalize the first word of a complete sentence. *The office is open.*
- Capitalize the first word of quoted material that is a full sentence: *Maureen said, "The accountant can't believe the audit is finished."* Do not capitalize the first letter of a quotation if it does not begin a complete sentence. *Andrew said that to finish the project late would mean "sudden death."*
- Capitalize the letter *I* when it stands alone: *I eat; I sleep; I work.*
- Capitalize the first letter of the main words in a title (book, play, headline, etc.): *Officials Question the Numbers in the Reports.* See **headline** entry.
- Capitalize the professional title of an individual when it precedes a proper noun: *Federal Reserve Board Chairman Ben Bernanke.* (Job descriptions are rarely capitalized, as in *copyeditor Matia Beirne.)*
- In correspondence, capitalize all titles in the address.
- Capitalize all words in the salutation, as in *To Whom It May Concern,* but only the first letter in a complimentary closing: *Yours truly.*
- Capitalize days of the week, months: *Thursday, April 15.*
- Capitalize all holidays – official, unofficial, religious, secular – including the word *Day,* as in *Martin Luther King Day.*
- On resumes, school subjects *(biology, chemistry)* are not capitalized unless they are languages: *English, Latin.* Only specific place names modifying a noun are capitalized: *European history.*
- Capitalize a noun not usually capitalized *(uncle)* when it is part of the proper noun: *Uncle Terry, Aunt Mary.*

- Capitalize *North, South, East, West* only if it is a region, not a direction. *They are planning to relocate to the South. Go south on Harpeth Street to find the office.* Capitalize directions if they are part of a proper noun, as in *the Lower East Side, South Street.* In an address, spell out and capitalize *North, South, East, West* when they appear before the street; abbreviate and capitalize when they appear after the street: *1200 South Maple Street* versus *1200 Maple Street S.*
- Capitalize words that precede numbers, as in *Page 12, Section 4, Version 3.*
- Capitalize words that are email or computer functions, as in *Hit the Send button.* The exceptions to this guideline are *cc* and *bcc.* When referring to the *cc* or *bcc* function in email, lowercase, as in *Be sure to cc Walter on your email* or *Marta cc'd the entire department on the memo.*

captcha. It means *Completely Automated Public Turing Test to Tell Computers and Humans Apart.* A captcha protects a website from bots. The captcha is usually in a box and has distorted letters/words/numbers (sometimes with a line running through them). Users are asked to type the phrase into a field to verify the user is human.

caption A caption is the blurb under (or next to) a photograph. It should describe what the reader cannot see by looking at the photograph. Try to keep it to one or two sentences. Write it in the present tense. Sometimes it makes sense to give some background for the photograph. Identify individuals pictured (from left to right or clockwise). A common error is that the spelling of proper nouns in the caption does not match the spelling in the text. Take extra time to check. Stand-alone photos (photographs that are not part of an article or text) usually have longer captions, but brevity should still be a consideration. Avoid irrelevant captions, as in *A man at work on the factory floor* or *An employee uses the company gym* or *A woman beams approval at her coworkers.* An informative caption reads: *Douglas Eich, a foreman at the Detroit plant, examines the new ergonomic adjustments made to the assembly line.* Don't assume the reader will see the connection between the photograph and the text.

carat This is a unit of weight for gemstones. Do not confuse this with *karat,* which measures the fineness of gold. *Her future husband gave her a 14-karat gold ring with a 2-carat diamond.* A *caret* (^) is a mark used by editors and proofreaders.

carbon copy, cc Use *cc* in all references unless the abbreviation could create confusion. If spelling out, write *copy* (you don't need the *carbon*): *Marta copied the entire department on the memo. Marta cc'd the entire department on the memo.* When referring to the *cc* function in email, lowercase it, as in *Be sure to cc Walter on your email.* (The *cc* and *bcc* are the exceptions to the guideline that computer and email functions should be capitalized, as in *the Send button.*)

carriers, shippers *Carriers* transport or convey goods. *Shippers* are the owners of the goods or receive goods for transport.

case-sensitive This takes a hyphen and means that it makes a difference whether letters are upper- or lowercase. Many passwords are *case-sensitive.*

cash flow, cash-flow Use two words when they act as a noun, as in *The company has difficulties with cash flow.* Write with a hyphen when used as an adjective, as in *The company has cash-flow difficulties.*

cash on delivery Use *c.o.d.* with periods for all references.

catalog This is the preferred spelling (not *catalogue*).

Catch-22 Capitalize the *C* and use a hyphen. This phrase, from the Joseph Heller novel of the same name, means an inherently illogical condition in a law, regulation or circumstance that creates a no-win situation. *The company is in a Catch-22: It cannot become profitable without investing more capital, but it cannot raise capital because it is unprofitable.*

cc See **carbon copy, cc** entry.

CD Use *CD* in all references. It stands for *compact disc* or *certificate of deposit.* *CDs* is the plural.

cellphone One word.

Celsius This is the temperature scale used in the metric system. If using this scale, specify *32 °C* (with a capital *C,* without a space before or after the degree symbol and without a period after the *C).* Use figures and the degree symbol. Use the word *minus,* not a *minus sign,* for temperatures below zero, as in *The pipes froze because it was minus 10 °C.*

Fahrenheit is the temperature scale used in the U.S. Note that *Fahrenheit* and *Celsius* are capitalized.

Also note that everyone has a temperature, usually 98.6°, so do not write that *Mark has a temperature.* Instead write *Mark has a high temperature* or *Mark has a fever.*

center on Use *center on,* as in *Marie's presentation centered on the upcoming RFP.* Do not use *center around.*

cents Spell out and lowercase *cents,* using numerals for amounts less than a dollar, such as *59 cents.* For slide shows, tables or other material using decimals, write *$0.59.* Use the currency symbol and a decimal for amounts greater than a dollar, as in *$62.39.* When exact figures are not essential, round numbers to avoid using decimals.

century Spell out the words *first* through *ninth* if they precede century, as in *ninth century.* Use numerals for higher numbers, as in *21st century.* Lowercase *century* unless it is part of a proper noun.

CEO See **chief executive officer** entry.

certainly, very Use *certainly* and *very* sparingly. Always aim to be concise. These words add little meaning to a sentence.

chair, chairman, chairperson, chairwoman These terms are lowercased unless written as an official title preceding a name; then capitalize: *Chairman John Lukas*. Do not use the term *chairlady*, unless it is an organization's formal title for an office. Some women prefer *chair* or *chairman* to *chairwoman*.

Chanukah This holiday has three spellings. *Hanukkah* (not *Chanukah* or *Hanukah)* is the preferred spelling. Capitalize all holidays – official, unofficial, religious, secular.

Chapter 11 Capitalize the *C* when referring to Chapter 11 bankruptcy protection. Also capitalize in *Chapter 7, Chapter 12, Chapter 13, Chapter 15,* all of which are bankruptcy categories.

charts, graphs Because space is at a premium in charts and graphs, use abbreviations you would not normally use in text, such as *bn* for *billion*. Develop style preferences that lend themselves to visuals and use them consistently (e.g., write *2013–18* instead of *2013–2018)*. Write titles that are concise and convey as much information as possible, as in *2013–18: Income by Region ($bn)*.

If you have a series of related charts in a slide show or other material, check all the elements for consistency, including type size and font; size, shape and punctuation for bullets; use of colors; size of graphics; use of decimal points; and spellings and use of names (e.g., *Goldman Sachs Group* or *Goldman Sachs* or *Goldman;* the shortest form usually).

check in, check-in Write without a hyphen when used as a verb. *He will check in with the Privacy Office before sending the email.* Write with a hyphen when used as an adjective. *Check-in times vary depending on whether the flights are domestic.*

checkout, check out One word, no hyphen, when used as an adjective or noun. *The line at the checkout counter was too long. The company simplified procedures so that checkout is much faster.* Write as two words when used as a verb. *I will check out of my hotel at noon.*

chief executive officer Whether to spell out or use the abbreviation *CEO* in the first reference depends on the audience. For *CEO*, capitalize all three letters. The plural is *CEOs*. Another alternative is *chief executive*. *The CEO sent a memo about the business-transformation program. The chief executive sent the memo.*

chief financial officer Whether to use the abbreviation *CFO* in the first reference depends on the audience. Capitalize all three letters. The plural is *CFOs*.

chief information officer Whether to use the abbreviation *CIO* in the first reference depends on the audience. Capitalize all three letters. The plural is *CIOs*.

chief marketing officer Whether to use the abbreviation *CMO* in the first reference depends on the audience. Capitalize all three letters. The plural is *CMOs*.

chief operating officer Whether to use the abbreviation *COO* in the first reference depends on the audience. Capitalize all three letters. The plural is *COOs*.

chief privacy officer Whether to use the abbreviation *CPO* in the first reference depends on the audience. Capitalize all three letters. The plural is *CPOs*.

chief technology officer Whether to use the abbreviation *CTO* in the first reference depends on the audience. Capitalize all three letters. The plural is *CTOs*.

childcare One word.

Chinese names In Chinese, names are written with the family name first, followed by the given name: *Sun* (family name) *Xiao* (given name). Although many English-language publications follow that style and would write *Sun Xiao*, this creates confusion about first and last names. To avoid such confusion when writing for business, put Chinese names in the same order as names written in English: given name first, followed by the family name: *Xiao Sun* or *Mr. Sun.*

chutzpah Often misspelled.

Cincinnati Often misspelled.

citation Unless it is a scientific or academic report, parenthetical documentation (instead of footnotes/bibliography) may work best for citing sources. Follow this style for parenthetical documentation: *Jenna Wortham cited a book, "140 Characters, A Style Guide for the Short Form," in a recent blog ("The Anatomy of a Tweet: Twitter Gets a Style Guide," New York Times, Feb. 13, 2009).*

cite, site *Cite* means to quote or name: *He cited his source in the bibliography. Site* means a place for a building: *They gathered at the building site for the inspection. Site* also means a location on the web: *The company's new site is highly interactive.*

cities If the city is synonymous with the state or is widely recognizable, then the city can stand alone in text. The following list of cities can stand alone (based on the style used by the AP for domestic cities and the New York Times stylebook for international cities). If a place name is not identifiable in context, then for clarification include the state or country.

United States:

Atlanta	Detroit	Milwaukee	St. Louis
Baltimore	Honolulu	Minneapolis	Salt Lake City
Boston	Houston	New Orleans	San Antonio
Chicago	Indianapolis	New York	San Diego
Cincinnati	Jersey City	Oklahoma City	San Francisco
Cleveland	Las Vegas	Philadelphia	Seattle
Dallas	Los Angeles	Phoenix	Washington
Denver	Miami	Pittsburgh	

International:

Algiers	Edinburgh	Macao***	Rome
Amsterdam	Frankfurt	Madrid	San Marino
Athens	Geneva	Manila	San Salvador
Bangkok	Gibraltar	Mexico City	Shanghai
Beijing	Glasgow	Milan	Singapore
Berlin	Guatemala City	Monaco	Stockholm
Bombay	The Hague	Montreal	Tel Aviv
Bonn	Havana	Moscow	Tehran
Brasilia	Hong Kong	Munich	Tokyo
Brussels	Istanbul	New Delhi	Toronto
Budapest	Jerusalem	Oslo	Tunis
Buenos Aires	Johannesburg	Ottawa	Venice
Cairo	Kolkata**	Panama	Vienna
Cape Town	Kuwait	Paris	Warsaw
Copenhagen	Lisbon	Prague	Zurich
Djibouti*	London	Quebec	
Dublin	Luxembourg	Rio de Janeiro	

*Djibouti is also the name of the country.

** Kolkata (Calcutta).

***Macao is also written *Macau*.

civil rights movement Lowercase names of political or quasi-historical movements if specific dates are not assigned (e.g., *cold war, westward movement, gold rush*).

class action, class-action No hyphen is needed for the noun, as in *Shareholders filed a class action alleging the company failed to disclose information about its foreign exchange hedging practices.* When used as an adjective, write it with a hyphen, as in *Shareholders filed a class-action lawsuit alleging the company. . . .*

clause This is a group of related words within a sentence that has both a subject and a predicate (a verb and all its auxiliaries, modifiers and complements).

An independent (or main) clause is a complete statement (if it stood alone, it would be a simple sentence). A dependent clause is not a complete statement and cannot stand alone.

C-level Capitalize the *C* and write with a hyphen, as in *C-level executives,* such as *CEO, CMO, CFO, CIO.*

cliche This is an expression or truism that has lost its originality through overuse. Try to avoid using cliches. If it is necessary to use one, don't put quotation marks around it. This stylebook has dropped the accent on the *e.*

click No need for the preposition *on* when used as an instruction for web links. *Click the button on the upper-right side of the page.*

clicks and mortar This term is used to refer to brick-and-mortar companies that have integrated a website with existing fulfillment, logistics and marketing. *Bricks and mortar* refers to businesses that have physical structures as opposed to e-tailers or virtual companies. Both phrases are often used as adjectives (in which case hyphens are used and the *s* is dropped), as in *The company is making the transition from successful brick-and-mortar retailing to a click-and-mortar business.*

clickthrough(s) Write as one word when used as a noun or adjective. *The site requires too many clickthroughs to find information. The web team is gathering metrics on the site's clickthrough rates.*

clock time Use figures, as in *We will meet at 9 a.m. in the conference room* (not *nine a.m.).* It is better to specify *a.m.* or *p.m.* than to use *o'clock.* Note the space between the number and *a.m.* If the time is on the hour, it is not necessary to include a colon and two zeros. Just write *9 a.m.* Use the colon for fractions of hours, as in *9.15 a.m.* If the *o'clock* form is used, spell out the number (*one* through *nine*), as in *nine o'clock,* not *9 o'clock.* (If *o'clock* appears in a headline or title, uppercase the *O* and *C.*)

cloud *The cloud* refers to resources and applications available on the internet from just about any internet-connected device. For instance, Gmail is considered in the cloud because you can access it from any device with internet access. According to Novell, "The cloud is a set of services and technologies that enable the delivery of computing services over the internet in real time, allowing end-users instant access to data and applications from any device with internet access." Do not capitalize *the cloud*.

Co. An abbreviation for *Company*.

co(-) Keep the hyphen when forming nouns, adjectives and verbs that indicate occupation or status. *The co-chairman of the annual fund-raiser was Michael Greene.* For other *co-* words, some are hyphenated and others aren't: *coauthor, cofounder, cooperate, coordinate, coworker, co-owner.* Check the dictionary if you are uncertain.

c.o.d. Use *c.o.d.* with periods for all references. It stands for *cash on delivery.*

collectibles Often misspelled (not *collectables).*

collective nouns A noun that denotes a unit (or collection) takes a singular verb and pronoun. *The committee is meeting to discuss its technology proposal. Headquarters is located on Elm Street. Human Resources is on the 22nd floor.* Usually collective nouns take singular verbs.

Colombia, Columbia Often confused. *Colombia* is the country in northwestern South America. *Columbia* is the university or its undergraduate college and also the name of many cities.

colon A colon (*:)* is a strong pause used to introduce related statements, quotations or lists. If the statement following the colon is a complete sentence, a proper noun or a quotation, begin it with a capital letter: *Sheila Nadata is rising rapidly in the company: She will be promoted to vice president next year.*

Otherwise use a lowercase letter: *Three positions will open up next month: account executive, administrative assistant and manager.* A business letter salutation generally takes a colon, as in *Dear Ms. Lesnikowski:*.

comma A comma *(,)* is a signal to pause in a sentence. Do not overuse commas. They are there to clarify meaning. Too many commas can make a sentence unwieldy. Follow these guidelines:

- When two long clauses are linked by a conjunction (e.g., *and, but*) and each clause can stand alone as a separate sentence, use a comma before the conjunction in most cases: *Bill will go to the meeting, but he must finish the proposal first. Mary likes her new job, and she plans to stay until she retires.* (For a comma to be used here, the subject must be included. Do not use a comma if the sentence reads *Mary likes her new job and plans to stay until she retires* [the *she* is missing]). If the two clauses are short, there is no need for a comma: *Andrei called in the trade and Nikolai executed it.*
- If the word or phrase is essential (restrictive) to the meaning of the sentence, then do not use commas around it: *Martin Scorsese's film "Hugo" is playing at the theater.* (He has directed more than one film.) When the word or phrase is not essential to the meaning of the sentence, it is placed between commas: *Mary's mother, Martha Byrne, lives next door.*
- The salutation of a personal letter takes a comma, as in *Dear Mary,*. (The salutation in a business communication generally takes a colon, as in *Dear Ms. Lesnikowski:.)*
- The complimentary close of a communication is followed by a comma: *Sincerely,* or *Yours truly,.* (The second word of a closing is lowercase, as in *truly.)*
- Use commas to set off parenthetical words: *I believe, therefore, we should hire an accounting company to conduct the audit. If, however, you disagree, feel free to seek the counsel of some other law firm.*
- An introductory phrase of five or more words is usually set off by a comma to show that it is subordinate to the main clause: *Because the manager had placed the proposal on the stage after the speech, he forgot to*

take it back to the office. After a short introductory phrase, use a comma if it is needed for clarity: *To Marie, Elizabeth seemed to be overwhelmed.* It is not necessary to place a comma in this construction: *After an hour we left the cafeteria.* (Many writers use commas after all introductory phrases. It is not incorrect to do so.)

- Use commas in a series (called the serial comma) to avoid confusion: *Pens, pencils, stapler, ruler, etc. are in the desk drawer* (note there is no comma after the word *etc.*). No comma is necessary before the *and* in a simple series (single items): *France's flag is red, white and blue.* The majority of business writers do not use the serial comma, unless confusion would arise without it: *Artem spoke about the tax liability, Ed spoke about taxes and tariffs, and Susan covered pricing and financing.* Only on rare occasions should you use the serial comma. Too many writers overuse the serial comma.

- A comma marks off a date when it appears in text: *She currently works in Chicago, but on September 6, 2013, she will relocate to Paris* (note the comma after the year). Do not insert a comma before the month and the year if it appears without the day: *In December 2015 Rob will retire.*

- Use a comma before a direct quotation to set the attribution off from the rest of the sentence: *Allen Markowitz said, "I will never hire an intern again."* Also: *"I will never hire an intern again," said Allen Markowitz.* However, do not use a comma if the quoted statement ends with a question mark or an exclamation point: *"When does the Hong Kong Stock Exchange close?" he asked.*

- Use a comma after an introductory clause. *If you want to take the survey, click here.*

- Do not use a comma at the start of a partial quotation: *Yuri said we needed "to start from scratch."*

- Use a comma in direct address: *Thomas, it was a pleasure meeting you at the conference Wednesday.*

- Use a comma to set off interjections: *Yes, I will go to the meeting with you.* But no comma is needed when you write *Rose Anna said yes to Tim.*

- Use a comma to set off a city or town: *Nancy Rine, Baltimore, and Luisa Beltran, Barcelona, Spain, represented the company at the meeting.* (Some cities can stand alone without a state or country. See **cities** entry.)

- Separate ages with two commas: *Bill Eckert, 59, plans to take early retirement.*
- Do not use a comma before a parenthesis, as in *Vinny will take the plane to New York (and the subway to Brooklyn).*
- Use commas to separate two or more adjectives if each equally modifies the noun alone: *He was the only short, slim participant in the study.* However, if the first adjective modifies the second adjective, no comma is necessary: *The facilities manager asked the janitor to cut down the tall blue spruce.*
- Use a comma when the first and last names are reversed: *Byrne, Myles.* Use a comma to separate a name from a title: *Myles Greene, president.* Use a comma for a personal name suffix: *Myles Greene, Jr.*
- Use a comma after the company name with *Inc.,* if a comma precedes *Inc.,* as in *We will visit SCI Systems, Inc., on our next trip.* Do not use a comma if the company name does not use a comma before *Inc.,* as in *Marissa applied for a job at Safeway Inc. last month.*

Commonwealth of Independent States Spell out in the first reference; then use *CIS.* This refers to 12 of the former republics of the Soviet Union.

company, companies If the word *company* or *companies* appears alone in a second reference, always spell out and lowercase. *The Brensis Co. will release the annual earnings report in a few weeks. The company did not specify the reason for the delay.* Use *it/its* when referring to a single company (not *they/their*). *The company launched its new web service* (not *their new web service*). *It announced the news in March* (not *They announced*).

company names The Fortune 500 communications executives surveyed for this stylebook agree on how to write company names: Spell out and punctuate the name exactly the way the company does in correspondence and in the first reference (Including *Inc., Ltd., S.A., P.L.C.* and other equivalents); use the shortened form afterward. *Nike, Inc., is a Fortune 500 company. Nike participated in the survey.* (Note the commas and the abbreviated form of *Inc.* in the first reference.)

To verify the correct spelling and punctuation, visit the company's website, check its marketing or other branded material (such as press releases, business cards) or consult "Standard & Poor's Register of Corporations, Directors and Executives." Hoover's Online is another reliable source (www.hoovers.com). Spend the extra time to make sure that the spelling and punctuation of company names are correct.

company-wide Use a hyphen for *company-wide, enterprise-wide, firm-wide, industry-wide. Nationwide, worldwide* are one word.

compare to, compare with Use *compare to* when describing resemblances between unlike things, as in *JoElyn compared the music to her practice of meditation.* Use *compare with* when examining similar things to determine their similarities or differences. *The staff compared the new software with the previous version.*

compass points In text, lowercase *east, west, north, south,* except when they designate regions, as in *the South,* or when they are part of a proper name, as in *the Lower East Side, South Street.* In an address, spell out and capitalize *North, South, East, West* when they appear before the street, but abbreviate and capitalize when they come after the street, as in *1200 South Maple Street* versus *1200 Maple Street S.*

complement, compliment *Complement* has noun, verb and adjective forms. It means a part that completes the whole. *The manager's writing skill complements his assistant's ability to calculate numbers.* Their skills are complementary. *Compliment* also has noun, verb and adjective forms, but it means either *flattery* or *free. He complimented her writing style. The magazine sent a complimentary tote bag to all new subscribers.*

complimentary close Words that appear at the end of correspondence and just before the writer's name are used as a polite ending. Capitalize the first letter of the close, but lowercase all other words, as in *Very truly yours.* Put a comma after the close. In choosing a close, take into account the degree of formality and familiarity. In an email to a colleague, for example, use *All the best, Best, Cheers,* but for a written communication to a client, use a more formal close, such as *Sincerely* or *Cordially.*

comprise, compose *Comprise* means to include. *The whole comprises the parts,* but *the parts compose the whole.* The distinction between *comprise* and *compose* is losing ground, but many grammarians still insist on it. *The IT department comprises 50 people.* (A common error is to write *The IT department is comprised of 50 people.* Do not use *is* with *comprise.*) *More than 50 employees compose the IT department.*

comptroller, controller Government financial officers are *comptrollers.* Financial officers in businesses are *controllers.* Both words are pronounced the same way.

computer functions Write computer or email functions with a capital letter. It is not necessary to use quotation marks. *I hit the Send button.* This guideline applies to other functions, as in *Nancy hit the Submit button after she finished the order* and *Make sure you hit Print just once.*

Congress Capitalize references to official governmental bodies, as in *U.S. Congress, French Congress.*

congressperson This term is preferred to *congressman* or *congresswomen,* as it avoids reference to gender. *The congressperson from Maine will lead the discussion.* Before a name, use *Rep.* (short for *representative*), as in *Rep. Donna Edwards of Maryland is the keynote speaker.*

conjunction It is a word that joins words, phrases or clauses, such as *and, but, not, since, although, when, yet, so.* Conjunctions come in many shapes and forms: *coordinating, subordinating, correlative.*

connoisseur Often misspelled.

connote, denote *Connote* means to suggest; *denote* means to mean explicitly.

consumer price index Spell out and lowercase in the first reference; use *CPI* afterward. The CPI measures price changes, excluding taxes. There is a difference between the CPI and the cost of living index (COL), which is the amount of money needed to pay taxes and buy goods and services necessary for a certain standard of living. Do not capitalize indexes when spelled out.

Continent, the Capitalize the *C* when referring to Europe.

continual, continuous *Continual* means over and over again; *continuous* means uninterrupted. They are not interchangeable. *The flu outbreak has caused continual absences among the employees. The continuous din of the copy machine gave her a headache.*

contractions They are considered informal in speech and writing, but for most business writing, contractions (e.g., *isn't)* are acceptable.

copacetic, copasetic Both spellings are correct. The origin of this word is unknown. It means satisfactory or acceptable.

copyright This refers to the protection given to the author of an original work, such as an article, book, painting, music, photograph. The symbol for a work protected by copyright is ©. *Copyright* is a noun; it is also a verb, as in *Lorna copyrighted the cantata she wrote last year.*

Corp. An abbreviation for *Corporation.*

corporate affairs Lowercase the names of departments within companies, unless it is already established practice to capitalize. Note that *corporate affairs* takes a singular verb because the term refers to the department. *Corporate affairs is responsible for community relations.* If that sounds awkward, rewrite the sentence, as in *The corporate affairs department is responsible for community relations.*

corporate America Do not use a capital *C* in *corporate*.

corporate communication(s) Lowercase the names of departments within companies, unless it is already established practice to capitalize. Note that *corporate communications* takes a singular verb because the term refers to the department. *Corporate communications is responsible for the annual report.* If that sounds awkward, rewrite the sentence, as in *The corporate communications department is responsible for the annual report.*

corporatespeak, corp-speak These terms are informal and refer to business jargon. Write *corporatespeak* as one word; use a hyphen with *corp-speak*.

corrupted Use this word to describe damaged files (rather than *corrupt*). *The IT department quarantined the corrupted files.*

cost of living, cost-of-living Spell out and lowercase in the first reference; use *COL* afterward. Hyphenate when the term is used as an adjective, as in *The company gave all employees a 2% cost-of-living adjustment.* The COL is the amount of money needed to pay taxes and buy goods and services necessary for a certain standard of living. There is a difference between the COL and the consumer price index (CPI), which measures price changes, excluding taxes. Do not capitalize indexes when spelled out.

cost-plus Use a hyphen.

could care less Write *couldn't care less* instead.

could have Do not use *could of, should of, must of, would of.* These constructions are incorrect but common in speech. Write *could have,* etc.

council, counsel A *council* refers to an administrative group and its members, as in *The Quality Council oversees the company's quality program.* The word *counsel* is both a verb and a noun. As a verb, it means to advise. As a noun, it means advice or guidance. *Counsel* is also used to refer to a lawyer, especially a trial lawyer. *The Quality Office will counsel* [verb] *departments on how to improve quality. The Quality Office will offer counsel* [noun] *on how to improve quality. In case of an emergency, directors should consult with counsel* [noun].

country Use *it/its* when referring to a country (not *they/their). Brazil increased its exports* (not *their exports) to China. It will also increase exports to Korea* (not *They will also increase).*

coup Note the spelling of this term, which refers to a noteworthy achievement or action or to a sudden takeover of leadership or power. *It was a coup for the Asian division to win a contract with the Chinese government. The CEO was ousted in a boardroom coup.*

couple This word takes a plural verb and pronoun if it is used in the sense of two people. *The couple were reunited at their alma mater.*

court cases Use either *v.* or *vs.* for *versus* in court cases, as in Hirsch *v.* 3Com or *Anderson* vs. *Leonard.* (Whichever abbreviation you choose for *versus,* use it consistently. Also note that the abbreviation is set in a different font from the rest of the case title.) If used in a headline, lowercase the abbreviation: Roe *v.* Wade Battle Begins. When not referring to court cases, spell out *versus* in text, as in *At the company softball game, it was the Titans versus the Bullets.*

courtesy titles In text, do not include *Mr., Mrs., Ms.* in the first reference to an individual, because the full name should be used, as in *Andrea Sholler will join the company March 5* (not *Ms. Andrea Sholler).* Afterward, the title can be used, as in *Ms. Sholler has extensive experience in business development.* Other options for subsequent references are to use the first or last name only, as in *Andrea has extensive experience . . .* or *Sholler has extensive experience. . . .* Many newspapers use only the last name in subsequent references, but many companies use a courtesy title.

For women, use *Ms.*, unless *Mrs.* is someone's preference.

In addresses, use *Mr.* or *Ms.* It simplifies matters to refer to all women as *Ms.*

The plural of *Mr.* is *Messrs.* The plural of *Ms.* is *Mss.* The plural of *Mrs.* is *Mmes.*

credit default swap Spell out the first reference to this financial instrument (no hyphen needed); use *CDS* afterward.

criterion, criteria *Criterion,* which means rule or standard, is singular. *The main criterion for hiring Isabel is her B-school degree. Criteria* is plural. *For this job, the criteria are a B-school degree and experience in the healthcare industry.* Make sure the verbs agree with the singular or plural form: *criterion is* and *criteria are.*

cross-border Write *cross-border* with a hyphen, as in *The company announced its third cross-border acquisition in a year.* In headings or headlines, capitalize the *B,* as in *Cross-Border Trading Explodes.*

crowdsource One word.

currency See **foreign currency** entry.

curriculum, curriculums *Curriculum* is singular. For the plural, *curriculums* is preferred to *curricula.*

cut-and-dried Not *cut-and-dry.*

cut back, cutback This term is two words when used as a verb, as in *The company cut back on spending to retain jobs.* Write as one word when used as a noun, as in *The company's spending cutbacks will enable it to retain jobs.*

cutthroat One word.

cutting-edge Use a hyphen with both the noun and adjective forms, as in *The new technology is cutting-edge* and *The company uses cutting-edge technology.*

cyber No hyphen is necessary for most variations of this word. *Cyberspace, cyberthreat.*

Cyber Monday Capitalize both words, no hyphen needed, in this reference to online shopping the Monday after Thanksgiving.

czar This spelling is preferred to *tsar.* It is not always a formal title and is sometimes used to refer to a person with a great deal of power, as in *The president appointed a new drug czar to combat drug trafficking.*

· D ·

"Do your readers a service by anticipating their questions."
– Jeff Cole, director of marketing communication
Dana Holding Corp.

dad Lowercase this word (as in, *Jane's dad is attending the picnic*), unless it substitutes for a proper name, as in *I think Dad is in the garage organizing his tools.* The same goes for *father/Father.*

dangling phrases A phrase dangles when it cannot logically modify the noun or pronoun to which it refers. The following sentences are examples of dangling phrases:

> *To apply for a promotion, a review must be submitted by your manager* (a review cannot apply for a promotion).
> *With much effort the project was completed just before the deadline* (the project cannot exert effort).

To correct these, change the subject of the main clause:

> *To apply for a promotion, you must have your manager submit a review.*
> *With much effort we completed the project just before the deadline.*

dash Use a dash to indicate a sudden break or change in thought, as in *Jane arranged to meet her new sales prospect – at Baltimore's most expensive restaurant – two hours before her flight left for Chicago,* or to set off a series of words, as in *Ryan packed everything – laptop, BlackBerry, Kindle, vitamins – in the bag he left at home.* Instead of making the distinction between em dashes (—) and en dashes (–), this stylebook now uses the en dash instead of the em dash to set off a phrase (with spaces on both side of the dash). A sentence should not be full of indiscriminate dashes; no more than two dashes should appear in a sentence. The en dash is also used to indicate the minus sign or for continuing numbers, as in 2013 – 2015.

data Most business writers use *data* as a collective noun because they perceive *data* as a unit, so it takes a singular verb. *The data is used to track customer spending habits. The data is highly confidential.* The singular of *data* is *datum.*

database One word.

dateline Many media stories begin with *datelines* (specifying where and when the reporting took place). Generally a dateline appears when the article originates from a place other than where the publication is based or when a wire service has been used.

daughter-in-law, daughters-in-law Add an *s* on *daughter,* not *law,* for the plural.

daycare Write as one word whether used as an adjective or noun. *He will drop his daughter off at the daycare center before work. He will drop his daughter at daycare.*

daylight saving time Often misspelled (it is not *daylight savings time).* Lowercase. In the U.S. the clock is set forward an hour on the second Sunday of March at 2 a.m. and set back one hour at 2 a.m. on the first Sunday in November.

daylong One word.

days sales outstanding Spell out in first reference; use *DSO* afterward. This means the average number of days that elapse between when a company books a sale and when it actually gets paid.

days of the week Spell out and capitalize the days of the week in text: *Sunday, Monday, Tuesday, Wednesday, Thursday, Friday, Saturday.* In tabular material, slide shows or charts and graphs, abbreviate days: *Sun., Mon., Tues., Wed., Thurs., Fri., Sat.* See **month** entry.

deal Use *deal* interchangeably with *transaction.*

dealbreaker One word.

dean Capitalize when it is a title preceding a name, as in *Dean Robert Scala will appear at the opening ceremony.* Otherwise, lowercase, as in *The dean of the law school resigned.*

debuted This is the past tense for *debut,* as in *The new software debuted in the second quarter.*

decades You may use either form: *1990s* or *'90s.* Be consistent throughout the entire communication.

decimal Try to avoid using more than two decimal points in text. Round the numbers and avoid decimals altogether when exact figures are not necessary. Be consistent throughout the entire communication.

decision-maker, decision-making Always write with a hyphen. *The team's top decision-maker is based in Hong Kong. The CEO demands timely decision-making from senior officers. The decision-making process involves too many people.*

degrees To indicate temperature, use figures and the degree symbol for all numbers except zero: *It is 76°* or *Do you think the temperature will rise above* *zero today?* Use a word, not a minus sign, for temperatures below zero, as in *The pipes froze because it was minus 10°.*

If a reference to the type of temperature scale is necessary, write *32 °F* with a capital *F,* without a space before or after the degree symbol and without a period after the *F.* (Use the same style for the *C* in *Celsius.)* Fahrenheit is the temperature scale used in the U.S.

degrees See **bachelor of arts, bachelor of science** entry; **master of arts, master of science** entry; **M.B.A.** entry; **Ph.D., Ph.D.s** entry; **L.L.B** entry, **L.L.D.** entry. Also **academic degrees** entry.

delist One word, no hyphen.

depart Always follow with a preposition: *He will depart after the weekend.* Avoid airline style: *He will depart Logan Airport.* Instead write *He will depart from Logan Airport.*

departments There is a great deal of inconsistency within companies on whether to upper- or lowercase department names. Unless it is established practice, lowercase department names, as in *human resources, finance, information systems, facilities, public relations.*

dependent Often misspelled (not *dependant).*

depression When the meaning is economic downturn, lowercase the *d.* Capitalize only when referring to the worldwide economic upheaval of the 1930s. *The central bank helped to avert a depression by lowering interest rates.*

desert (n.), desert (v.), dessert (n.) Misspellings often occur. The first noun means an arid area (or in the case of *just deserts,* it is what you deserve). *The Mojave Desert has two different spellings in the dictionary. Desert* also means to abandon. *The soldier refused to desert his troop. Dessert* is the final course of a meal. *We had apple pie for dessert.*

diacritical marks Avoid using them because they don't transmit well. Some examples of diacritical marks are the *acute accent (é), grave accent (è), umlaut (ü), circumflex (ê), tilde (ñ), cedilla (ç)*.

dialog, dialogue Use *dialog* when referring to a computer *dialog box;* use *dialogue* in other instances.

different from Use the preposition *from*. It is preferred to *different than*. *These numbers are different from the preliminary estimates.*

digital age Lowercase references to this age because a specific date is not assigned to it, even though *Wired Style* states the digital age began in 1984 after Apple produced the first Macintosh computer.

digitize, digitized, digitizes, digitizing These forms are preferred to *digitalize, digitalized, digitalizes, digitalizing*. These terms mean to put into digital form.

dilemma Often used incorrectly. A *dilemma* is more than just a problem. It is the inability to choose between two or more difficult alternatives.

directions In text, lowercase *east, west, north, south,* except when they designate regions, as in *the South,* or if they are part of a proper noun, as in *the Lower East Side, South Street*. In an address, spell out and capitalize *North, South, East, West* when they appear before the street, but abbreviate and capitalize when they come after the street, as in *1200 South Maple Street* versus *1200 Maple Street S*.

disbursement Often misspelled.

disc, disk Often confused. Follow the New York Times style guidelines: Use *disc* for automobile brakes, phonograph records and related terms (*disc jockey*), optical and laser-based devices (*compact disc*). Use *disk* for magnetic devices used with computers (*hard disk*) and the injury to the back (*slipped disk*).

disinterested This word has a different meaning from *uninterested. Disinterested* means neutral or impartial. *The companies signed an arbitration agreement to ensure that disinterested parties handle all disputes.* The word *uninterested* means not interested in something or indifferent toward it.

disintermediate It means to eliminate the go-between person or company.

dive, dived, diving Do not write *Brendan **dove** into the pool.* The preferred form is *dived.*

division Lowercase *division* when referring to parts of the government or corporations. *The food products division increased earnings by 12%.*

.doc, .docx Use the period before the names of file extensions. *Please consolidate the comments into a .docx file, so I can review everything at once. You need to create an error-free .doc file before submitting it for review.*

Dodd-Frank Act Use this shortened version of the legislation in all references; note the hyphen. It can be used interchangeably with *Dodd-Frank law,* but lowercase the *l.* The full name of this financial reform legislation is *Dodd-Frank Wall Street Reform and Consumer Protection Act.*

dollar Use figures with the *$* sign. Note there is no space between *$* and the number, as in *$4 million.*

- The rule to spell out numbers under 10 does not apply to money. *The binder costs $7.*
- Avoid redundancy. Write *$1 million,* not *$1 million dollars.*
- For amounts without a figure, always lowercase *dollars: The bond issue was denominated in dollars.*
- Use singular verbs with specified amounts. *More than $100,000 is expected when making the first payment.*

- For amounts less than $1 million, follow this style: *$9, $34, $500, $2,500, $50,000, $365,000.*
- For amounts more than $1 million, follow this style: *$2.3 million, $4.57 billion.*
- For communications with an international orientation or audience, put *US* before *$* (*US$2.1 billion),* since many countries use dollars. Note that spaces are not needed on either side of *$* and periods are not used in *US,* which differs from the usual abbreviation for the United States, which is *U.S.* See **foreign currency** entry.
- Abbreviate *million* as *mn* and *billion* as *bn* for charts and graphs.

dollar-a-year, dollars a year Use hyphens and write *dollar* without an *s* when used as an adjective, as in *The million-dollar-a-year exhibit draws people from all over the world.* When used as a noun, write without hyphens, as in *The company spends millions of dollars a year on health benefits.* Note the *s* in *dollars.*

When using specific numbers, write *The $84 million-a-year exhibit draws people from all over the world.* Note that no hyphen is needed between the *$84* and *million,* although the rest of the phrase is hyphenated because it modifies.

He earns more than $150,000 a year. No hyphens are needed in this case. The same rules apply for other currencies and other uses of *dollar,* such as *dollars a month, dollars a week, dollars a day.*

domain This is the suffix in web addresses that identifies the type of organization, as in *.com* (general use), *.edu* (educational institution), *.org* (organization), *.gov* (government).

do's and don'ts Write *do's* with an apostrophe to avoid confusion with the word *does* or *dos* (the acronym for *disk operating system).* Note that *don'ts* does not take a second apostrophe.

dotcom, dot-com Write as one word or use a hyphen; just be consistent.

double-check Use a hyphen.

double-click Use a hyphen.

double digit(s) Write as two words when used as a noun, as in *The company expects revenue to grow in the double digits for the next three years.* Note the *s* in *digits*. Hyphenate when used as an adjective, as in *The company expects double-digit revenue growth for the next three years.* Note *digit* is without the *s* in the preceding sentence.

Dow Jones industrial average Spell out in the first reference, capitalizing only *Dow Jones;* use *the Dow* afterward.

download, upload *Download* means to retrieve an application or file from a network or the internet to a PC or mobile device. *Upload* means to transfer a file to a server or the internet. *Upload* as a noun is a word for those transmitted files. Other forms are *downloadable* and *uploadable.*

downside One word. *Upside* is also one word.

downtime One word. *The site has not experienced any downtime. Uptime* is also one word.

Dr. When referring to physicians or dentists, put the title *Dr.* before the name: *Dr. Laura D'Annibale.* If you want to use the *M.D.* title, write *Laura D'Annibale, M.D.* Do not write *Dr. Laura D'Annibale, M.D.* It's redundant. The same holds for *D.D.S.* (dentist) and *Ph.D.*

drugmaker One word.

DSL Use *DSL* in all references for *digital subscriber line.* Do not write *DSL lines,* which is redundant.

due to the fact that This is a wordy construction. Use *because* instead. Remember to be direct and to keep writing short and simple.

Rudolf Flesch, the author of "The Art of Readable Writing," recommends: "Avoid all prepositions and conjunctions that consist of more than one word. Aside from *in as much as,* this includes *with regard to, in association with, in connection with, with respect to, in the absence of, with a view to, in an effort to, in terms of, in order to, for the purpose of, for the reason that, in accordance with, in the neighborhood of, on the basis of* and so on. There's not a single one of these word combinations that can't be replaced by a simple word like *if, for, to, by, about* or *since.*"

DVD Write *DVD* in all references; the plural is *DVDs. DVD* stands for *digital video recorder.*

· E ·

e- This prefix is short for *electronic* and now forms innumerable words: *e-book, e-business, e-commerce, e-learning, e-reader.* Lowercase the *e* and note that many *e-words* still use a hyphen. If you choose not to hyphenate an *e-word,* such as *email,* be consistent. Capitalize *e-words* at the beginning of a sentence, as in *E-learning is becoming the method of choice for managers who want to pursue their studies.*

each When the subject of the sentence begins with *each,* it takes a singular verb. *Each of the investment bankers speaks Japanese.* When *each* follows a plural subject, however, it takes a plural verb: *They each want the same thing.*

each other, one another Use *each other* when referring to two people. *They looked at each other in disbelief.* Use *one another* when referring to more than two people. *Sandra, Christine and Alice will help one another with the project.* To form the possessive of *each other,* write *each other's. They read each other's reports and synthesized the findings into a single document.*

eager This means desirous. *Fran was eager to complete her degree.* Do not use *eager* in place of *anxious,* which means worried, full of anxiety. *He was anxious about the product launch.*

Earth Capitalize when written as a proper noun, such as *Earth, Venus, Mars* or *Earth Day.* Lowercase if it is not a proper noun, as in *The new CFO seems down to earth* or *The earth was dry from lack of rain.*

eBay Inc. Lowercase the *e* and capitalize the *B.* If used at the beginning of a sentence, capitalize the first letter. *EBay announced corporate earnings for the fourth quarter.*

economic, economical *Economic* refers to the subject of economics. *Economical* means thrifty.

economic indicator Lowercase the names of indicators, as in *housing starts, consumer price index.* It is a statistic used, along with other indicators, to measure the state of general economic activity. Common leading indicators are building permits (suggesting the future volume of new construction), common stock prices, business inventories, consumer installment debt, unemployment claims and corporate profits. Other types of indicators move in line with the overall economy (coincident indicator) or change direction after the economy does (lagging indicator).

editorial An editorial is an opinion piece in a publication, which reflects the views of the publisher. An oped expresses the personal viewpoints of individual writers.

e.g. It means *for example* and stands for *exempli gratia* in Latin. This abbreviation is generally used for parenthetical material. It is lowercased, has two periods, is not italicized and is followed by a comma. *The design company has many Asian clients (e.g., Hyundai Mobis, Dongfeng Motor Group, HCL Technologies).* The abbreviation *e.g.* is not interchangeable with *i.e.,* which means *that is* (or *in other words)* and stands for *id est.*

either/or Use *either/or* when referring to a choice between two things. *The company will list on either Nasdaq or the Korea Stock Exchange. Neither/nor* is the negative form. *Neither the CFO nor the CIO is authorized to speak to the media.* When all the elements in an *either/or* construction are singular, use a singular verb: *Either Coleen or Megan is expected to work on the project.* When all the elements in an *either/or* construction are plural, use a plural verb: *Either the desks or the file cabinets have to be moved.* When the construction mixes both singular and plural nouns, the verb should agree with the noun closest to it: *Either the receptionist or the administrative assistants have to come in Saturday.*

elder, eldest Unlike *older* and *oldest,* these terms are generally reserved for persons (not things). Use principally with reference to seniority, as in *elder statesman, elder brother.*

eldercare One word. This refers to care for the elderly, as in *Robin is researching eldercare options for her mother.*

ellipsis The *ellipsis* (. . .) designates an omission of material. Use three periods in place of the omitted material. If the material deleted includes a final period, type four periods (. . . .).

else This word is often unnecessary, as in this construction: *No one else but Dylan is expected to arrive late.* Write instead *No one but Dylan is expected to arrive late.*

email, e-mail Write with or without a hyphen; just be consistent. This stylebook prefers no hyphen in all references. Write email and computer functions with a capital letter, as in *Christine hit the Reply-to-All button.* See Chapter 5 for more information on email.

emailable Material that can be sent via email. *She created an emailable file that contained text and photos.*

embargoed This is the past tense of the verb *embargo. The company embargoed the press release until Monday.*

embarrass Often misspelled.

emcee The word *emcee* is preferred to *MC*, short for *master of ceremonies*.

emeritus This designation implies that a person has retained a title after retiring. Place it after the formal title and lowercase. *Dr. Cathy Chiavetta, professor emeritus of chemistry at Lehigh, addressed the conference.*

emigrate When someone leaves a country, use *emigrate*. *His ancestors emigrated from Ireland.* When someone enters a country, use *immigrate*. *His ancestors immigrated to Brazil.*

emoji Lowercase this Japanese word for picture characters and icons used in email and texting. The plural is *emojis*. *She downloaded an emoji app to her phone. She tends to overuse emojis in her messages.* Avoid *emojis* in most business correspondence.

emoticon Avoid *emoticons* in most business correspondence. These are symbols intended to communicate tone or emotion, as in :-o, :) or :(. *Emoticon* is derived from the words *emotional icon*. See Chapter 5 for more information.

endnote It is documentation that places information about the writer's sources outside the body of the text. This appears at the end of the text under the heading "Notes." Endnotes are placed before the bibliography. Parenthetical documentation is an alternative to endnotes and footnotes: *Employment at large companies rose 29% ("Small Companies Create More Jobs? Maybe Not," New York Times, Feb. 25, 2012).* Include links when possible.

end to end, end-to-end Hyphenate when it precedes a noun, as in *The auditors conducted an end-to-end test of the new technology.* Omit hyphens in this case: *The auditors tested the new technology end to end.*

ensure, insure *Ensure* means to guarantee. *The airline canceled the flight to ensure passenger safety. Insure* refers to insurance. *The company insured its computer equipment for $12 million.*

enterprise-wide Use a hyphen for *enterprise-wide, company-wide, firm-wide, industry-wide. Nationwide* and *worldwide* are one word.

entrepreneur Note the spelling.

envelop (v.), envelope (n.) The verb means to encase completely. *The police will envelop the plaza before the president speaks.* The noun refers to a paper container, especially for letters.

Environmental Protection Agency Spell out in the first reference; use *EPA* afterward.

ePub Short for *electronic publication.*

Equal Employment Opportunity Commission Spell out in the first reference; use *EEOC* afterward.

eras The names of *eras* or *periods* are uppercased but not the words *era* and *period: Colonial era, Obama era, Romantic period.*

ergonomics This takes a singular verb, as in *Ergonomics is responsible for reducing repetitive stress injuries.* When it modifies or describes a noun, it should be written without the *s: ergonomic chair, ergonomic workstation.*

esquire This title used by lawyers comes after the name and is capitalized and abbreviated, as in *Clara Marshall, Esq.* Note the comma. It is never used when another title appears before or after the name. (It is incorrect to write *Ms. Clara Marshall, Esq.)* In most cases it's not necessary to use this title unless the individual lawyer prefers it.

essential clauses, nonessential clauses See **comma** entry.

et al. This abbreviated Latin phrase (*et alii*) means and others. Use it sparingly; many readers won't be sure of its meaning. No italics are necessary. This abbreviation is also used in bibliographies after an author's name if there are more than three authors.

etc. An abbreviation for *et cetera*, meaning and so on and so forth. Use it sparingly. Do not place a comma after *etc.* when it occurs in the middle of a sentence: *She brought her laptop, cellphone, books, etc. to the conference.*

Ethernet Capitalize this term. It refers to a LAN that allows two or more stations to share connectivity.

euphemism When mild, bland or indirect terms are substituted for harsh, direct or blunt words, a euphemism occurs. *A series of technical infrastructure changes has resulted in modified product-launch dates* is a euphemism for *We missed the deadline.*

euro Currency used by 17 of the 27 European Union nations. It is lowercased, just as *dollar, yen* and *renminbi* are lowercased. The plural form varies depending on the language. In English, write *euros,* since adding the letter *s* is how plurals are formed in English and the Bank of England writes *euros.* Do not put a space between the symbol and the number, as in *The shoes cost €200.*

European Union Spell out *European Union* when used as a noun, as in *The European Union was established in 1991.* When used as an adjective, spell out *European Union* in the first reference; use *E.U.* afterward. *The European Union countries issue an E.U. passport.*

eurozone Lowercase the *e* and write as one word. This term is for countries whose currency is the euro; it can be used interchangeably with *euro area* (two words).

every day, everyday Use two words when referring to time. *He exercises every day.* Write as one word when describing something ordinary or routine. *She wears her everyday clothes for gardening.*

every one, everyone Use two words when referring to individual items or persons. *Every one of the computers crashed.* Write as one word when used as a pronoun referring to all persons. *Everyone met at noon for the teleconference.* Because *everyone* is singular, it should take singular verbs and pronouns, as in *Everyone must carry his or her own luggage* (not *Everyone must carry their own luggage*).

every time Always two words.

exaggerate, exaggeration Often misspelled. Connotative words that give little meaning to the text are terms of exaggeration, as in *wonderful, terrific, sensational, incredible, fabulous, unbelievable.* Exercise restraint with these terms.

excerpt An excerpt is always *from* a speech, essay, article, book. Do not use the preposition *of* with *excerpt. The excerpt from the book was provocative.*

exclamation point Use the exclamation point sparingly. But in sentences where an answer to a question is not expected, use the exclamation point instead of the question mark, as in *Wouldn't it be great if we received bonuses this year!* See **quotation marks** entry.

executive summary Lowercase. In a long document an executive summary is a brief synopsis of the key points, placed at the beginning of the document. For the sake of brevity, try to keep it to one page.

extranet Lowercase. This refers to a private network that uses internet technology to link businesses with suppliers, customers and other businesses.

· F ·

"Always ask, 'So what?' after you've written it, and don't send it
if you don't have a good answer."
Peter Thonis, senior vice president, external communications
GTE Corporation (now Verizon)

50-50 Write with a hyphen and numerals (rather than *fifty-fifty*). *The project has a 50-50 chance of gaining board approval.*

401(k) Lowercase the *k* and put into parentheses. Note there is no space between the *401* and the *(k)*. Use *401(k)s* for the plural and *401(k)'s* for the possessive.

Facebook Capitalize. Also written *FB* for short.

face to face, face-to-face This refers to communication that is not electronic. Avoid the abbreviation *f2f* or *F2F*, which many readers will not recognize. *They met face to face for the first time in Paris.* Write with hyphens when used as an adjective. *Face-to-face negotiations are not necessary to close the deal.*

facilities Use *facilities* when referring to a department within a corporation responsible for the physical structures. Lowercase the names of departments within companies, unless it is already established practice to capitalize.

Note that this usage of *facilities* takes a singular verb because it refers to the department. *Facilities is overseeing the renovation.* If that sounds awkward, rewrite the sentence, as in *The facilities department is overseeing the renovation.*

facsimile, fax Use *fax* when referring to the office equipment, the faxed document and the process. The term *facsimile* is dated and may confuse readers.

factoid This means an invented fact believed to be true because of its appearance in print. It also means a brief or usually trivial news item.

Fahrenheit This is the temperature scale used in the U.S. Use figures and the degree symbol for all numbers except zero: *It was 98° in Utah yesterday. Do you think the temperature will rise above zero today?* Use a word, not a minus sign, for temperatures below zero, as in *The pipes froze because it was minus 10°*. If a reference to the type of temperature scale is necessary, then write *32°F* (with a capital *F,* without a space before or after the degree symbol and without a period after the *F).*

fall Lowercase *fall,* which is interchangeable with *autumn.* Lowercase all seasons.

Fannie Mae Note the spelling of *Mae.* Spell out *Federal National Mortgage Association* in the first reference; use *Fannie Mae* afterward.

FAQ See **frequently asked question** entry.

farther, further Use *farther* when referring to concrete distance, as in *The farther he traveled from Beijing, the more he needed his translator.* Use *further* when the meaning is additional or continued, as in *The manager needs further training if she is to be promoted.*

fast track, fast-track Write *fast track* (no hyphen) when used as a noun, as in *The promotion puts Daniel Cregan on the fast track for the CIO position.* This stylebook favors using *fast-track* with a hyphen as a verb, as in *The director decided to fast-track development of the new software.*

father Lowercase *father* unless it substitutes for a proper noun. *His father used to work for IBM. Tell Father we cannot play golf today.* The same goes for *dad.*

fax, facsimile Use *fax* when referring to the office equipment, the faxed document and the process. The term *facsimile* is dated and could confuse readers.

fax numbers Follow these guidelines:

- For the U.S. and Canada, start with *1* and use periods or hyphens to separate the numbers, as in *1 422.111.1111* or *1 422-111-1111.* This stylebook prefers periods; whichever style you choose, use it consistently.
- If writing international fax numbers for a U.S. audience, give the U.S. international access code *(011),* followed by the country and city codes, as in *011 44 111 111 1111.* Use spaces instead of punctuation (periods or hyphens) for international numbers. International numbers vary as far as punctuation goes and also in terms of how numbers are grouped. In addition, not all countries use seven numbers.
- If writing international numbers for an international audience, do not include *011* since this is the international access code from the U.S.

Follow the same guidelines for telephone numbers.

faze Do not confuse this word with *phase.* Use *faze* when the meaning is to disturb or embarrass, as in *The setback did not faze the legal team.*

February Often misspelled.

federal Lowercase when referring to government *(federal agents),* unless it is part of a proper noun, as in *Federal Reserve Board.*

Federal Communications Commission Spell out in the first reference; use *FCC* or *the commission* afterward.

Federal Home Loan Mortgage Corporation Spell out in the first reference; use *Freddie Mac* afterward.

Federal Reserve Board Note it is *Board*, not *Bank*. Spell out in the first reference; afterward use *Federal Reserve, the Fed* (capital *F*), *the Reserve* (capital *R*), *the board* (lowercase *b*). The term *central bank* (lowercased) is another alternative, though it is used less frequently.

Federal Trade Commission Spell out in the first reference; use *FTC* afterward.

FedEx This stylebook favors using *FedEx* (formerly *Federal Express*) as a verb. *Please FedEx this package for me.*

female, male Use these terms as adjectives: *She was the only female CEO at the conference.* For nouns, use *woman* and *man* instead: *She was the only woman at the conference.*

fever, temperature Use *fever* to indicate an undue rise in temperature. *Three employees went to the nurse's office complaining of a fever.* *Temperature* refers to the degree of heat. Everyone has a temperature but not necessarily a fever. The terms are not interchangeable.

fewer, less Use *fewer* when referring to things or people that can be counted. *The OPEC countries are pumping fewer barrels of oil under the new quotas* (barrels can be counted). Use *less* for quantities that cannot be counted or can be considered as a whole. *The OPEC countries are pumping less oil under the new quotas* (oil cannot be counted). *I had less than $10,000 in my 401(k) account* (an amount). *The workstation has a life span of less than 24 months* (a block of time).

Filipinos Use this term for people from the Philippines. *Filipina* is the feminine form.

film Put the names of films in quotation marks, not in italic font. See **movie, television titles** entry.

firefighter, fireman *Firefighter* is preferable as it avoids reference to gender.

firm-wide Use a hyphen for *firm-wide, company-wide, enterprise-wide, industry-wide. Nationwide* and *worldwide* are one word.

first, firstly Use *first* in an enumeration. *The first item on the agenda is the proposed acquisition; the second item is executive compensation.* Avoid *firstly, secondly, thirdly.* Use *first, second, third* instead, as in *First we will discuss the proposed acquisition* (not *Firstly we will discuss . . .*).

first-come-first-served Use hyphens and a *d* in all cases, as in *Breakfast is first-come-first-served.*

first in first out Spell out in the first reference; use *FIFO* afterward. Write *first in first out* with hyphens when used as an adjective, as in *The company changed to first-in-first-out accounting years ago.*

fiscal, monetary Use *fiscal* when referring to budgetary matters: *The company's fiscal year begins in October.* The fiscal year is the 12-month period a company or the government uses for bookkeeping purposes. Use *monetary* when referring to the money supply. *The goal of the central bank's monetary policy is to keep a lid on inflation.*

five nines Either spell out *five nines* or write *99.999%* for this expression, which indicates reliability and uptime in a computer system, as in *The system is noted for its five nines.*

fixed income, fixed-income Use the hyphen when this phrase modifies, as in *fixed-income securities.*

flack Avoid this pejorative term that refers to a publicist.

flak Note the spelling of this term that refers to criticism. *The company took a lot of flak for its delay in announcing the product recall.*

flex-fuel Note the hyphen. This refers to any vehicle that can use more than one source for power, as in *It is a flex-fuel vehicle; the latest model runs on biofuel and gasoline.*

flip-flop Write with a hyphen. *If the company flip-flops again on its pricing policy, we will not renew the contract.*

fluorescent Often misspelled.

f.o.b. Lowercase and use periods. Use *f.o.b.*, which stands for *free on board*, in all references: *The goods from China were shipped f.o.b.*

following For clarity, use *after* instead of *following* in this construction: *After the meeting she went to the third floor.*

font Use font styles (e.g., bold) to make communications user-friendly, but don't overuse; otherwise the fonts lose their impact and the content starts to look busy. Also be aware that when applied to more than a few words, bold and italics render text more difficult to read. Put punctuation following bold or italicized words in the same fonts.

food Usually lowercase food names (*bread, butter)*, except when they are brand names or trade names, such as *Inka Chips.* Capitalize proper nouns or adjectives when they distinguish a particular type of food, such as *Manhattan clam chowder, Muenster cheese.* If the proper noun in the food name does not depend on its distinction for its meaning, lowercase it: *french fries.*

Food and Drug Administration Spell out in the first reference; use *FDA* afterward.

foreign Be mindful when using this word, especially in communications written for a global audience, as it creates a distinction between one location and others. For example, for a Swedish-based multinational company with offices around the world, avoid writing *The company's foreign offices will be closed Jan. 1*, because it relegates all offices outside Sweden to a separate category. Better to write *The company's global offices will be closed Jan. 1*.

foreign country Just write *country*.

foreign currency Spell out the full name of a currency if no value is cited, as in *The company invested hundreds of billions of yen in the project*. If quoting a value, either spell out the currency, as in *The company invested 400 billion yen* (the name of the currency comes after the value), or use the currency symbol: *The company invested ¥400 billion* (the symbol precedes the value).

Note that all countries have two ways to write their currency: a symbol and a three-letter international code. The International Organization for Standardization establishes these three-letter abbreviations, which are called ISO 4217 codes. For Japan's yen, the symbol is ¥ and the ISO code is *JPY*. The symbol for the U.S. dollar is $ (also written *US$*) and the ISO code is *USD*. The abbreviations for the Australian dollar are *A$* and *AUD*. For the euro, they are € and *EUR*.

Decisions on how to write currencies depend on the audience, the context and the medium. If your audience will recognize the symbols, use them. Otherwise, spell out the full names of currencies or use the three-letter codes.

If you are writing a communication citing multiple currencies more than once, the three-letter codes are an option. If your audience is financial and likely to know the codes, use them in the first reference. If your audience might be unfamiliar with the codes, spell out the currency in the first reference, followed by the ISO code in parentheses; use the codes afterward.

Whichever approach you choose for writing currencies, use it consistently. Don't mix styles in a single communication.

Also keep in mind that if you're writing an email, currency symbols other than $ (e.g., £, ¥, €) may not transmit properly to the recipient, making the full names or the ISO codes a better choice.

If it is necessary to convert values from one currency to another, use the latest available exchange rate or, for historical data, the exchange rate prevailing at the relevant date. When you need to include both currency values, put one of the two in parentheses, as in *The company issued a bond valued at €1 billion (US$1.3 billion)*. Note that no space goes between the symbol and the numerals.

foreign exchange Spell out in formal documents, such as annual reports. In other communications, spell out in the first reference; use *FX* or *forex* afterward. Do not hyphenate *foreign exchange* even when used as an adjective, because the meaning is clear without the hyphen. *The company, which operates abroad, is exposed to fluctuations in foreign exchange rates. The finance department tracks FX rates for 60 markets. The website has real-time forex quotations.*

foreign particles Lowercase *de, da, la, von* and other particles when they appear in foreign names. *The marketing director is Rosita de la Paz.* Uppercase the particle only if it begins a sentence, as in *De la Paz joined the company last year.*

foreign words and phrases Use these judiciously and be sure they won't confuse readers. *The exchange of business cards is de rigueur when doing business in Japan.* Avoid putting foreign words into italics.

for example Use this phrase carefully. It should not be used to clarify an unclear statement that precedes it. Rather, use the example to reassert the preceding statement and deepen understanding. The Latin equivalent of *for example* is *e.g.,* which stands for *exempli gratia.* In general, use this abbreviation for parenthetical material. It is lowercased, has two periods, is not italicized and is followed by a comma. *The design company has many Asian clients (e.g., Hyundai Mobis, Dongfeng Motor Group, HCL Technologies).* The abbreviation *e.g.* is not interchangeable with *i.e.,* which means *that is* and stands for *id est.*

former, latter *Former* means the first of two. *He interviewed the manager and the account executive and determined the former had more experience. Former* also means ex-. *The former mayor of Detroit was a Democrat. Latter* means the second of two. *Latter* also refers to nearer to the end. *He devoted the latter half of the meeting to a discussion of the budget.*

form of address A word or phrase used as the polite way of speaking or writing to someone. Most business correspondence still requires a degree of formality in forms of address. In a blind mailing the best practice is to address individuals formally, using *Dear Mr., Dear Ms.,* etc. If the gender is uncertain, write *Dear Chris Smith* rather than *Dear Chris.*

formulas Not *formulae.*

Fortune 500 companies For the most recent list, go to www.fortune.com.

forward Not *forwards.*

Fourth of July The other preferred forms are *July Fourth* and *Independence Day.*

fractions Follow these guidelines:

- If fractions consist of whole numbers and fractions, use figures. *Wayne Anderson poured 2¾ gallons into the mold.*
- When fractions in amounts less than 1 appear in text, spell out and hyphenate. *Approximately one-third of employees work remotely.*
- For ages or pairs of dimensions, use numerals plus fractions, as in *Children must be at least 2½ years old to be admitted to the preschool in town.*
- In tabular material, use figures, preferably expressing fractions with decimal points (*5.5* instead of *5½*). Use the multiplication symbol instead of the word *by* in tabular material (*5¾ × 3½*) if decimals are not used.

free gift Avoid this expression, which is redundant. No one pays for a gift.

freelance One word without a hyphen is the preferred form. The noun is *freelancer,* as in *We are accepting bids from freelancers.*

frequent-flier miles Often misspelled. Note the hyphen.

frequently asked question Spell out in the first reference; use *FAQ* afterward. The plural is *FAQs,* with a small *s.*

Friday Spell out and capitalize days of the week.

friend This word has become a verb, as in *Friend me on Facebook.* The opposite is *unfriend.* The past is *friended.*

fulfill, fulfilled, fulfilling Often misspelled.

full (-) Hyphenate when used to modify. *She is a full-time employee.* Do not hyphenate otherwise. *We would like you to work full time.*

further, farther Use *further* when the meaning is additional or continued, as in *The manager needs further education if she is to be promoted.* Use *farther* when referring to concrete distance, as in *The farther he traveled from Beijing, the more he needed his translator.*

FY This is the abbreviation for *fiscal year,* as in *FY 2014.*

FYI Capitalize all three letters. This is informal for *for your information.* Spell out in formal communications.

· G ·

"I frequently use Google to see what other folks are using."
– Cynthia Hanson, senior copy editor
Franklin Templeton Investments

GAAP Spell out this acronym in first reference. It means *generally accepted accounting principles.* GAAP includes the standards, conventions and rules accountants follow in recording and summarizing and in preparing financial statements.

game-changer, game-changing Use a hyphen in all instances to avoid confusion. *The acquisition has the potential to be an industry game-changer. The company rolled out another game-changing product.*

game plan Two words.

garnish, garnishee *Garnish* is a lien on property or wages to satisfy a debt. *Garnishee* is the person served with a legal garnishment. *Garnish* also can mean to decorate or adorn.

gatekeeper One word. *The CEO's assistant is an excellent gatekeeper for her boss.*

gateway One word. *Hong Kong is the gateway to the company's Asia-Pacific operations.*

gay For sexual orientation, *gay* is the preferred usage when referring to homosexuals. In specific references to lesbians, however, *lesbian* may be preferred. Sexual orientation is not pertinent to most business writing. The same is true for age, race and gender.

GDP See **gross domestic product** entry.

gender Do not always assume maleness in writing. Revise sentences if necessary to address this issue. Rather than *Each executive must carry his own bag,* rewrite the sentence in the plural, as in *Executives must carry their own bags.*

General Accountability Office Spell out in the first reference and use *GAO* afterward.

generally accepted accounting principles See **GAAP** entry.

Generation D, X, Y Note the capitalization in these three *Generation* terms.

Generation D: This is used for the digital generation (which is lowercased); a similar term is *Millennial Generation* (capitalized), which describes students entering the workforce as of 2000.

Generation X: This is used for people born in the 1960s/1970s. The shortened version is *Gen Xers* or just *Xers,* but this is usually too informal for business writing.

Generation Y: This is used for people born in the late 1970s/1980s.

genus, species Usually, but not always, the genus name is uppercased and the species name is lowercased, as in *Esox lucius.* Both words are italicized. Always check the dictionary or use a stylebook. If it is not a scientific document, use familiar names when writing for a general audience, as in *The roses are in bloom,* not *The* Rosa caroliniana *are in bloom.*

geographic names Follow these guidelines:

- For states, note the difference between standard state abbreviations and the two-letter Postal Service abbreviations (*Calif.* versus *CA*). See the **state abbreviations** entry for a list of both types of abbreviations.
- In text, use standard state abbreviations when cities or towns are included, as in *Needles, Calif.* If a city is synonymous with the state or is widely recognizable, then the city can stand alone in text. See **cities** entry.
- Use the Postal Service abbreviations only for full addresses. Capitalize both letters without periods. Do not use a comma between the state abbreviation and the ZIP code.
- Spell out the names of states and U.S. territories when used alone in text.
- If a non-U.S. place name is not identifiable in context, include the country as well.
- Abbreviate U.S. and U.K. as nouns and adjectives. *The sales manager is based in the U.S. and covers all North America. The U.K. office is located in London.*

get The principal parts of this verb are *get* (present), *got* (past), *got* or *gotten* (past participle). Both forms of the past participle are acceptable: *Mary had gotten the email before she went to the meeting* and *Mary had got the email before she went to the meeting.*

gibe It means to jeer or mock. Do not confuse with *jibe,* which means to conform to standard.

GIF Use *GIF* in all references. It stands for *graphics interchange format* and refers to the file format for web-based images.

globalization The American English spelling is with a *z.*

going forward No hyphen is needed. Do not write *going forwards.*

goings-on Use a hyphen. *The report covered the industry's goings-on for the year.*

go-live Use a hyphen. *The go-live date for the software implementation is Mar. 21.*

good, well Make the distinction between *good* and *well. Good* describes a noun, as in *He is a good manager.* Also use *good* with so-called linking verbs, such as *be, appears, seems,* as in *He is good at his job. Well* describes the verb, as in *He works well under pressure.* (*Well* describes how he works.) Also use *well* as an adjective, usually referring to a state of health, as in *The doctor expects her to be well after she takes the antibiotic for 10 days.*

   Hyphenate *well-* phrases before a noun, as in *well-dressed executive, well-read student.*

goodbye One word, no hyphen.

Google Capitalize when referring to the company, as in *Last year, Google changed its privacy policy.* When used in the verb forms, uppercase, as in *Google, Googling* and *Googled. The HR manager Googled the prospective employee.* Avoid the verb form in formal writing.

go-to Use a hyphen. *Christopher is the go-to person for questions on the software rollout.*

government Lowercase, even when a specific government is meant: *U.S. government, Colombian government.*

governor Lowercase this word unless it precedes a name, as in *Gov. Andrew Cuomo.* Before two names, write *Govs.,* as in *Govs. Cuomo and Gregoire.*

GPS Use the abbreviation in all references, as in *GPS navigation devices.* It stands for *global positioning system.*

grade, grader Hyphenate when used to form a noun (*third-grader*) and an adjective (an *11th-grade student*).

No hyphen is needed with the phrase *grade level*. *Finance hired a new manager with a grade level of 42.*

graduate With the verb *graduate,* use the preposition *from,* as in *Denis graduated from business school last year,* not *Denis graduated business school last year.*

gram It is a basic unit of weight in the metric system.

grassroots One word.

gray, grey Use the American English *gray.* The British spelling is *grey.* Note, though, the dog is a *greyhound.* The bus is also *Greyhound.*

great Avoid overusing this word. Like other words of exaggeration, *great* becomes meaningless when used too often in writing.

Great Britain Use this interchangeably with Britain. But note that Great Britain is not interchangeable with *England* or with the *U.K.* Great Britain comprises England, Scotland and Wales. Northern Ireland is not part of Great Britain. The U.K. comprises Great Britain and Northern Ireland.

Great Depression Capitalize when referring to the depression of the 1930s.

Great Lakes There are five Great Lakes: *Lake Superior, Lake Huron, Lake Michigan, Lake Erie, Lake Ontario.* Always capitalize.

Great Recession Capitalize. It refers to the recession that began in 2007 and lasted until 2009, according to the National Bureau of Economic Research.

greenback A one-word nickname for the U.S. dollar. Avoid using *greenback* in formal writing.

gross domestic product Spell out and lowercase in the first reference; use *GDP* afterward. It is the total of all goods and services produced by a nation.

gross national product Spell out and lowercase in the first reference; use *GNP* afterward. It is the total of all the goods and services produced by a nation, including citizens working abroad.

groundbreaking One word. *In a groundbreaking alliance, the two companies agreed to a joint marketing campaign in Asia.*

group Write with singular verbs and pronouns. *The group meets twice a month to review its schedule.*

guru This term commonly refers to a specialist, expert, teacher or mentor.

· H ·

hacker This term is used by some to mean a smart programmer and by others to refer to someone engaged in illegal or mischievous manipulation of computer software. The verb is *hack,* as in *He couldn't hack into the company's systems because the security was so tight.*

half, half(-) It is not necessary to use the preposition *of* with this word, although both constructions are correct: *half the battle, half of the battle.* Most phrases using *half* are hyphenated (*half-dozen, half-hour*), but exceptions exist (*halfway*), so it's a good idea to check the dictionary.

handheld One word, no hyphen. *The company's margins for handheld devices keep shrinking.*

handpicked One word, no hyphen. *Martin is the CEO's handpicked successor. The CEO handpicked his successor.*

handset One word, no hyphen. *The company's new handset has cutting-edge design and functionality.*

hangar, hanger Note the spelling. *Hangar* refers to the building; *hanger* is for hanging clothes.

hanged, hung A person is *hanged* (suicide or execution); clothes are *hung* on the line. The past tense of *hang, hanged* is used only to refer to death by hanging: *He was hanged during the civil unrest of the '60s.* Use *hung* for the past tense in all other cases: *The HR department hung fund-raising posters on each floor of the building.*

Hanukkah This holiday has three spellings. *Hanukkah* (not *Chanukah* or *Hanukah)* is the preferred spelling. Capitalize all holidays – official, unofficial, religious, secular.

harass, harassment Often misspelled.

harebrained Not *hairbrained.*

hashtag One word. Originally used for Twitter messages, it refers to a word or phrase preceded by the # symbol to indicate a topic users may be interested in, such as *#yoga.*

Hawaii Do not abbreviate in text, but use *HI* (capitals without periods) with full addresses, including ZIP code. *HI* is the two-letter Postal Service abbreviation. Seven other states are not abbreviated in text: *Alaska, Idaho, Iowa, Maine, Ohio, Texas, Utah.* See **state abbreviations** entry.

he, him, his, thee, thou It is no longer necessary to capitalize these pronouns when referring to a deity.

headcount One word.

heading When writing a long communication, it is generally useful to break it up with headings. Choose a style for headings and use it consistently throughout the document.

- Decide whether to capitalize only the first word or each of the main words in the heading: *Status of new safety requirements* or *Status of New Safety Requirements.*

- Decide how to differentiate the heading: bold, capitals, larger type.
- Decide whether the headings will be flush left or centered.
- Ensure that spacing above and below the heading is consistent.

headline Write most headlines in the present tense (and put them in quotation marks when citing them). Briefly describe what the article is about or highlight a significant fact in the article (without distorting the article's essence). Space is usually a factor in headlines, so the fewer words the better. Writing a good headline takes extra effort, so remember the following rules:

- For capitalization in headlines, follow these guidelines: Capitalize the first and last words in a headline. Capitalize all principal words (nouns, pronouns, verbs, adjectives, adverbs) and all other words of four or more letters (such as *About, Though, Between, Against*). Lowercase articles (such as *the, a, an*), conjunctions (such as *and, or, but*) and prepositions (such as *of, with, from, for, by*). Also lowercase the *to* in infinitives (such as *to Drive, to Work*). Remember, the word *is* is a verb, so capitalize it in headlines.
- When using hyphenated or compound words in headlines, capitalize the word following the hyphen, as in *Cross-Border Trade Increases, Sales of Over-the-Counter Medicine Rise.*
- Be sure spelling and numbers in headlines are exactly the same as the information in the text.
- Single quotation marks are often used with quoted words if the headline is in large, bold type. This is a graphic decision. Establish a style and use it consistently.
- Use standard English (do not shorten the word *neighborhood* to *nabe;* better to find an alternative word).
- Keep it short and simple.
- Use short, active verbs and make sure an omission of words (such as the articles *a, an, the*) does not confuse the reader.
- Draw the reader into the material with good headlines.
- Avoid foreign phrases in headlines.

- Avoid sensational headlines.
- In headlines referring to court cases, lowercase *vs.* or *v.*

headquarters This noun can take a singular or plural verb. This stylebook favors a singular verb: *Headquarters is in Dublin.* This stylebook also favors using *headquarter* as a verb form, even though it may be considered nonstandard. *The company is headquartered in Dublin.*

heads-up Write with a hyphen. This means advance warning or alert. *I gave the boss a heads-up that we might not meet the quarterly budget numbers.*

healthcare This noun can be one or two words. This stylebook favors the one-word form.

healthful, healthy It is acceptable to use these words interchangeably, according to "The American Heritage Dictionary." Both words mean conducive to good health. If you are concerned with making the distinction, this is what "Merriam-Webster's Dictionary of English Usage" says: "*Healthful* means 'conducive to health' and *healthy* means 'enjoying or evincing health'. . . . *Healthy,* since its introduction in the middle of the 16th century, has been used much more frequently than *healthful,* so, if you observe the distinction between *healthful* and *healthy,* you are absolutely correct, and in the minority. If you ignore the distinction, you are absolutely correct, and in the majority."

he is a man who This construction is wordy, according to Strunk and White. *He is a man who* is easily replaced with the single word *he.* One word is better than five. Be concise in business writing.

here When *Here* begins a sentence and is followed by a verb, make sure the verb agrees with the subject that comes after it, as in *Here comes the judge* or *Here is the book you wanted* or *Here are the brochures for the conference. Here* is an adverb, not a noun.

heretofore, hitherto Both words mean *until now.* Avoid using them in business writing not concerned with legal matters.

highflying One word.

high-tech Write with a hyphen. Use this short version of *high-technology* in all references; same for *low-tech.*

highway designations Follow this format: *U.S. Route 9, state Route 17, U.S. Route 66, Interstate 95* (in later references, use *I-95*). When a letter is attached to a number, capitalize it, but do not use a hyphen: *Route 9S.*

high yield No hyphen is needed whether used as a noun, as in *The bonds have a high yield,* or as an adjective, as in *The bank underwrote the company's high yield debt offering.*

hike This is used widely as a noun or verb to designate a sudden or abrupt increase in price or salary. *The government hiked public-sector salaries to compensate for the previous month's spike in inflation.* In some documents (such as an annual report), it may be too informal; use *increase* or *raise* instead.

his or her Avoid the assumption of maleness, as in *Each speaker will use slides with his presentation.* To avoid the wordy *his or her* construction (*Each speaker will use slides with his or her presentation),* it is often better to rewrite the sentence in the plural: *Speakers will use slides with their presentations.* Business writers should pay attention to gender issues.

Hispanic(s) Person who traces his or her ancestry to a Spanish-speaking country. *Hispanic* is the broadest term. The term *Latino* is less formal but may be preferred by some because it de-emphasizes the tie to Spain.

historical references Capitalize important historical events or periods, such as *the Renaissance, the Depression, the French Revolution, Prohibition.* Lowercase indefinite periods, as in *nuclear age*. Also lowercase centuries, such as *the 20th century*.

hoi polloi It is a term meaning the common people, not the elite. (Although many writers insert *the* with this expression, it is not necessary because the Greek word *hoi* means *the).*

hole-in-one, holes-in-one Hyphenate and add an *s* to *hole* for the plural.

holiday Capitalize all holidays – official, unofficial, religious, secular – including the word *Day,* as in *Martin Luther King Day.*

homemaker This one-word term is preferred to *housewife,* which defines by marital status as well as gender.

homepage, home page This can be written as one or two words; just be consistent.

hopefully Avoid writing *Hopefully we will have the survey results by May.* Although many writers use *hopefully* this way and some stylebooks find it acceptable, it is a pet peeve of strict grammarians, who insist that adverbs modify verbs (not the whole sentence, which is how *hopefully* is working in this construction).

hors d'oeuvre Often misspelled. The singular is *hors d'oeuvre,* and the plural can be either *hors d'oeuvre* (same as the singular) or *hors d'oeuvres.* This stylebook favors *hors d'oeuvres.*

hot button, hot-button Use two words, without a hyphen, when it acts as a noun; use a hyphen when it modifies, as in *hot-button issue.*

hotline Lowercase and write as one word, even though some stylebooks write this as two words (*hot line).*

hotspot One word. *She found a wifi hotspot near the university. The newest hotspot for Korean tacos is on 10th Street.*

hours For time of day, use figures, as in *We will meet at 9 a.m. in the conference room* (not *nine a.m.*). Note the space between the number and *a.m.* Lowercase *a.m.* and *p.m.* with periods. If the time is on the hour, it is not necessary to include a colon and two zeros. Just write *9 a.m.* Use the colon to separate minutes from hours, as in *9:15 a.m.* It is better to specify *a.m.* or *p.m.* than to use the *o'clock* form. If the *o'clock* form is used, spell out the number (*one* through *nine*), as in *nine o'clock*, not *9 o'clock*.

hover This verb is used in conjunction with *mouse*, as in *Hover the mouse over the image to see the information box.* Other variations of this concept are *mouse over* and *roll over*, as in *Mouse over the image to see the information box* or *Roll over the image.*

however This word works better in the middle of a sentence than at the beginning: *We cannot finalize the report until Monday. We will, however, give you a draft to review over the weekend.* Note the commas on either side of the word.

how-to, how-tos Use a hyphen.

HTML Use *HTML* in all references. *HTML* stands for *Hypertext Markup Language*, the codes and formatting instructions for interactive internet documents.

http://www In a web address, it is not necessary to include the protocol *http://* as long as *www* is part of the address, as in *www.nytimes.com.* If *www* is not part of the address, then include *http://*.

Also, when a web address has a protocol other than *http://* (e.g., *ftp*, *https*), then include that protocol.

humankind This is sometimes used as a gender-free alternative to *mankind,* but it sounds a bit contrived in business writing. When possible, use an alternative, such as *human beings.*

human resources Spell out and lowercase in the first reference; use *HR* afterward. *The new head of human resources called a meeting with the entire HR department.* Many companies capitalize the names of departments, but unless it is already established practice, lowercase department names.

Note that *human resources* and *HR* take a singular verb because the terms refer to the department. *Human resources **is** responsible for the employee survey.* If that sounds awkward, rewrite the sentence, as in *The human resources department is responsible for the employee survey.*

hundredth Often misspelled.

hybrid An automobile that can use more than one source of energy, such as gasoline and electric.

hyperbole This is a figure of speech that uses exaggeration for effect, as in *Tara waited an eternity for the report.*

hyperlink No hyphen is needed for this word. *The hyperlink takes readers to the company's annual report. Link* is a shorter alternative to *hyperlink.*

hypertext No hyphen is needed for this word.

hyphen A *hyphen* links words and is often inserted to establish clarity. It has no space on either side of it. Many communications professionals surveyed for this book noted that they often use their stylebooks to check hyphenation on particular words. Use hyphens:

- To link two or more words that serve as an adjective: *collective-bargaining talks, cross-border transaction, 28-year-old manager, $4 billion-dollar* *company, 2-for-1 stock split.* But avoid overuse. If the meaning of a phrase is clear without a hyphen, don't use one: *best seller list, real estate agent, income tax form, foreign exchange rates.*

- To join two or more words to form a single idea: *African-American.*
- To separate double letters: *semi-independent, pre-existing.*
- To avoid writing words that may be unclear without a hyphen: *re-form.*
- To form words with the prefixes *ex-, self-: ex-banker, self-explanatory.*
- To join a single letter to another word: *X-rated, y-axis, T-shirt.*
- To form a title that joins two equal nouns: *secretary-treasurer.*
- At the end of a word or number to avoid repetition: *The 65- and 66-year-old employees retired last week. The second- and third-quarter results will be released next month. The medium- and long-term goals must be linked.* These are suspensive hyphens.
- To spell out numbers when they cannot be written as numerals, for instance, at the beginning of a sentence, as in *Twenty-five.*
- To spell out fractions in amounts less than 1 in text. *Approximately one-third of employees work remotely.*
- To break words at the end of lines by syllable.

Other points to remember:

- A common error is to use hyphens in phrases with the word *very* and adverbs ending in *-ly.* Do not use hyphens with such phrases: *eagerly awaited proposal, newly elected board member, highly controversial report.*
- Note that many combinations that are hyphenated before a noun are not hyphenated when they come after the noun: *a full-time job* versus *She worked full time.*
- Use an *en dash* in place of a hyphen in a compound adjective if one element consists of a hyphenated word: *quasi-corporate–quasi-government body, self-employed–ex-accountant.* This can make a sentence unwieldy, but occasionally it is unavoidable.
- When using hyphenated words in headings or headlines, capitalize the word following the hyphen, as in *Cross-Border Trade Increases.*

hyphenated Americans *Hyphenated Americans* is a pejorative term. Do not use it when referring to American immigrants or their descendants.

hyphenated names To alphabetize a hyphenated name, treat the name as one word, so that *Madeleine Kurtz-Adler* is alphabetized under *K,* not *A.* The same applies to compound last names, as in *Martin Van Buren,* which is alphabetized under *V,* not *B.*

· I ·

I Using the first-person *I* can change the tone in writing. Always write with your audience in mind. See Chapter 4 for more on the use of *I*.

icon Always lowercase, regardless of the meaning. *He deleted the icon for Acrobat Reader. Joel Good, a conservative icon, was uncomfortable while speaking to the union.*

ID Use *ID* in the first reference as long as it is clear in context. It stands for *identification. After the merger the company will issue new ID cards.*

Idaho Do not abbreviate in text, but use *ID* (capitals without periods) with full addresses, including ZIP code. *ID* is the two-letter Postal Service abbreviation. Seven other states are not abbreviated in text: *Alaska, Hawaii, Iowa, Maine, Ohio, Texas, Utah.* See **state abbreviations** entry.

i.e. This abbreviation stands for *id est,* which is Latin for *that is* (or *in other words*). In general, use *i.e.* for parenthetical material. It is lowercased, has two periods, is not italicized and is followed by a comma. *The designer developed the new company's* *branded materials (i.e., letterhead, signage, business cards).* It is not interchangeable with *e.g.,* which means *for example* and stands for *exempli gratia.*

if In *if* clauses that describe hypothetical situations, use the following verb tense (called the *subjunctive): If I were you, I'd go to the meeting.* See **subjunctive** entry.

ifs, ands or buts No apostrophes are needed in this expression.

illegal Use *illegal* only if a law has been broken. It is not applicable to the breaking of contracts.

illicit, elicit These words differ in meaning. *Illicit* means illegal or prohibited, as in *The company fired the director because of his illicit trading activities. Elicit* means to bring forth or draw out, as in *What response did the manager elicit when he reported the budget shortfall?*

IM, IMed, IMing Use the short form in all references; stands for *instant message/messaged/messaging.*

immune from Note the use of *from* (not *to). The company is immune from weak market conditions in Europe and Asia.*

impact *Impact* as a noun means a strong effect: *The dollar's depreciation is having a positive impact on exports. Impact* is also a verb, used frequently in business communications. *How will the price war impact margins?* Strict grammarians consider using *impact* as a verb as technical jargon.

imply, infer These words have similar meanings, but a distinction exists between actor and reactor. Writers and speakers *imply* (suggest or convey an idea without stating it), while readers and listeners *infer* (they draw conclusions or figure out what is being suggested). *Mike implied layoffs were imminent. The staff inferred from Mike's comments that layoffs were imminent.*

inasmuch as This term is two words.

in between, in-between The first is an adverb or preposition, as in *Bob is in between jobs at the moment.* The second is an adjective or noun, as in *The social media companies, the traditional media companies and the in-betweens were at the conference.*

inbox One word. *Outbox* is also one word.

Inc. In the first reference to a company, write and punctuate this exactly as the company does (*Incorporated* or *Inc.,* with or without a comma before it). In the second reference, it is not necessary to include this part of the formal name. The same applies to *Ltd., S.A., A.G., Mfg., Mfrs., SpA, N.V., GmbH* and other corporate appellations.

Use a comma after the company name with *Inc.* if a comma precedes *Inc.* in the official company name, as in *Wal-Mart Stores, Inc., announced its earnings.* Do not use a comma if the company name does not use a comma before *Inc.,* as in *Tara works for Newell Rubbermaid Inc. at its headquarters.*

incentivize This stylebook favors using this word (the noun is *incentive*), as it is commonly used in business. *The compensation policy is designed to incentivize leadership behaviors.* The opposite, *disincentivize,* though correct, is not used as frequently.

incidence This word means *rate* or *prevalence,* as in *The company detected a high incidence of internet usage.* Avoid confusion with *incidents,* which means specific occurrences. *The IT team discovered 200 incidents involving security breaches.*

including This word implies a partial list. *The firm has capital markets experience in sectors including technology, healthcare and entertainment.* If the subject is negative, as in *No one* (the subject), *including John Forde, will be laid off next year,* it is better to use *not even,* as in *No one, not even John Forde, will be laid off next year.*

index Write the plural as *indexes: Both indexes, the S&P 500 and the Hang Seng, were down for the third quarter. Indexes* is preferred to *indices* for the plural.

indiscreet, indiscrete Use *indiscreet* when the meaning is lacking judgment or prudence (*indiscretion* is the noun). *Indiscrete* means not separated into distinct parts. A more commonly used variation of this word is *discrete. She organized the white paper into discrete sections by topic.*

industry-wide Use a hyphen for *industry-wide, company-wide, enterprise-wide, firm-wide. Nationwide* and *worldwide* are one word.

infarction, infraction Do not confuse these terms. *Infarction* is a medical term referring to an area of tissue that dies because of an obstruction of the blood supply. *Infraction* is a term meaning violation.

infinitive An infinitive is a verb form that usually can be identified by the word *to,* as in *to eat, to purchase, to win, to write.* Nowadays it is acceptable to split infinitives by putting a word in the middle, as in *to easily purchase.* The constructions that result from never splitting infinitives are often awkward. But don't put too many words between the *to* and the verb, or the reader may lose track of the verb.

information services Spell out and lowercase in the first reference; use *IS* afterward. *The new head of information services called a meeting with the entire IS department.* Many companies capitalize the names of departments, but unless it is already established practice, lowercase department names.

Note that *information services* takes a singular verb because the term refers to the department. *Information services is responsible for software development.* If that sounds awkward, rewrite the sentence, as in *The information services department is responsible for software development.*

information technology Spell out and lowercase in the first reference; use *IT* afterward. *The new head of information technology called a meeting with the* *entire IT department.* Many companies capitalize the names of departments, but unless it is already established practice, lowercase department names.

initial When an individual prefers two initials to a first name, use periods and no space between the initials: *P.T. Barnum, T.C. Boyle.* Avoid using the first initial in place of the first name. *Russell Bleemer* is preferable to *R. Bleemer.*

initialism An *initialism* is an abbreviation pronounced by letter, as in *IRS* (for *Internal Revenue Service* and pronounced *I-R-S)* or *CBOE* (for *Chicago Board Options Exchange* and pronounced *C-B-O-E).* Most initialisms are capitalized without periods.

An initialism is not the same as an acronym, which is a word formed from the first letter or letters of a series of words. Acronyms are pronounced as single words, as in *NASA, NATO, NOW.* If the acronym is longer than four letters, capitalize the first letter and lowercase the remaining letters, as in *Nasdaq, Unctad.* Company names are an exception to this guideline. Follow a company's style. Most acronyms do not require periods. When acronyms cross over and become generic terms, lowercase them, as in *radar, modem, captcha, abend (abnormal end of task).*

To write initialisms or acronyms, follow this guideline: Spell out the entire phrase in the first reference; use just the initialism/acronym afterward: *John Andrews is employed by the Brotherhood of Locomotive Engineers and Trainmen. He works at BLET headquarters in Cleveland.* If an initialism or acronym is widely recognizable, however, it's not necessary to spell out in first reference, as in *Nasdaq.*

in line, on line People wait *in line.* To wait *on line* is a regional preference in the New York area. Use *in line* outside New York. When referring to skating, *inline* is one word. Write *online* as one word, as in *Nelson buys electronics online* or *Esther coordinates the company's online sales program.*

inoculate Often misspelled; it has a single *n* and a single *c.*

input, output Use *input* as a noun, meaning something (such as information) put into a system to achieve output (a result). *Input* also means a contribution of information, a comment or a viewpoint, as in *We need input from customers to determine whether the product modifications meet their needs. Input* can also be used as a verb. *Diane input the salary information on a spreadsheet.*

in regard to There is no *s* at the end of *regard* in this phrase. A common error is to write *in regards to.*

insource One word, no hyphen; opposite of *outsource.*

institution Capitalize the full name and always follow the institution's style in the first reference; use the abbreviation or shortened name afterward, as in *She is an economist at the National Labor Relations Board. She has worked at the NLRB for five years.* Use *it/its* when referring to an institution (not *they/their*). *The World Bank held its meeting in Santiago* (not *their meeting*). *It invited all Latin American countries to attend* (not *They invited*).

insure, ensure *Insure* refers to insurance. *The company insured the computer equipment for $2 million. Ensure* means to guarantee. *The airline canceled the flight to ensure passenger safety.*

interesting Use this word sparingly. Let the reader judge whether something is interesting. This also applies to terms like *funny, fascinating, stimulating, awe-inspiring, unique.*

interface Used as a verb, it means to meet and exchange ideas. *The manager needs to interface more with her staff.*

interjection An exclamation that expresses strong feeling: *Bravo! Kudos! Scram!*

Internal Revenue Service *Internal Revenue Service* and *IRS* may be used interchangeably.

internet Lowercase and use in the first reference. Use *the net* interchangeably afterward.

A web address is a URL (for *uniform resource locator*). Include it when referencing a website readers might want to consult. Follow capitalization, no matter how idiosyncratic it may be, because some addresses are case-sensitive. Write the sentence so that normal punctuation (a comma, for instance) does not cause confusion. It is not necessary to include the protocol *http://* as long as *www* is part of the address, as in *See www.yourdomain.com for more information.* If *www* is not part of the address, then include *http://*.

Also, when a web address has a protocol other than *http://* (e.g., *ftp, https*), then include that protocol.

internet service provider Spell out in the first reference; use *ISP* afterward.

intranet Lowercase. This is part of an organization's internal network, which is usually linked to the internet.

intriguing Nowadays this word is used to mean fascinating or alluring. Its original meaning suggested subterfuge, an underhanded scheme.

investor relations Spell out and lowercase in the first reference; use *IR* afterward. *The new head of investor relations called a meeting with the entire IR department.* Lowercase the names of departments within companies, unless it is already established practice to capitalize.

Note that *investor relations* takes a singular verb because the term refers to the department. *Investor relations is responsible for financial information.* If that sounds awkward, rewrite the sentence, as in *The investor relations department is responsible for financial information.*

IOU Write *IOU* in all references. It comes from the pronunciation of *I owe you.*

Iowa Do not abbreviate in text, but use *IA* (capitals without periods) with full addresses, including ZIP code. *IA* is the two-letter Postal Service abbreviation.

Seven other states are not abbreviated in text: *Alaska, Hawaii, Idaho, Maine, Ohio, Texas, Utah*. See **state abbreviations** entry.

IP Spell out *intellectual property* in the first reference; use *IP* afterward. Also stands for *internet protocol,* as in *IP address*.

iPad, iPhone, iPod, iTunes Lowercase the *i* and uppercase the first letter in the word that follows it for Apple products. The exception is when one of these words starts a sentence. *ITunes released a software update last week*. (If *ITunes* at the beginning of a sentence jars the eye, then recast the sentence, as in *Apple's iTunes.)*

IPO Spell out *initial public offering* in the first reference; use *IPO* afterward.

IQ Use *IQ* in all references. *He probably has a high IQ, but his interpersonal skills are lacking. IQ* stands for *intelligence quotient*.

it Use *it* to refer to a company, a department within a company, an organization, a school or a country. *The company had an outstanding year. It* (not *They) increased sales by 30%*.
  Other ways to use *it:*

- To refer to something previously mentioned, as in *I saw "Mysteries of Lisbon" last weekend; it was fabulous*.
- To refer to someone whose identity is unknown, as in *Someone left this package on my desk, but I don't know who it was*.
- To refer to a general condition or state of affairs, as in *He couldn't take it anymore, so he resigned*.
- To emphasize a word that is not the subject of the sentence, as in *It is incredible that he finished the project so quickly*.
- To refer to an animal, as in *It bit my leg*.
- To refer to a ship, as in *The ship sailed Friday; it is fully booked*. It is outdated to use *she*.

italics The first edition of this stylebook recommended italics to differentiate certain words. We now recommend quotation marks, which are easier to type and transmit over portable devices. Italicizing words adds time to the writing process, and italics can get lost if material is read on BlackBerrys, iPhones and other portable devices. To set off a word or phrase, quotation marks are a better bet, but use them sparingly. *I looked up the word "verisimilitude" in the dictionary.* (Italics, however, are used in this stylebook to illustrate examples and cast words as words.)

In addition, this stylebook no longer recommends using italics for the titles of periodicals and foreign phrases because of the technology. Just set the name of the newspaper/periodical as a proper noun, with caps and without the italic font or quotation marks, as in the New York Times (notice the lowercase *the*). Most other stylebooks follow this guideline. For books, television and movie titles, use quotation marks.

It is Sentences beginning with *It is, There is, There are* can become monotonous. Rewrite and combine sentences to show a closer connection: *Relationships are everything is a deeply rooted business maxim* as opposed to *There is a maxim in business that relationships are everything. It is deeply rooted.*

it's, its Confusing these forms is one of the most common mistakes in writing. *It's* is the contraction for *it is* or *it has. It's your turn* or *It's been a productive week. Its* indicates possession in the singular. *The board made its decision at the July meeting. The company will release its new technology next year. The IT team made its recommendations after the budget numbers were finalized.*

-ize This stylebook favors using *-ize* to create verbs from nouns because these forms are useful in business. Examples include *finalize, prioritize, optimize, incentivize.*

· J ·

"If a style standard is chosen, it's important to apply that style across the board in all written communication."
— Kristine Pavletich, public relations specialist
Bemis Company, Inc.

Japanese names In Japanese, names are written with the family name first, followed by the given name: *Matsumoto* (family name) *Kazuyuki* (given name). Although many English-language publications follow that style and would write *Matsumoto Kazuyuki,* this creates confusion about first and last names. To avoid such confusion when writing for business, put Japanese names in the same order as names written in English: given name first, followed by the family name: *Kazuyuki Matsumoto* or *Mr. Matsumoto.*

jargon This is the language of the inner circle, often exclusionary in nature. In some instances certain terms may be appropriate and necessary in business writing, but for a wider readership, include explanations. Do not assume all readers know the terms. See Chapter 2 for more details.

Java Capitalize when it is a reference to the computer language or the island in Indonesia. Lowercase the informal term when it refers to a cup of coffee.

Jeep, jeep Uppercase the four-wheel-drive vehicle used by civilians because it is a trademark, but lowercase the military vehicle.

Jehovah's Witness Use an apostrophe and capitalize *Witness*. It refers to a member of a religious denomination founded in the U.S.

jibe Note the spelling (not *jive*). It means to conform to standard. Do not confuse with *gibe,* which means to jeer or mock.

job titles Lowercase job titles when they come after a name: *Rhonda Price, managing director.* Uppercase when the title precedes the name: *Managing Director Rhonda Price.* Lowercase when no name is used, as in *The managing director will speak at the meeting.* Note the difference between a job description (*technologist*) and a job title (*information systems manager*).

Johns Hopkins University Often misspelled. (It is not *John Hopkins University.*)

joint venture, joint-venture Do not hyphenate when used as a noun, as in *The companies formed a joint venture to develop the technology.* Write with a hyphen when used to modify, as in *The companies signed a joint-venture agreement.* Spell out in the first reference; for subsequent references *JV* is an alternative.

jpeg Use *jpeg* in all references. This book favors writing it in lowercase, although some stylebooks write it with all caps. It stands for *Joint Photographic Experts Group* and is a file format for web-based images (particularly photographs). The plural is *jpegs.*

judge Use this title in all references. Capitalize it if it precedes a person's name. *He will meet with Judge Myles Markowitz today.* Note that for the Supreme Court, the title is *justice.*

judgment Use the American English spelling (*judgment*), not the British spelling (*judgement*).

judicial, judicious *Judicial* means pertaining to courts or law. *Judicious* means wise.

juggernaut Note the spelling of this word for a powerful, relentless force. *SK Telecom decimated its competition and is a mobile phone juggernaut.*

jump-start Write this term with a hyphen. *Fayza wants to jump-start the product launch by offering rebates.*

junior, senior Use the abbreviation *Jr.* or *Sr.* with names of people. Use a comma before *Jr.* or *Sr.* For instance: *Robert Downey, Jr.* In a listing by last name, the *Jr.* or *Sr.* comes last: *Downey, Robert, Jr.*

Spell out and lowercase *junior* or *senior* to designate a member of the class.

junk mail Lowercase this term, which refers to *unsolicited mail.*

jury-rig, jury-rigged Hyphenate this phrase, which means to assemble for a temporary purpose. *Jerry-rig(ged)* is similar in meaning and is probably a blend of *jerry-built* and *jury-rigged.*

justice The Supreme Court uses the title *justice* instead of *judge.* Capitalize *justice* only if it precedes a person's name. *He interviewed Justice Sonia Sotomayor. He will interview Sonia Sotomayor, who has been a justice of the Supreme Court since 2009.* The New York State Supreme Court and its Appellate Division also use *justice* instead of *judge.* Check to make sure the title is appropriate.

juvenile delinquent This term refers to someone under the age of 18 who is guilty of a criminal offense. Do not capitalize.

· K ·

K Use *K* (capitalized) as an abbreviation for thousand, especially in headlines and headings to save space. *The new process will save the company $400K.* Do not put a space between *K* and the number. *K* is also an abbreviation for *kilobyte*, as in *128K*. Use the *K* for all references.

karat Measures the fineness of gold. Do not confuse this term with *carat*, which is a unit of weight for gemstones. *Her future husband gave her a 14-karat gold ring with a 2-carat diamond.* A *caret* (^) is a mark used by editors and proofreaders.

ketchup This spelling is preferred to *catsup* or *catchup*.

Keynesian Relating to the economic theories of John Maynard Keynes, especially those theories advocating government monetary and fiscal programs designed to increase employment and stimulate business activity.

keynote One word, used as both an adjective and noun. *The new chairman will be the keynote speaker at this year's customer forum. The new chairman will give the keynote at this year's customer forum.*

Keystone Kops Often misspelled.

keystroke One word.

keystroke guideline The fewer keys it takes to form a word, the better. In most instances, this stylebook favors the keystroke guideline – as long as clarity is not jeopardized. In making this decision, determine who the readers are and what degree of formality you want to convey. This stylebook follows this suggestion from "The Chicago Manual of Style": "Anything that reduces the fussiness of typography makes for easier reading."

keyword Write as one word in the sense of a word used in performing an online search, as in *The HR department has a list of keywords for identifying risk management professionals in LinkedIn.*

kids Slang for *children*. It is generally too informal for business communications.

kilo(-) Words formed with *kilo* are not hyphenated, such as *kilometer* and *kilowatt*.

kilobyte Use *K* for *kilobyte* for all references. There is no space between the number and the *K,* as in *128K.* A kilobyte equals 1,024 bytes.

kindergarten, kindergartner These words are often misspelled (as *kindergarden* and *kindergardner).*

kind of, sort of These are colloquial expressions for *rather. She was kind of disappointed with her raise* is too informal for writing. *She was rather disappointed* *with her raise* is better, but both are qualifying terms that are often unnecessary. It is preferable to be more direct and write *She was disappointed with her raise*.

These phrases can also mean type of, as in *What kind of car are you buying?* Do not insert the article *a* in this construction, as in *What kind of **a** car are you buying?* Check for agreement in these constructions: *That kind, those kinds*.

king Lowercase *king* when it is not part of a name, as in the *king of England*, but uppercase it if it precedes the name: *King Charles*.

kiosk This is a place that gives customers or employees access to computers. *The store has kiosks that enable customers to order out-of-stock items online.* A *kiosk* is also a newsstand.

Kleenex Uppercase this term, which is a trademark.

knock-on Write with a hyphen, as in *The delay in the rollout will have multiple knock-on effects*. This term is more British than American.

knot Do not write *knots per hour.* It is implied because a knot equals 1 nautical mile per hour.

know-how Write with a hyphen.

knowledgeable Often misspelled.

known as No quotation marks are necessary in this construction: *The business reengineering consultants, known among the staff as the Hit Squad, are scheduled to begin working next year.* (No quotation marks around *Hit Squad*.)

Korean names In Korean, names are written with the family name first, followed by the given name(s): *Hong* (family name) *Ji Hoon* (given names). Although many English-language publications follow that style and would write *Hong JiHoon*, this creates confusion about first and last names. To avoid such confusion when writing for business, put Korean names in the same order as names written in English: given name(s) first, followed by the family name: *Ji Hoon Hong* or *Mr. Hong.*

kosher Lowercase this term, which refers to the dietary laws of Judaism. Informally this term can mean legitimate or proper.

kudos This means praise or credit. No verb is needed, as in *Kudos to Sarah for surpassing this month's sales quota.* If a verb is used, the verb is singular. *Kudos goes to Sarah for surpassing this month's sales quota.*

kW Use a lowercase *k* and an uppercase *W* for the abbreviation for *kilowatt.*

Kwanzaa Note the spelling of this African-American cultural festival, which begins Dec. 26 and ends Jan. 1. This celebration is based on African harvest customs.

· L ·

lady While a synonym for *woman,* this word has a patronizing and antiquated tone. Reserve the use of *lady* for nobility.

laissez-faire Note the hyphen. This French term is frequently used in the sense of hands-off or indifferent. *The regulators are scrutinizing the company because of its laissez-faire approach to risk management.*

LAN Use *LAN* in all references. It stands for *local area network,* a network that connects computers over a limited distance.

languages Capitalize the names of languages and dialects: *English, Mandarin, Latin, Spanish, Catalan, Gujarati, Arabic, Cajun.*

laptop One word.

largess This spelling is preferred to *largesse.* It is a generous bestowal of gifts.

last in first out Spell out in the first reference; use *LIFO* afterward. Write *last in first out* with hyphens when used to modify, as in *The company changed to last-in-first-out accounting years ago.* This is a method of inventory accounting.

later The *on* isn't necessary with *later.* Write *I will see you later,* not *I will see you later on.*

Latino(s)/Latina(s) A *Latino* is a person who traces his ancestry to a Spanish-speaking country. *Latina* is the feminine form. *Latinos* is the plural when it includes both genders.

Latino is less formal than *Hispanic* (which is a broader term), but *Latino* may be preferred by some because it de-emphasizes the tie to Spain. Note that Brazil is not a Spanish-speaking country.

latitude, longitude Do not use the degree symbol for *latitude* and *longitude.* Instead use these forms: *45 degrees north latitude, 22 degrees west longitude.* *Latitude* is the distance north or south of the equator, designated by parallels, as in *17th parallel.* The distance east or west of Greenwich, England, is *longitude,* designated by meridians, as in *Greenwich meridian.*

latter, former *Latter* means the second of two. *He interviewed the manager and the account executive and determined the latter had more experience. Latter* also refers to nearer to the end. *He devoted the latter half of the meeting to a discussion of the budget. Former* means the first of two. *Former* also means ex. *The former mayor of Detroit was a Democrat.*

lawyer It is a generic term that covers all members of the bar. It is often used interchangeably with *attorney,* who is someone authorized to act for another. But note that an attorney does not have to be a lawyer.

lay, lie Distinguishing the correct tense of these verbs can be tricky.

The *lay* form takes a direct object, as in *Lay your laptop on the table.* The tenses are *lay, laid, laid.*

Lie, which means *to recline,* never takes a direct object, as in *Lie on the bed before you faint.* The tenses are *lie, lay* (as in, *Mary lay down and slept soundly),* *lain* (as in *He loves naps, but he hasn't lain down all day).*

lay off, layoff Lay off is two words when used as a verb, as in *The company will lay off 500 employees to cut costs.* Write as one word when used as a noun, as in *The lay-off is intended to cut costs.* These terms apply to the removal of employees to reduce a workforce or cut costs, not for terminations because of job performance.

LCD Use the abbreviation, which stands for *liquid-crystal display,* in all references, as in *LCD TV.*

lead, led Note that *lead* is the present and *led* is the past tense of this verb. *She leads the staff meeting each week. She led the staff meeting last week.* When referring to the metal, the spelling is *lead,* as in *lead paint, lead poisoning.*

lead-up Write with a hyphen, as in *The team worked long hours in the lead-up to the annual meeting.*

lecture If a lecture has a formal title, write the title with capital initials and use quotation marks.

LED Use the abbreviation in all references. It stands for *light-emitting diode,* an energy-efficient light used in many apps and lamps.

left-click Use a hyphen.

left-handed Use a hyphen.

legacy Use this to refer to previous systems. *The company is consolidating its legacy systems onto a single platform.*

legislative body Capitalize *Congress, Senate, House of Representatives, Assembly, Legislature, Parliament, State Council, Duma,* etc. in references to a specific body.

lend This is a verb. *The bank lends to companies with a superior credit rating.* Use *loan* for the noun. *The bank is processing the loan.*

letters When a single letter appears in text, use quotation marks instead of italics: *Place an "x" next to your preference.* If the letter stands for a capitalized word, capitalize the letter; if it stands for a lowercase word, lowercase the letter.

leveraged buyout Spell out in the first reference (note that *buyout* is one word); use *LBO* afterward.

LGBT Use the initialism in all references if the audience is familiar with it; otherwise spell out in the first reference, which stands for *lesbian, gay, bisexual, transgender;* use *LGBT* afterward. *The LGBT Committee announced the company would begin offering partner health benefits next year.*

liable This is not just a probability but an undesirable one. *The company is liable to be sued if the tainted food is not removed from the stores.*

liaison Often misspelled. The verb is *liaise. Min is her department's compliance liaison; she liaises with the regulatory staff on a daily basis.*

libel It means injurious to a company or individual's reputation. Do not confuse with *slander,* which is a spoken statement that belittles another person.

life and death The expression is not *life **or** death.*

likable Often misspelled.

like Use *like* for comparisons. *She runs like a gazelle. Like* in this construction introduces just a noun. Use *as* instead of *like* to introduce phrases with a subject and verb. Write *The union went on strike as we expected.*

When used to refer to an approval rating on a social networking site, write with quotation marks for clarity, as in *Guests from across the Americas "like" us on Facebook.*

limousine Often misspelled.

LinkedIn Capitalize both *L* and *I* and note the absence of a space in the name of this social networking site for professionals.

liquefy Often misspelled.

livable Often misspelled.

L.L.B. Use *L.L.B.* in all references. It stands for *bachelor of laws.*

L.L.C. Refers to a *limited liability corporation. L.L.L.P.* refers to a *limited liability limited partnership.*

L.L.D. Use *L.L.D.* in all references. It stands for *doctor of laws.*

loan This is a noun. *The bank is processing the loan.* Use *lend* for the verb. *The bank lends to companies with a superior credit rating.*

loath, loathe *Loath* means unwilling or reluctant, as in *Megan Byrne was loath to predict how employees would react to the announcement. Loathe* means to feel intense dislike or disgust, as in *She loathes the Monday-morning meetings.*

local Often this term is unnecessary, as in *She was rushed to a local hospital.* Just write *She was rushed to a hospital.*

local area network Use *LAN* in all references. This refers to a network that connects computers over a limited distance.

local of a union Use a figure and capitalize when giving the name of a union subdivision: *Local 25 of the UAW.* Lowercase *local* when it stands alone. Observe the local's name preference (in punctuation, capitalization, etc.).

login, log in One word when used as a noun, as in the username/password combination. *My login expired last week.* Two words when used as a verb. *I will log in to the office system when I get home.*

logjam One word. *The change of leadership should break the negotiating logjam.*

logo Use *logo* in all references. It is short for *logogram* and *logotype.* Most companies have guidelines to protect how their logos are used, both externally and internally (e.g., for business cards, ID cards, slide presentations). Pay attention to how logos are used.

logoff, log off One word when used as a noun or adjective. *She finished the work and did a remote logoff. The logoff procedure is easy and fast.* Two words when used as a verb. *I will log off the system before going home.* Same for *logout, log out.*

long distance, long-distance When used as a noun, no hyphen is needed. *It is a long distance from Moscow to Novosibirsk.* Write with a hyphen when used as an adjective. *The company cut its long-distance calling costs 20% last year.*

lowercase It is a verb, noun and adjective and refers to letters that are not capitalized. It is one word, no hyphen. The same goes for *uppercase.* Note the difference in how it is used: *Lowercase the word chairman. The word chairman is lowercased* (with a *d).*

low-tech Write with a hyphen. Use this short version of *low-technology* in all references; same for *high-tech.*

Lunar New Year Capitalize all three words; refers to the Asian festival.

-ly Do not use a hyphen between adverbs ending in *-ly* and the adjectives they modify, as in a *highly complex formula,* a *badly damaged box,* a *fully informed participant.*

· M ·

*"We provide online references and guidelines for style and
for formatting manuals, letters, brochures and training materials. We also
conduct classes in writing for new employees. As a large company (4,000 plus in
the U.S.), we need to do this to maintain consistency in the branding
of the corporate publications."*
– Glenn Wells, editorial consultant
Aflac

M.A., M.S. See **master of arts, master of science** entry.

Mac This word is from *Macintosh,* the computer manufactured by Apple Computer. The plural is *Macs.* Other variations are *MacBook* and *iMac.* Note the capitalizations (not *MacIntosh*).

Mac/Mc When alphabetizing words beginning with *Mac/Mc,* do so as though all letters were lowercased: *MacDougal, Mackey, McDonald.* Do not treat *Mac/Mc* as separate alphabetical entries.

mad, angry These words are not interchangeable. Use *mad* when meaning insane, *angry* when the meaning is irritation.

Mafia The preferred term is *organized crime.*

magazine, newspaper, publication names Capitalize the names of publications, following their style, as in *the Financial Times, the Huffington Post, the New York Times, POLITICO, the Daily Beast, the Miami Herald.* (Italics are used here only to illustrate examples.) No need to capitalize *the* in the title of a publication. Use quotation marks for the titles of articles, as in *"Ten Ways to Improve Your Speaking Skills."*

mail carrier Use this instead of *mailman,* as it avoids reference to gender. Another alternative is *postal worker.*

mailroom One word.

Maine Do not abbreviate in text, but use *ME* (capitals without periods) with full addresses, including ZIP code. *ME* is the two-letter Postal Service abbreviation. Seven other states are not abbreviated in text: *Alaska, Hawaii, Idaho, Iowa, Ohio, Texas, Utah.* See **state abbreviations** entry.

majority, plurality Often confused. A *majority* means more than half of the total number. A *plurality* refers to the number of votes cast for the winning choice if this number is not more than half of the total votes cast.

Depending on the construction, *majority* can take either a singular or a plural verb. *The majority of union members have voted to strike* or *The majority has voted to strike.*

male, female Use *male* and *female* as adjectives: *He was the only male yoga instructor.* Use *man* or *woman* as a noun: *He was the only man in the yoga class.* Do not refer to gender unless it is pertinent.

malware One word; use the abbreviated form in all references. It is short for *malicious software,* meaning software that infects computers.

maneuver Often misspelled.

man-hour Avoid terms that refer to gender; just write *hour*. This applies to *manpower* as well; instead use *personnel, labor, workforce*. Note that *workforce* is one word.

manpower Avoid terms that refer to gender. Depending on the context, alternatives include *labor, workforce, human resources, talent, staff.*

many, much Use *many* with nouns that can be counted, as in *How many days do you need to set up the office?* Use *much* with quantity in bulk or things that can't be counted. *How much time do you need to set up the office?*

marcom This is informal. It is an abbreviated form for *marketing communications,* often used to refer to departments within companies. It takes a singular verb, as in *Marcom writes all brochures, fact sheets and customer communications.*

Martin Luther King Day Capitalize *Day.* This is a U.S. federal holiday held on the third Monday in January. Capitalize all holidays – official, unofficial, religious, secular.

mashup, mash-up Can be written as one word or with a hyphen. This stylebook favors one word in all instances, whether used as a noun or adjective. Whichever version you choose, use it consistently. It means a mixture of content or elements. *The report is a mashup of ideas from developers in Asia. The mashup report includes data and video content.*

Mass Capitalize when referring to the Catholic ceremony. Use *celebrated* rather than *said. The Mass will be celebrated at 10 a.m.*

masterful, masterly *Masterful* means domineering or overpowering. *Masterly* means skillful.

master of arts, master of science Lowercase both these terms. They can be abbreviated, but it is better to write out in text, as in *Teresa has a master of science* or *Teresa has a master's degree.* When using the initials, write *M.A.* or *M.S.* In resumes, degrees are often uppercased, as in *Bachelor of Arts* or *Master of Science.*

maverick Lowercase this word, which sometimes refers to a highly independent individual who resists the mainstream.

May Day, mayday The first term refers to May 1, which celebrates the coming of spring and is a labor holiday in many countries. The second term, which is one word, is an emergency signal, which comes from the French phrase *m'aidez,* meaning help me.

M.B.A. Use *M.B.A.* in most cases. It stands for *master of business administration.*

MC The preferred form is *emcee. MC* is short for *master of ceremonies.*

m-commerce Write this short form of *mobile commerce* with a hyphen. Use it in all references if your audience will understand; otherwise spell it out the first time. *The company's m-commerce revenue increased 20% last year.*

measurements Use figures instead of spelling out the numbers. *The recipe called for 6 cups of flour and 2 cups of sugar.* Do not abbreviate measurements in text, although it is acceptable to use abbreviations in tabular material, as long as their meanings are clear, such as in recipes: *2 tsp. salt.*

measurement tables Always check the conversion between metrics (the International System of Units) and the U.S. Customary Units. Consult a dictionary or the internet for metric conversion.

media This stylebook favors using *media* as a collective noun so that the verb is singular. *The media is expected to comment extensively on the chairman's sudden resignation.*

media relations Lowercase the names of departments within companies, unless it is already established practice to capitalize.

Note that *media relations* takes a singular verb because the term refers to the department. *Media relations is responsible for the press release.* If that sounds awkward, rewrite the sentence, as in *The media relations department is responsible for the press release.*

Medicaid, Medicare Capitalize both. *Medicaid* is a federal-state program designed to pay for healthcare for the needy. *Medicare* is the federal healthcare insurance program for people age 65 and over, as well as for the disabled. Both Medicaid and Medicare cover some of the costs associated with healthcare.

megabyte Use *MB* in all references in technical writing. In other writing, spell it out in the first reference; use *MB* afterward.

megahertz Use *MHz* in all references in technical writing. In other writing, spell it out in the first reference; use *MHz* afterward. Note the capitalization.

memento Often misspelled. (Not *momento.*)

memo, memorandum, memorandum The shortened form, *memo,* is preferred to the longer forms in all references.

menswear This is the preferred form. It is often written as *men's wear.*

mergers and acquisitions Spell out in the first reference (including the word *and*); use *M&A* (no spaces) afterward. When used as an adjective, the spelled-out term takes hyphens and drops the *s*'s. *The firm has extensive merger-and-acquisition experience in the biotech industry* or *The firm has extensive M&A experience in the biotech industry.*

meridians It designates *longitude,* the distance east or west of Greenwich, England, as in *Greenwich meridian.* See **latitude, longitude** entry for additional information.

metaphor A metaphor is a comparison between dissimilar terms that gives the phrase a whole new meaning, as in *spaghetti code* (unstructured computer program code that is impossible to follow). Do not mix metaphors. A mixed metaphor occurs when the comparison between the dissimilar terms is too outlandish for association, as in *a playground of red tape*.

metric measurements Although metric measurements (the International System of Units) are increasingly recognized in the U.S., it is still necessary to list the U.S. equivalent in parentheses. For specifics, consult a metric conversion chart or the measurement table in most dictionaries or on the internet. For international communications, it may be useful to follow this suggestion from "Wired Style": "Use the measurement system of the place you're writing about." But still provide an equivalent for U.S. readers.

micromanage No hyphen is needed for this term, which refers to a style of managing that is too hands-on and detail-oriented.

mid- Many *mid-* words use a hyphen: *By mid-year we will know the results of the market survey.* Check the dictionary if unsure.

middle age, middle-aged Do not capitalize. Use a hyphen and a *d* in *aged* when used like an adjective, as in *The middle-aged man began a second career.* This term usually refers to people between 40 and 65 years of age.

middle initials They are often a part of a name, so in the first reference include them when they are offered or relevant, as in *Booker T. Washington.* If two people in one organization have the same name, use the middle initial to distinguish between them.

midnight Write *midnight,* not *12 midnight.* Midnight is a transition phase, so it is technically incorrect to write *12 a.m.,* but "The U.S. Government Style Manual" states it is acceptable to use *12 a.m.* for *midnight* and *12 p.m.* for *noon.* The new day begins at 12:01 a.m. Also write *noon,* not *12 noon.*

mike Lowercase; acceptable to use in all references for *microphone*. Another option is *mic.*

mile A mile equals 5,280 feet, 1,760 yards or 1,609 meters.

miles per hour Use *mph* in all references.

Millennial Generation Note the capitalization in this term, which describes students entering the workforce as of 2000.

millennium Remember that *millennium* has two *l*'s and two *n*'s. The preferred plural is *millenniums,* not *millennia.*

million, billion Use the word *billion* or *million* instead of writing out the zeros. A billion is equal to a thousand million. (FYI: A billion in Britain, Canada and Germany is equal to a million million [a *trillion* in the U.S.])

Use figures with the words *million* and *billion,* as in *The surplus was $2 billion* (note it is not *$2 billions*). Use decimals instead of fractions: *2.5 million* rather than *2½ million.* Do not use a hyphen to join the figures and the word *million* or *billion,* even in the following example: *The board approved the $1 million investment.* Use hyphens after the word *million* or *billion* when the amount forms a phrase that modifies, as in *The meeting is a $2 million-a-year event.*

For slide shows, charts, spreadsheets, etc., abbreviate *million* to *M* or *mn* (without periods). Abbreviate *billion* as *B* or *bn* (without periods). *Total Value of Deal: $10B* (no space between the number and *B*) or *Total Value of Deal: $10bn* (no space between the number and *bn*).

mindset One word. *His mindset remains positive, despite the complaints from customers.*

minuscule Often misspelled. (Not *miniscule.*)

minus sign Use the minus sign with negative numbers for charts, slide shows, etc., writing it with an en dash if possible; otherwise use a hyphen.

The alternative is to put negative numbers in parentheses. Whichever style you choose, use it consistently.

Use a word, not a *minus sign,* to indicate temperatures below zero: *minus 10°* or *40° below zero.* In text, spell out the word *minus,* as in *We will receive the shipment, minus the spare parts, next week.*

minutiae Often misspelled. It means small details and is the plural of *minutia.*

mips Spell out *millions of instructions per second* in the first reference, except in technical writing. Use *mips* afterward. Note it is lowercased.

miscellaneous Often misspelled.

missteps Note the double *s.*

mobile It is acceptable to use this shortened version of *mobile phone,* unless it will create confusion, as in *Call me on my mobile if you can't reach me at the office.* The term *mobile* is more prevalent in British English, whereas *cell* or *cellphone* is more common in American English. *Call me on my cell if you can't reach me at the office.*

modifier A modifier is any word or phrase that describes a noun, pronoun or verb. Modifiers function as either adjectives or adverbs. Modifiers make the meaning more exact, as in *tall man, part-time employee, 2-for-1 stock split, billion-dollar deal.* Keep modifiers close to the words they describe.

mom Lowercase *mom* unless it serves as a proper noun. *Your mom is waiting out in the lobby. Don't forget to tell Mom we love her!*

momentarily This adverb means either *for a moment* or *moment by moment.* A frequent error is to use it to mean *at any moment.* Write *The support person will be online in a moment,* not *The support person will be online momentarily.*

Monday Capitalize days of the week.

Monday morning quarterback No hyphen is needed for this term. It describes a person who second-guesses.

money Do not use the plural of money (*moneys* or *monies*). It sounds awkward to most readers. See **foreign currency** entry.

month Abbreviate *Jan., Feb., Mar., Apr., Aug., Sept., Oct., Nov., Dec.* in text as long as they are followed by numerals: *Dec. 27, Jan. 29, Sept. 7.* Do not abbreviate *May, June* or *July,* even if followed by a numeral: *June 16.* Spell out the month if it appears alone or with just the year: *December, October 1984.* Tabular material follows a different style.

monthlong One word.

Moody's Note the apostrophe in the name of this credit rating agency.

more important, more importantly Use these phrases interchangeably, as in *More important, all managers must attend the conference* and *More importantly, all managers must attend the conference.*

more perfect Avoid this phrase. Something is either perfect or not.

more than Use *more than* when referring to amounts (instead of *over*), as in *The consultant makes more than $200 an hour.* Exact figures are always better than estimates. If exact figures are unavailable, *about* is an alternative, as in *The consultant makes about $200 an hour.*

morph This verb means to change or evolve. It is derived from *metamorphosis. The online image morphs from a dollar sign into a euro sign.*

mother Lowercase *mother* unless it serves as a proper noun: *The CEO's mother is a major stockholder. Tell Mother her broker is on the telephone.* The same goes for *mom.*

mouse, mouses Note the plural for the hand-operated device for using a computer.

mouse over, mouseover Write as two words when used as a verb, as in *Mouse over the title of the song and click play.* Write as one word when used as an adjective or noun, as in *The mouseover text was highlighted in blue. He created a simple mouseover for the site.*

movie, television titles Use quotation marks for titles of movies and television shows (no need to italicize). Follow headline style and capitalize the first letter of the main words (but lowercase articles [*the, a, an*], conjunctions [*and, or, for, nor*] and prepositions, unless they are more than four letters or they are the first or last words of the title or subtitle. Also lowercase the *to* in verb forms, as in *to Speak*). Examples: *"The Tree of Life," "Midnight in Paris," "Bagdad Cafe," "The Last Picture Show."* For television shows and individual episodes, use quotation marks, as in *"Blind Spot"* on *"Homeland."* (Italics are used here only to illustrate examples.)

MP3, MP3s Capitalize the *MP* in all instances.

Mr., Mrs., Ms. In text, do not include these titles in the first reference to an individual. Use the full name, as in *Andrea Sholler* (not *Ms. Andrea Sholler*) *will join the company effective March 5.* Afterward the title can be used, as in *Ms. Sholler has extensive experience in business development.* Other options for subsequent references are to use the first or last name only, as in *Andrea has extensive experience . . .* or *Sholler has extensive experience.* Whichever style you choose, use it consistently. Many newspapers use the full name first, then just the last name in later references. For women, use *Ms.* unless *Mrs.* is a known preference.

In addresses, use *Mr.* or *Ms.* It simplifies matters to refer to all women as *Ms.*

The plural of *Mr.* is *Messrs.* The plural of *Mrs.* is *Mmes.* The plural of *Ms.* is *Mss.*

much, many Use *much* with quantity in bulk or things that can't be counted. *How much time do you need to set up the office?* Use *many* with nouns that can be counted, as in *How many days do you need to set up the office?*

multi(-) Do not hyphenate words beginning with *multi* unless followed by an *i* or unless the word could be confusing. *The company signed a multiyear, multicurrency agreement in November* but *The World Bank announced the initiative would be a multi-agency effort.*

Murphy's law Note the apostrophe. This law states that if something can go wrong it will.

music Use quotation marks for the titles of songs, popular as well as classical (*"Layla," "Ave Maria"*). Also use quotation marks for national anthems (*"The Star-Spangled Banner"*). Follow headline style. For operas use quotation marks, as in *"Don Giovanni."* Many musical compositions do not have descriptive titles but are identified by the name of a musical form. When used as the title of a work, the name of the form and the key are usually capitalized but not put in quotation marks, as in *Sonata in C.*

Muslim This is the preferred term to describe adherents to Islam. Do not differentiate between *black Muslims* and *Muslims.*

Myspace Capitalize the *M.* The company no longer uppercases the *S.*

· N ·

9/11 Use this shortened reference to *Sept. 11, 2001,* if the audience will be familiar with it, as in *In the aftermath of 9/11, Ground Zero is being rebuilt.* Otherwise write out *Sept. 11, 2001.*

NAACP Use *NAACP* in all references, even though it is more than four letters. It stands for the *National Association for the Advancement of Colored People.*

names Follow these guidelines. Pay particular attention to the correct spelling of personal names. People don't like to see their names misspelled or their titles cited incorrectly, so double-check both.

- In the first reference, use full names, as well as initials if given or relevant: *Carlos Estrella, Martin S. Simmons, Coleen Byrne.* Include the person's title if it is relevant. Capitalize the title only if it precedes the name, as in *Managing Director Tom Smith;* lowercase if it follows the name, as in *Tom Smith, managing director.*
- In text, do not include *Mr., Mrs., Ms.* in the first reference. Write *John Banville* (not *Mr. John Banville*). Use *Mr., Mrs., Ms.* for addresses. For subsequent references, decide whether to use first names, last names or

names with titles. For example: *John Banville is the guest speaker. John is an acclaimed author* or *Banville is an acclaimed author* or *Mr. Banville is an acclaimed author.* Whichever style you choose, use it consistently for every name throughout the communication.

- Do not use abbreviations for names (as in *Thom.)* unless that is the person's preference.
- As long as the identity is clear, refer to people as they prefer to be known, as in *Bill Gates.*
- Use *Jr., Sr.* or *III* if part of the name, as in *Daniel R. Lesnikowski, Jr.* Note that names with Roman numerals, as in *Thomas Walsh III,* do not take a comma. In an alphabetical listing by last names, put the *Jr., Sr.* or *III* last, as in *Lesnikowski, Daniel R., Jr.*

nano Most *nano* words do not need a hyphen, as in *nanosecond. Nano* is a prefix denoting one-billionth of a unit.

NASA Use *NASA* in all references. It stands for the *National Aeronautics and Space Administration.*

Nasdaq Use *Nasdaq* in all references. Note that only the first letter is capitalized. (If an acronym is longer than four letters, uppercase the first letter and lowercase the remaining letters.) *Nasdaq* stands for *National Association of Securities Dealers Automated Quotation System.*

Nasdaq composite index Capitalize only the word *Nasdaq* when referring to this index. Write out *Nasdaq composite index* in the first reference; use *Nasdaq composite* afterward. Do not refer to the index simply as *Nasdaq* because this would be a reference to the entire market.

nation, national Lowercase these terms unless they are part of a formal name. *The nation is relieved the economy is growing again. The National Security Council meets this week.*

national anthem Put a specific national anthem in quotation marks.

National Institutes of Health Spell out in the first reference (note the *s* at the end of *Institutes);* use *NIH* afterward. This is an agency within the Department of Health and Human Services and is the primary biomedical research arm of the federal government.

nationality Capitalize the proper names of nationalities, as in *Chinese, Japanese, Irish, Polish, Colombian, Nigerian, Syrian, Swedish;* lowercase racial descriptions, as in *black* or *white.* Also capitalize terms such as *African-American, Asian-American, Italian-American.*

National Labor Relations Board Spell out in the first reference; use *NLRB* afterward.

National Organization for Women Spell out in the first reference; use *NOW* afterward. Note it is *for Women,* not *of Women.*

nationwide *Nationwide* and *worldwide* are both one word. Use a hyphen *for company-wide, enterprise-wide, firm-wide, industry-wide.*

NATO Use *NATO* in all references. It stands for *North Atlantic Treaty Organization.*

Navy Capitalize when referring to the U.S. forces (as in *Navy policy, the Navy, the U.S. Navy);* lowercase when referring to naval forces, as in *the Dutch navy.*

Negro(es) Use this term only if it is part of a proper noun or in historical contexts. *African-American* is generally the preferred term when talking about black Americans.

neither/nor This means not either of two. It is not interchangeable with *none* or *not one. Neither the CFO nor the CIO is authorized to speak to the media.*

After a *neither/nor* construction, use a singular verb if both subjects are singular; use a plural verb if both subjects are plural; if one of the subjects is singular and one is plural, use the number of the one nearer the verb, as in *Neither the director nor her managers know how to use the new software.*

net, the Spell out *internet* in the first reference; use *the net* interchangeably afterward.

net income Lowercase *net income,* the amount left after taxes are paid.

newsfeed One word. *She subscribes to a digital newsfeed from Asia.*

newspaper, publication names Do not capitalize *the* in a publication's name, as in *the Huffington Post* (see **magazine, newspaper, publication names** entry). Do not place the name of the publication in an italic font or in quotation marks.

newsstand One word.

New Year's Day It can also be referred to as the *New Year.* (Lowercase *new year* if it refers to the 12-month period.) Other examples: *Chinese New Year, Jewish New Year, Lunar New Year.* Since the New Year is the first day of the calendar year and a holiday, write *Happy New Year* (not *Happy new year* or *Happy New Year's*).

New Year's Eve Capitalize all three words.

New York Stock Exchange Spell out in the first reference; use *NYSE, the stock exchange, the exchange* or *the Big Board* for other references. Its parent company is NYSE Euronext.

nicknames If nicknames are preferred, honor them: *Bill Gates, Steve Jobs, Jimmy Carter, Babe Ruth.* It is not necessary to put the nickname in quotation marks if it is a substitute for the name, as in *the Oracle of Omaha (Warren Buffet)* or *the Wizard of Menlo Park (Thomas Edison)*.

night, nite Both variations appear in the dictionary, but in business correspondence, write *night,* as *nite* is informal.

nighttime One word.

nitty-gritty Write with a hyphen. This means specific details, as in *We need to get down to the nitty-gritty of the rollout plan.*

no, yes It is not necessary to use quotation marks, except in direct discourse: *He answered yes to the question. Rose said yes to Tim. "No," he grumbled as he hung up the telephone.*

No. Use this abbreviation for the word *number* only with an accompanying figure, as in *Her office is No. 15 on the second floor.* Capitalize the *n* in *No.*

No. 1 Use *No. 1* (rather than spell out *number one*) in all references, as in *The company ranked No. 1 for safety* or *Ida's No. 1 fear about using a credit card online is identity theft.* The same holds for other numbers, as in *The No. 2 internet service provider announced plans to merge with the No. 3 cable company.*

no-brainer Write with a hyphen. This informal term refers to something that is obvious or easy or requires little thought. *John's decision to take the position at headquarters was a no-brainer.*

noes and yeses This form is preferred to *nos and yeses.*

non(-) Most words starting with *non* need no hyphen, as in *nonbinding, noncompliance.* But if the word might be confusing without a hyphen, use a hyphen, as in *non-negotiable.* Also use a hyphen when *non* precedes a word with a capital letter: *non-American, non-Canadian.*

none When it refers to *no one* or *not one,* it should take a singular verb, as in *None of the oranges was ripe.* Just as often the plural form is appropriate, as in *None of the workers were present at the ribbon-cutting ceremony.* Use the plural, except when emphasizing the idea of *not one* or *no one.*

no-noes Use this form instead of *no-nos.*

nonprofit One word. It is preferable to *not-for-profit.*

noon Write *noon,* not *12 noon.* Also write *midnight,* not *12 midnight.* See **midnight** entry.

noteworthy One word.

not-for-profit Use *nonprofit* instead.

notwithstanding One word.

noun A noun is a word that names a person, place, thing, idea or quality. Using nouns as verbs is common practice (e.g., *access, impact, bullet, fast-track*) in business writing. Even though many of these constructions are considered nonstandard, this stylebook favors them because they are useful.

number Use a singular verb when *number* stands alone, as in *The number is not available yet.* Use a plural verb after *a number of,* as in *A number of employees are scheduled to attend the workshop.*

number, amount Use *number* for things that can be counted one by one, as in *She put a number of coins on the counter* or *The number of days spent on the reports varies each quarter.* Use *amount* for things that cannot be counted one by one, as in *The amount of time spent on the reports varies each quarter.*

number cruncher Lowercase this term.

numbers Spell out numbers under 10 in text; use figures for numbers 10 and above. There are exceptions to this general rule:

- Use figures for ages of people and animals; building numbers; headlines, slide shows, charts and other tabular material; some financial contexts (as in *The index edged up 2 percentage points);* figures that include decimals *(2.8 inches of rain);* results from voting; percentages *(1%, 10%);* measurements *(2 tsp.);* data-driven references *(8 bits);* references to money *($2 million, 5 pence);* time of day *(1 a.m.);* days of the month; degrees of temperature; latitude and longitude; dimensions; numbered expressions *(Page 1);* sports points or scores.
- Use figures in a series, even if one of the numbers is below 10: *The director has 3 assistants, 10 managers and 12 account executives reporting to her.*
- Use the word *billion* or *million* instead of writing out the zeros. Do not use a hyphen to join the figures and the word *million* or *billion,* even in the following example: *The board approved the $1 million investment.* If the amount is used as an adjective, use hyphens only after the amount, as in *The meeting is a $2 million-a-year event.*
- Round long numbers. In general, round off figures in the millions to one decimal place *(4.5 million),* those in the billions to two places *(6.58 billion)* and those in the trillions to three *(4.768 trillion).* Be mindful that rounding numbers can be misleading.
- When fractions in amounts less than 1 appear in text, spell out and hyphenate: *Approximately one-third of employees work remotely.* If fractions consist of whole numbers and fractions, use figures. *Wayne Anderson poured 2¾ gallons into the mold.*
- For ages or pairs of dimensions, use numerals plus fractions, as in *Children must be at least 2½ years old to be admitted to the preschool in town.*
- In tabular material, use figures, preferably expressing fractions with decimal points *(5.5 instead of 5½).* Use the multiplication symbol instead of the word *by* in tabular material *(5¾ × 3½)* if decimals are not used.
- For recipes, use numbers, including *1* through *9,* as in *8 fluid ounces.*

- For numbers in names, use Roman numerals (without a comma): *John M. Dawson III.* In an alphabetical listing by last name, the number comes last: *Dawson, John M. III.*
- Spell out all numbers that begin a sentence: *Eighty-four employees attended the conference.* Use hyphens between words that form one number: *twenty-three, forty-one.*
- Spell out casual expressions: *Thanks a million.*
- For ordinal numbers, spell out *first* through *ninth.* Use figures starting with *10th.* If an ordinal number is part of a name, use figures: *1st Fleet.*
- Use words or numerals according to an organization's practice: *3M, Twenty-First Century Foundation.*
- When numbers are used to designate sections, chapters, pages, etc., capitalize the word that precedes the number, as in *Chapter 4, Page 6, Version 7, Section 8.*
- Remember: Always take the time to ensure that all the numbers cited are correct and, if appropriate, add up. Also be sure any numbers appearing in graphs, charts, headings or captions match the numbers in the text. Pay extra attention to making sure the numbers are accurate. Miscalculating the numbers can turn out to be expensive.

· O ·

*"Generally people are able to construct their ideas in a
fairly well-organized fashion. The biggest problem we have is forgetting the
audience and using jargon that is meaningless to that audience or else not
providing adequate context so that the jargon or acronyms can be understood."*
– Scot Roskelley, communications director, mid-America Region
Aetna

observance, observation These words are not interchangeable. *Observance*
is the act of complying with prescribed rites, while *observation* is something
that is noted. *In observance of the holiday, the banks will be closed. His observation that the company needs to develop an internet-centric model met with
agreement.*

occasion Often misspelled.

Occupational Safety and Health Administration Spell out in the first reference; use *OSHA* afterward.

occupational titles Lowercase job titles when they come after a name:
Christina Greer, managing director. Uppercase when the formal company title
precedes the name: *Managing Director Christina Greer.* Lowercase all titles/job
descriptions when no name is used, as in *The receptionist resigned Monday* or
The chairman asked for a status report on the new legislation.

Occupy Wall Street Capitalize and spell out in the first reference; no need to use quotation marks. Write *OWS* in subsequent references. If your audience will be familiar with the shortened version, write *Occupy* capitalized in all references. *The article reported that Occupy Wall Street has impacted communications programs at many corporations.*

occur, occurred, occurring (v.), occurrence (n.) Often misspelled.

ocean Lowercase *ocean* if it stands alone, but uppercase it if it is part of the name of one of the five oceans: *Pacific Ocean, Atlantic Ocean, Indian Ocean, Antarctic Ocean, Arctic Ocean.* When more than one ocean is mentioned, style has changed so capitalize the plural form, as in *the Atlantic and Indian Oceans.*

o'clock It is better to specify *a.m.* or *p.m.* than to use the *o'clock* form, as in *We will meet at 9 a.m. in the conference room* rather than *We will meet at nine o'clock in the conference room.* Note the space between the number and *a.m.* If the time is on the hour, it is not necessary to include a colon and two zeros. Just write *9 a.m.,* not *9:00 a.m.* Use the colon to separate minutes from hours, as in *9:15 a.m.* If the o'clock form is used, spell out the number, as in *nine o'clock,* not *9 o'clock.*

off Do not write *off of.* The *of* is unnecessary. *She fell off the stage,* not *She fell off of the stage.*

offboard One word. The opposite is *onboard.* *The client relations department offboards companies that no longer subscribe to the service.*

offsite One word. *The company's senior management team had an offsite meeting in January.*

Ohio Do not abbreviate in text, but use *OH* (capitals without periods) with full addresses, including ZIP code. *OH* is the two-letter Postal Service abbreviation. Seven other states are not abbreviated in text: *Alaska, Hawaii, Idaho, Iowa, Maine, Texas, Utah*. See **state abbreviations** entry.

OK This is informal (capitals without periods). The past is *OK'd*. To ensure consistency in a communication, change any *O.K., okay* or *ok* forms to *OK*.

old-boy network, old-girl network Use a hyphen, but do not capitalize these terms, which refer to an informal system of mutual assistance. *The old-girl network at Colgate helped Elise get a job.*

omission Often misspelled. There are several ways to indicate omission in text. See **ellipsis** entry. See **apostrophe** entry.

on It is not necessary to use *on* before a date or day of the week. *She heard about the promotion Tuesday.* If, however, confusion would occur, include *on: Harold met Mary on Friday.*

on account of Use *because* instead.

onboard One word. The opposite is *offboard. The human resources department onboards new personnel.*

one When using *one* in the sense of a person (as a pronoun), do not substitute *his* or *her* later in the sentence. Write *One does not need one's calculator to figure out the sum* (not *One does not need his calculator to figure out the sum*). In American English, this form is considered overly formal and is rarely used in business writing.

one(-) In text hyphenate *one-* in fractions: *one-third, one-half.* The same applies for other fractions: *two-thirds, five-eighths.* Use figures for slides, tabular material, etc.

one another, each other Use *one another* when referring to more than two people. *Martha, Tara and Alice will help one another with the project.* Use *each* *other* when referring to two people. *They looked at each other in disbelief.* To form the possessive of *one another,* write *one another's. They read one another's reports and synthesized the findings into a single document.*

onetime, one-time *Onetime* means ex- or former, as in *The onetime management consultant now works at the Fed. One-time* with a hyphen means once, as in *The company marketed the sale price as a one-time offer.*

ongoing One word. Alternatives are *continuing* and *developing.*

on line, in line To wait *on line* is a regional preference in the New York area. People wait *in line* in other parts of the country. Use *in line* outside New York.

online Always write *online* as one word. *The company offers various online services. Luisa went online to find the address.*

online shorthand These informal abbreviations are common in email, texting and IMing, but avoid them in formal business communications. Abbreviations that are widely recognized include *BTW (by the way), LOL (laughing out loud), IOW (in other words)* and *BRB (be right back).* See Chapter 5 for more information.

onscreen One word. *You can view the document onscreen and then send it to the legal department for review.*

OPEC Use *OPEC* in all references. It stands for *Organization of Petroleum Exporting Countries.*

oped, op-ed, OpEd This word for an article that expresses the writer's personal viewpoint is both a noun and adjective. It can be written various ways. Choose one style and use it consistently. This stylebook favors *oped.* (Italics are used here only to illustrate the example.) *The CEO wrote an oped on the China-Japan* *currency agreement in the Financial Times.* Note that an oped differs from an editorial, which is an opinion piece that reflects the publisher's views.

operations Note that *operations* takes a singular verb when used to refer to a department. *Operations is responsible for trade processing.* If it sounds awkward, rewrite the sentence, as in *The operations department is responsible for trade processing.* Lowercase the names of departments within companies unless it is already established practice to capitalize.

ophthalmologist, optometrist, optician The first is a doctor who treats eye disease. The second measures the eye to prescribe glasses. The third makes the glasses.

opt in, opt-in Write it as two words as a verb; hyphenate as a noun or adjective.

ordinal number A number indicating position in a series or order is an ordinal number. The ordinal numbers are *first (1st), second (2nd), third (3rd)* and so on. In text, spell out *first* through *ninth;* use the numeral form for higher numbers (*10th, 20th*). The exception is for addresses or tabular material, when *1st* through *9th* should be used. Also use figures if an ordinal number is part of a name: *1st Fleet.*

organization, institution In text, always follow the organization's style in the first reference. Refer to an organization by its shortened form afterward. If the word *company* or *companies* appears alone in a subsequent reference, always spell it out and lowercase. *The Brensis Company, Inc., will release the annual earnings report in a few weeks. The company will issue a press release.* For internal parts of an organization, lowercase, as in *personnel, corporate affairs, accounting, operations, human resources,* unless it is already established practice to capitalize. These departments take singular verbs. Use *it/its* when referring to an organization or institution (not *they/their). The World Bank held its meeting in Santiago* (not *their meeting*). *It invited all Latin American countries to attend* (not *They invited*).

Oriental Use *Asian* instead.

orthodontics Use a singular verb.

orthodox Capitalize only when it is part of the name of a religion, as in *Eastern Orthodox Church*. Do not capitalize when the meaning is traditional, as in *Her orthodox approach to staff meetings is inappropriate for a company composed mostly of telecommuters.*

ounce Spell out in text, but it is acceptable to abbreviate to *oz.* for tabular material. A fluid ounce equals 2 tablespoons or 6 teaspoons. An ounce in weight is equal to 28.35 grams.

outbox One word. *Inbox* is also one word.

outline style The bulleted list has overtaken outline style in business writing, but for long enumeration outline style may be a better choice. Follow this example for outline style (format from "The Chicago Manual of Style"):

   I.   Executive summary
   II. Ideas for implementing a program
        A.   Role of facilities and human resources departments
             1.   Risk manager's assessment
             2.   Facilities manager's cost assessment
        B.   Outsourcing
             1.   Bid accepted from XYZ Company
             2.   Timeframe for implementation
                  a)   XYZ Company will complete first stage in January
                       (1)   Facilities department timeframe

(2) Construction proposal
    (a)   Areas affected by construction
    (b)   Noise level and inconvenience

outsource One word, no hyphen. Opposite of *insource*.

over Do not use *over* when referring to amounts. Instead use *more than,* as in *The consultant makes more than $200 an hour.* Exact figures are always preferable. If exact figures are unavailable, *about* is an alternative, as in *The consultant makes about $200 an hour.*

overall One word. Most *over(-)* words do not use a hyphen, but check the dictionary if you are uncertain.

over the counter, over-the-counter Spell out in the first reference; use *OTC* afterward. Do not use a hyphen when used as a noun, as in *She bought the medication over the counter.* Write with hyphens when used as an adjective, as in *The numbers exclude over-the-counter trades.*

overuse One word.

oxymoron It is a combination of contradictory terms, as in *deafening silence, jumbo shrimp.*

· P ·

page number Capitalize the word *Page,* as in *Page 1* story and *Page B15.* In tabular material, abbreviate, as in *P. 5* or *pp. 4, 9, 10.* Lowercase the abbreviation for pages, which is *pp.* If it begins a sentence, use *Pp.*

page view Two words. The viewing of a webpage by one visitor. The plural is *page views.*

pan- Use a hyphen in words formed with *pan* and proper nouns, as in *The company's pan-Asian strategy fails to take into account differences among the individual markets.*

paperwork One word.

paradigm This word means a pattern or example that may be copied. *The legislation will create a new paradigm for the regulation of financial markets.* When referring to computers and technology, *paradigm* means "an archetypal example or pattern that provides a model for a process or system," according to "Microsoft Computer Dictionary." While some grammarians insist it should be reserved for technical writing, it is often used in business communications.

paradox A seemingly contradictory statement that may in fact be true. *The paradox is that inertia may be more exhausting than vigorous activity.*

paragraph A paragraph typically deals with one idea or topic. Paragraphs are designed to develop an idea, so the size of a paragraph varies. Most range between three and five sentences. The one-sentence paragraph can be effective, but avoid overuse. Long paragraphs can put off some readers, especially in online materials, so refrain from writing paragraphs that consistently exceed five or six sentences. Paragraphs begin on a new line. They are indicated either by an indent or by a blank line of space before the paragraph that is flush left (without an indent).

paragraph number Capitalize the word *Paragraph,* as in *Paragraph 3.*

parallel Often misspelled. When used in reference to location, parallels designate latitude, the distance north or south of the equator, as in *17th parallel.* Use figures, as in *Operation Timber will take place at the 4th parallel north.* Meridians designate longitude, the distance east or west of Greenwich, England, as in *Greenwich meridian.* See **latitude, longitude** entry.

parameters This word is often used when *perimeter* (meaning the outer boundary) is the intended meaning. The origin of the word *parameter* is from science, meaning a factor that determines what is possible or what results. While some grammarians insist it should be reserved for technical writing, it is often used in business communications. *The board expanded the project's parameters to include the entire organization.*

parentheses Use *parentheses ( )* to enclose an explanation or clarify material. Do not use parentheses and brackets *[ ]* interchangeably. See **brackets** entry. To punctuate parentheses:

If an entire sentence is in parentheses, put a period (or question mark or exclamation point) inside the parentheses. *Employees mistakenly thought their pensions were secure. (Industry insiders knew otherwise.)* With a question mark: *Employees mistakenly believed their pensions were secure. (Did industry insiders know otherwise?)*

If the phrase in parentheses is entirely within the sentence, the punctuation goes outside the parentheses. *She did not confirm her leave of absence with the manager (which explains why they were looking for her Monday).* The punctuation goes outside, even if the material within the parentheses could stand as a complete sentence. *She did not confirm her leave of absence with the manager (they were looking for her Monday).* Note that the first word in the parentheses is not capitalized because the parenthetical material is part of the sentence.

Do not precede an opening parenthesis with a comma, semicolon or colon.

Use parentheses sparingly.

parenthetical documentation This method for citing sources is informal but generally preferred in business writing. Follow this style, which cites a quote from a newspaper article: *"I've always felt that companies should give back to people and communities" ("Keep Management Simple," New York Times, Feb. 26, 2012).* (Italics are used here only to illustrate the example.) In academic and scientific writing, usually footnotes and endnotes are preferred to parenthetical documentation to cite sources.

part from, part with Use *part from* for persons and *part with* for things. *She will part from her colleagues with regret. He is reluctant to part with his old laptop.*

partial quotes See **quotation marks** entry.

partner This word is both a noun and verb. *Our joint-venture partner is based in Vietnam. We partner with a company based in Vietnam.*

part time, part-time This takes no hyphen when used as an adverb, as in *He works for the company part time.* Write with a hyphen when it is used as an adjective, as in *She has a part-time job with an advertising agency.*

passenger lists Arrange alphabetically according to the last name and include full addresses if available. Use a paragraph break for each name.

passive voice Avoid using verbs in the passive voice and write in the active voice whenever possible. In the passive voice, the action is done to the subject, as in *The account executive was corrected by the sales manager.* In the active voice, the subject acts. *The sales manager corrected the account executive.* The emphasis changes. The active voice is stronger and more direct. It is preferred in most business writing.

While the active voice is preferred, there are instances where the passive voice is necessary. Richard Lauchman, author of "Plain Style: Techniques for Simple, Concise, Emphatic Business Writing," says, "The passive is often necessary and writers who believe it is 'bad' or 'weak' will often emphasize the wrong idea." See Chapter 4 for more information.

password One word.

password-protect(ed) Write with a hyphen. *The IT department password-protects all sensitive materials. The onboarding information is in the password-protected section of the website.*

pastor Lowercase because it is not a formal title. A pastor in the Catholic Church leads a parish. A Lutheran or Baptist pastor is a minister who leads a congregation. In the Catholic, Lutheran and some other Protestant religions, the first reference should read *pastor Dennis Cohan of St. Catharine Roman Catholic Church* or *Rev. Dennis Cohan, pastor of St. Catharine Roman Catholic Church.*

patrolman Most police departments use the term *police officer,* which avoids reference to gender. Capitalize either term if it precedes the name, as in *Patrolman James Whitcomb* or *Police Officer Joan Petersson.*

PayPal One word; uppercase both *P*'s.

PC Use *PC* for *personal computer* in all references. The plural is *PCs*. *PC* is also used informally to stand for *politically correct*.

pd., p.d. The first is an abbreviation for *paid;* the second is an abbreviation for *per diem,* which means *per day.* Do not use the *p.d.* abbreviation for a general audience, as it is not recognizable to some readers.

PDA Use *PDA* in all references; capitalize all three letters. It stands for *personal digital assistant,* a handheld device with a microprocessor for organizing personal information.

pdf Use *pdf* in all references. This book favors writing it in lowercase, although some stylebooks write it with all caps. It stands for *Portable Document Format,* a format created by Adobe Systems that preserves the look of an original document (both typeface and images), so that no matter which computer or printer is used, the document will look the same. As an aside, do not submit resumes in pdfs, unless requested by the employer.

P/E See **price-earnings ratio** entry.

per annum Write *p.a.* (lowercased with periods) instead of *per annum* in reports, slide shows and other internal communications. In formal communications, *yearly, a year* and *annually* are preferable to both *p.a.* and *per annum.*

percent Use the symbol (%) instead of the word *percent.* The exception is when a sentence begins with a number, in which case both the number and the word *percent* must be spelled out. *Forty percent of the budget goes to salaries.* (Note that many stylebooks spell out *percent,* as in *5 percent.* Most business publications do not.)

Percent takes a singular verb when standing alone: *The director said 10% was insufficient.* When a word follows *% of,* it takes a singular or plural verb depending on the word that follows: *Approximately 20% of her time is spent on customer service. Sixty percent of employees bike to work.*

Use decimals instead of fractions, as in *7.5%.* For amounts less than 1%, put a zero before the decimal, as in *0.3%.* Repeat % with each individual number, as in *He has tabulated 30% to 60% of the study.*

A common error is to confuse *percent* with *percentage point.* If the company grew market share from 35% to 40%, write *We grew market share to 40%, up 5 percentage points from last year,* not *We grew market share to 40%, up 5% from last year.*

period This is the final stop in a sentence. Periods are also used for many abbreviations. In internet and email addresses, it is called a *dot.*

period, era Do not capitalize *period* when referring to a specific timeframe, as in *the Romantic period.*

periodicals See **magazine, newspaper, publication names** entry.

perk Use *perk* (not *perq*) in all references. It is a shortened form of *perquisite,* which is a fringe benefit.

personal names See **names** entry.

personnel Note the spelling. When used to refer to employees in general, it takes a plural verb, as in *All personnel are invited to the holiday party.* When referring to a department within a company, lowercase and use a singular verb, as in *This year personnel is coordinating the holiday party.*

Peter Principle Note the capitalization. This theory is from a book of the same name by Laurence J. Peter and Raymond Hull that claims employees are promoted until they reach their level of incompetence.

Ph.D., Ph.D.s Note the punctuation. This title for someone who holds a doctorate goes after the name. Mention the area of specialty when appropriate, as in *Arturo Salazar, Ph.D. in economics, will discuss public-private partnerships.*

The abbreviation *Dr.* can also be used for people with Ph.D.s, as in *Dr. Arturo Salazar,* but it is redundant to write *Dr. Arturo Salazar, Ph.D.*

phish(ing) Note the spelling. This refers to an email scam through which the sender attempts to obtain confidential information from the recipient.

phone Use this interchangeably with *telephone.*

Photoshop Capitalize the name of this Adobe product for photo editing, which is frequently used more informally as a verb, as in *The design department routinely Photoshops executive photos.* Do not use this as a verb in formal communications.

PIN Use *PIN* in all references. It stands for *personal identification number,* so don't write *PIN number,* which is redundant.

pixel Use *pixel* in all references. It is the shortened form for *picture element* and refers to the dots that make up an image or character on a computer or TV screen. Resolution improves as the number increases.

play both ends against the middle No hyphens are needed. This statement means to maneuver opposing forces to personal advantage.

plays No need to italicize the titles of plays. Capitalize the principal words, as in *Death of a Salesman.*

plural Double-check the endings of plurals in the dictionary if uncertain. If using foreign words, don't assume the plural is formed by adding an *s.* For example, the plural of the *Italian lira* is *lire.*

plural nouns as adjectives A plural noun can often lose its *s* when modifying another noun, as in *mutual fund industry* (versus *mutual funds industry).* In some cases, it is more common to retain the *s,* as in *systems analyst* (not *system analyst), operations manager* (not *operation manager).*

plus Use a singular verb with the construction *108 plus 233 is 341.*

plus fours The four-digit add-on ZIP codes. Note the hyphen, as in *90452-2511.*

podcast One word, lowercase.

podium, pulpit, rostrum, lectern Pay attention to the prepositions (*on, in, behind*) for these terms. A speaker stands **on** a *podium* or *rostrum,* **in** a *pulpit* or **behind** a *lectern.*

poem Individual poems that are part of a collection take quotation marks, as in *Walt Whitman's "Song of Myself."* (Italics are used here only to illustrate the example.)

policeman, police officer Use *police officer,* which avoids reference to gender. Capitalize when it precedes a name, as in *Police Officer Sylvester Leonard.*

police stations Lowercase *station,* as in *56th Street station.*

policyholder One word.

policymaker It is one word, as in *If the economy starts to overheat, Fed policymakers will take steps to dampen inflation.*

political parties Capitalize, as in *Democratic Party, Republican Party, Labor Party, Nationalist Congress Party, Green Party, Socialist Party.*

political party labels For a U.S. senator, write *Sen. Michael Bennett, Democrat from Colorado* or *Sen. Michael Bennett, D-Colo.* Use standard state abbreviations with this form. See **state abbreviations** entry.

For a representative from the U.S. Congress or a state legislature, *congressperson* is preferred to *congressman* or *congresswoman,* as it avoids reference to gender. Before a name, use *Rep.* (short for *representative*), as in *Rep. Kevin McCarthy, Republican from California; Rep. Donna Edwards, Democrat from Maryland.* An alternative is *Rep. Kevin McCarthy, R-Calif.; Rep. Donna Edwards, D-Md.* Use standard state abbreviations with this form. See **state abbreviations** entry.

There are no short forms for *assemblyman/assemblywoman.* They are not capitalized, unless preceding a name.

Ponzi scheme Capitalize the *P.*

pop-up Write with a hyphen when used to modify. *The pop-up ads were so disruptive she logged off the site. The pop-up store will be at the lower Manhattan location for a month.*

portal A site serving as an entry to the web. It also means entryway. According to James Joyce, "Mistakes are the portals of discovery."

Portuguese names Some people from Portuguese-speaking countries use both their mother and father's family names. Note that the father's surname comes last. For example, in the case of *Amanda Teixeira Netto,* the mother's name is *Teixeira* and the father's name is *Netto.* For shortened references to the person's last name, write *Ms. Netto* or *Netto.* It is also correct to list both family names in shortened references, if that is how the person is known, as in *Ms. Teixeira Netto* or *Teixeira Netto.*

When alphabetizing Portuguese names in which both family names are used, use the father's surname, as in *Netto, Amanda Teixeira.*

Many married women retain their father's name before the husband's name. If *Amanda Teixeira Netto* married *Joao Macedo,* she could be known as *Amanda Netto Macedo.* In second references, write *Ms.* or *Mrs. Macedo* or *Macedo.*

To alphabetize in this instance, write *Macedo, Amanda Netto.*

Note the difference from Spanish, where the mother's name comes last. See **Spanish names** entry.

possessives See **apostrophe** entry.

Postal Service Use *Postal Service* interchangeably with the *United States Postal Service* or *USPS*.

Post-it Capitalize the *P,* use a hyphen and lowercase the *i* when referring to the trademarked paper product. The plural is *Post-its*. *Sticky Notes* is another name for this product, also trademarked, which is why it is capitalized.

post office Lowercase *post office* because it is not a formal name. A postmaster is the person in charge of a post office. Lowercase unless it is part of a formal title.

pounds and pence Spell out when the amount is indefinite. *The company invested millions of pounds in an infrastructure upgrade.*

When writing specific numbers for material that may be read on portable devices, avoid the £ symbol and spell out *pound* or write *GBP.* For print documents, use the symbol (£) with figures. *The company invested £10 million in an infrastructure upgrade.* Note there is no space between £ and the number.

Spell out *pence* and *penny* (which is singular for *pence)* when they appear alone in sums: *1 penny* (not *1 pence), 4 pence.* See **foreign currency** entry.

PowerPoint Capitalize both *P*'s.

pre(-) Most words beginning with *pre-* do not need a hyphen, as in *precursor, prepaid.* But use a hyphen when *pre-* is followed by the letter *e,* as in *pre-eminent, pre-existing.* Also use a hyphen if the letter following *pre-* is capitalized, as in *pre-Darwinian, pre-Facebook.*

predominant, predominantly These are the preferred spellings (not *predominate* and *predominately).*

prefixes Usually words with these prefixes are one word: *pre-, post-, over-, under-, intra-, extra-, infra-, ultra-, sub-, super-, pro-, anti-, re-, un-, non-,* *semi-, pseudo-, supra-, meta-, multi-* and *co-,* as in *superabundant, cofounder, infrared, extramarital, semiautomatic, multithreaded, intravenous, reintroduce, nonstandard.*

prepositions A preposition is used to relate a noun or pronoun to some other word in the sentence, as in *at, by, in, from, above, against, toward, with.* It is acceptable to end a sentence with a preposition, as in *The consultant said the hardware incompatibility problem is nothing to be concerned about.* If the sentence sounds awkward, revise it to avoid ending with a preposition, as in *The consultant said we had no reason to be concerned about the hardware incompatibility problem.*

presently It means in a little while or soon, but because it can also mean currently or now, *currently* is clearer when the meaning is now.

presidency Lowercase in all instances.

president For organizations, uppercase the word *President* only if it precedes a name, as in *President Armand D'Agostino will meet with the board this afternoon.* If no name is used, lowercase *president,* as in *D'Agostino is the company's president.*

Presidents Day Capitalize both words and do not use an apostrophe. This holiday commemorates the birthdays of George Washington and Abraham Lincoln.

preventive It is the preferred term, not *preventative.*

price-earnings ratio Spell out *price-earnings ratio* in the first reference; use *P/E ratio* or just *P/E* afterward. Note this takes a slash (/) and both letters are capitalized.

prime rate Do not capitalize. It is the lowest rate of interest on a bank loan offered to preferred borrowers.

principal, principle These terms are often confused. *Principal* means main party, owner, chief or leader. *French law firms represent the principals in the merger.* *Principal* also means the amount, excluding interest or premium, due on a loan or to a security holder at maturity. *The government has started paying down principal on its foreign debt.* *Principal* is also used as an adjective, as in *His principal contact at the firm is in marketing.*

Principle means a truth or belief, as in *The department's guiding principle is customer satisfaction.*

print out, printout Use two words for the verb, as in *Julio will print out the document for Margaret.* Write as one word when used as a noun. *Julio will give Margaret a printout of the document.*

privately held This does not take a hyphen, regardless of how it is used. *The company is privately held* or *It is a privately held company.* The same is true for other words ending in *ly*, as in *highly complex formula, remarkably astute analyst.*

private sector, private-sector No hyphen is needed when used as a noun, as in *The former ambassador now works in the private sector.* Write with a hyphen when used as an adjective, as in *The former ambassador now works at a private-sector foundation.* The same holds for *public sector.*

privilege Often misspelled.

proactive No hyphen is needed.

producer price index Spell out in the first reference; use *PPI* afterward. This measures prices paid to producers for their goods.

professor Always lowercase before a name and never abbreviate as *prof.*

pronoun A pronoun is a word used in place of a noun or noun phrase, as in *I, you, he, yours* (all personal pronouns), *who* (a relative or interrogative pronoun), *these* (a demonstrative pronoun), *each* (an indefinite pronoun), *himself* (a reflexive pronoun).

proposition Lowercase unless it refers to a specific ballot question. When a figure appears with *proposition,* capitalize and abbreviate, as in *Voters have many unanswered questions about Prop. 12.*

prostate, prostrate Do not confuse these terms. The first refers to the prostate gland; the second refers to the act of reclining.

protester Often misspelled (not *protestor).*

publication names Do not capitalize *the* in a publication's name, as in *the Huffington Post* (see **magazine, newspaper, publication names** entry). Do not place the name of the publication in an italic font or in quotation marks.

Public Broadcasting Service Spell out in the first reference; use *PBS* afterward. This is a nonprofit association, not a network of public television stations.

public schools Lowercase unless used with a figure, as in *Public School 9.*

public sector, public-sector This takes no hyphen when used as a noun, as in *She works in the public sector.* Write with a hyphen when used as an adjective, as in *She has worked in public-sector organizations for her entire career.* The same holds for *private sector.*

pullout Write as one word when used as an adjective, as in *The pullout section of the brochure will include photographs.*

punctuation Its primary purpose is to help readers understand the written word. Style may vary from one organization to the next, but the key issues are clarity and consistency. Avoid using punctuation for effect, as in *She quit without giving notice!!!*

push back, pushback Write as two words when used as a verb. *Carol will push back about her performance review.* Write as one word when used as a noun meaning to counter or provide feedback that is contrary. *The CFO anticipates pushback from the salespeople about the new expense account policy.*

· Q ·

Q1, Q2, Q3, Q4 These abbreviations can be used for *first quarter (Q1), second quarter (Q2),* etc. in slide shows, charts, tabular material and other documents, depending on the audience and degree of formality. Include the year if necessary. *In Q1 2016 the company plans to launch its new product line.* In formal documents, such as annual reports, do not use the abbreviation. *In the first quarter of 2016, the company plans to launch its new product line.*

Q&A Use *Q&A* in all references. It stands for *question and answer.* The plural is *Q&As.* If writing a Q&A for a formal document, choose a style that is readable and clear. Often the question is in bold or italics and the answer is in normal (roman) type.

QR code Always use the abbreviation and capitalize this reference to a type of barcode; stands for *Quick Response.*

Quakers Use this for Religious Society of Friends in all references.

quandary Often misspelled.

quart Spell out in text, but abbreviate as *qt.* in tabular material. A quart equals 32 ounces or 2 pints. To convert to liters, use a conversion chart.

quasi, quasi- This is a separate word when used with a noun, as in *a quasi success*. Hyphenate when used as an adjective, as in *quasi-official policy*. It means to resemble something.

queen Lowercase unless it appears before a name as an official title, as in *Queen Elizabeth*.

question mark Use a question mark (*?*) at the end of a direct question, as in *What time is it?* Do not use a question mark after an indirect question, as in *I wonder what time it is*. See **quotation marks** and **parentheses** entries.

questionnaire Often misspelled.

quick This is an adjective, as in *Nawal is a quick study*. A common error is to use it as an adverb, as in *Come quick*. Write *Come quickly* instead.

quick-and-dirty This expression refers to making a rough estimate or getting a task done quickly, without worrying about details. *The client asked for a quick-and-dirty report to expedite the budget request.*

quid pro quo Use this term only if it will be familiar to readers. It is Latin for an equal exchange or substitution. It has two plural forms, *quid pro quos* and *quids pro quo*. This stylebook favors *quid pro quos*. Choose one form and be consistent.

quincentenary It is the 500th anniversary. *Quincentennial* is an alternative. Offer an equivalent in parentheses if readers may not know these terms.

quindecennial It means occurring every 15 years or a 15th anniversary. This is an unfamiliar word to many readers, so use it judiciously.

quitclaim One word. It is the transfer of a title, right or claim to another.

quotation marks Follow these guidelines:

- Use double marks (" ") for direct quotations of speech or writing. *CFO Thomas Rider said, "We plan to close the German office because of shrinking demand for our products in Europe." The memo said, "It has been a year of change at our company."*
- Use single marks (' ') for a quotation within a quotation. *"The CFO explained that 'shrinking demand for our products in Europe' was the reason for closing the German office," said the managing director.*
- Use quotation marks the first time to introduce a new word in text, as in *The analyst told the investor about the "whisper numbers." The whisper numbers boosted the investor's interest.*
- When single and double quotation marks fall together, separate them with a space, as in *"The CFO explained that the reason for closing the German office was 'shrinking demand for our products in Europe,' " said the director.*
- If quotation marks occur within single quotation marks, use double quotation marks, as in *Kathleen said, "John told me, 'The "whisper number" had a negative impact on the stock.' "*
- With indirect quotations, do not use quotation marks, as in *Thomas Rider discussed the reason for closing the German office.*
- For multiple paragraphs of quoted material, begin each paragraph of the quoted material with quotation marks, but use ending quotation marks only at the end of the quoted material. Put the attribution for the multiple-paragraph quotation at the beginning or in the first paragraph of the quotation, not at the end. Another option is to set off long quotations from the text as block quotations, in which case they are not enclosed in quotation marks but indented. In a block quotation, change any single quotation marks to double marks.
- For unusual wording or unfamiliar expressions, use quotation marks, as in *HR was not amused when the job seeker used "WYSIWYG" in her cover letter.*

- Use quotation marks for the titles of speeches, chapters, lectures, paintings, songs (popular and classical), national anthems, articles in periodicals, short stories, poems, movies, books, individual episodes in television shows. Do not put the names of publications, newspapers, magazines, etc. in quotation marks.
- If a term is used differently from its original meaning, put it in quotation marks, as in "Gang of Four" when referring to Erich Gamma, Richard Helm, Ralph Johnson and John Vlissides, authors of the book, "Design Patterns" (as opposed to the Gang of Four associated with Mao's Cultural Revolution).

Punctuation with quotation marks for American English:

- A period goes inside quotation marks that end a sentence in American English. *Lynn said, "The report is due Friday."* The first chapter of the book is entitled *"Passionate Curiosity."* (Italics are used to illustrate the example, not because the chapter title should be italicized.)
- A comma goes inside quotation marks when the quotation does not end the sentence. *"I need to call my agent," said Kevin. If you want to be known as a "player," join the M&A group. The best chapters of the book are entitled "Be a Coach, Not a Critic," "Creating a Sense of Mission" and "So What Is Leadership?"*
- A comma precedes a direct quotation when the attribution comes first, as in *Kevin said, "I need to call my agent." The memo said, "It has been a year of change at our company."*
- Do not use a comma at the start of a partial quotation. *Michelle said we needed "to start from scratch."*
- A question mark goes inside quotation marks if it is part of the direct quotation, as in *"Where is the money?" asked Tyson.*
- A question mark goes outside the quotation marks if the whole sentence containing the quotation is a question, as in *What did he really mean when he said, "The project is mostly on schedule"?*

- An exclamation point goes inside the quotation marks if the quoted words are an exclamation, as in *Simpson told the reporters, "Buzz off!"* No period is necessary in this case.
- An exclamation point goes outside the quotation marks if the whole sentence is exclamatory, as in *Simpson actually admitted the experience was "humbling"!*
- A colon and a semicolon always go outside the quotation marks, as in *Nora said, "I have a migraine"; she added, "I need a vacation."*

quotations Accuracy is the primary consideration when quoting an individual. Never take a statement out of context. If the person quoted is cast in a negative light, the quotation should be exact – verbatim. Otherwise, clean up grammar and spelling.

quote, quotation *Quote* is the verb, though writers often use it as a noun. The noun is *quotation. Don't quote me on those numbers. He gave me the quotation over the phone,* not *He gave me the quote over the phone.*

· R ·

rabbi Lowercase *rabbi* unless it is a formal title that precedes a name, as in *Rabbi Levy.* The only other formal title in the Jewish congregation is *cantor,* the individual who leads the congregation in song, as in *Cantor David Klein.* Lowercase *cantor* when it is not a formal title, as in *The cantor was unable to come to the Bar Mitzvah.*

race Unless relevant to the material, avoid identifying individuals by race. Lowercase all racial descriptions, as in *black, white.*

radio station Use the letters without periods, as in *WNYC.* If the station may not be familiar to readers, write *radio station KEXP.*

railroad If it is part of a name, capitalize it; otherwise, lowercase *railroad.* Double-check railroad company names for the official spelling.

rainmaker One word. This refers to someone who generates business for an organization, bringing in clients and money.

RAM Use *RAM* in all references. It stands for *random access memory.*

ratio Use figures and hyphens, as in *a 3-to-1 ratio*.

R&D Spell out *research and development* in the first reference; use *R&D* afterward (with the *ampersand [&]* and no spaces).

really Avoid this word when possible in business writing. It rarely adds meaning. The same holds for *very*.

real time, real-time Write as two words when used as a noun, as in *The website allows customers and service representatives to communicate in real time*. Write with a hyphen when used as an adjective, as in *The company's goal is to provide real-time account information to all customers*.

Realtor Use *real estate agent*, the generic term, unless the individual is a member of the *National Association of Realtors;* then write *Realtor*, which is a service mark.

rebut, refute These are not interchangeable. *Rebut* means to take issue; *refute* means to disprove.

recession Lowercase. This is an economic downturn that may be temporary or may continue into a depression (also lowercased).

recipes Always use figures. It is acceptable to abbreviate measurements in lists or tabular material to save space, such as recipes: *½ teaspoon of sugar (½ tsp. sugar), 2 tablespoons of butter (2 T. butter)*.

record In the sense of setting a record, do not use *new*. Write *The sales department set a record this month*, not *The sales department set a new record this month*. The *new* in this sentence is redundant.

recordkeeping, record-keeping Can be written as one word or with a hyphen. This stylebook favors one word. Whichever version you choose, use it consistently. *The finance department is reviewing all recordkeeping procedures*.

recur, recurred, recurring Often misspelled.

red herring Facts, statements, accusations, actions that are used to draw attention away from the main point and throw the reader or opponent off balance. This is also used to refer to a preliminary statement or prospectus that is filed with the Securities and Exchange Commission.

redline The verb is one word, as in *The bank cannot redline this neighborhood* or *The technologist redlined my specifications.*

redundancy Avoid unnecessary repetition in all writing. The following are examples of redundancies: *$500 million dollars, new record, ATM machine, PIN number, absolutely necessary, rarely ever, consensus of opinion, close proximity, surround on all sides, Dr. Heidi Waldorf, M.D.*

reengineer No hyphen is needed.

refer back When using the construction *refer back,* make sure the *back* is necessary for clarification. In some cases, the *back* is redundant because the prefix *re-* means *back.*

regardless There is no such word as *irregardless.* It is a double negative. Write *regardless* instead.

regional names Uppercase the names of recognized regions, as in *New England, the Pacific Northwest, Latin America, Southeast Asia, the Middle East, the Baltics, Western Europe, North Africa.*

registered trademark When a product is a registered trademark, it means it is recorded and verified by an authorized association. Registration puts on public record the exact details of the claim. Follow the trademarked names' punctuation and capitalization, as in *Coca-Cola, Gold Medal, iPad, PayPal.* The symbol for it is ®, but the symbol is not required in general text, although some companies require it in advertising and marketing materials.

reign, rein *Reign* is a period of rule or dominance, as in *He had a short reign as CEO. Rein* is used for expressions such as *give free rein to, pull in the reins* and *rein in. Yevgeny gave his staff free rein to develop the new software.* (Literally, *rein* means the strip of leather attached to the bit in a horse's mouth.)

release time Follow this boldface style if a press release is embargoed until a specific time: *For release 9 a.m. ET.*

religious references Many religious references are capitalized; however, do not capitalize pronouns (e.g., *he, thou, thee*) when referring to a deity.

renminbi Lowercase and note the spelling of China's currency. *Renminbi* is often used interchangeably with *yuan,* although technically the terms differ. The *renminbi* is the currency and *yuan* is the main unit of the currency. This stylebook favors *renminbi,* which is what the Bank of China uses. *The company uses renminbi for its trade financing.* The abbreviation for *renminbi* is *RMB,* the three-letter international code is *CNY* and the currency symbol is ¥.

repellent This is the preferred spelling.

representative When referring to members of Congress, use the abbreviation *Rep.* before a name, as in *Rep. Donna Edwards of Maryland is the keynote speaker.* Lowercase for other uses, as in *The representative from Maryland is the keynote speaker. The company's sales representatives attended a weeklong training program.*

rescission Often misspelled (not *recision*). It means the act of making void (from *rescind*).

research and development Spell out in the first reference; use *R&D* afterward (with the *ampersand [&]* and no spaces).

restrictive clauses See **comma** entry.

resume No longer necessary to use the accents.

rethink No hyphen, whether used as a noun or verb. *The company's recent rethink shows the risk of an overly aggressive acquisition strategy. The new internet team will rethink the company's web strategy.*

return on investment Spell out in the first reference; use *ROI* afterward.

retweet This Twitter reference can be used as a noun, as in *I didn't get the retweet.* It also can be used as a verb, *John frequently retweets useful information. RT* is the short form.

Rev. Capitalize and abbreviate as a title that precedes a name, as in *Rev. Al Green.* Lowercase *reverend* when it is not followed by a name. *The reverend will hold a meeting at 4 p.m.*

RFP Spell out *request for proposal* in the first reference; use *RFP* afterward. The plural is *RFPs.*

rhythm Often misspelled.

right-click Write with a hyphen.

right-handed Write with a hyphen.

rise Use *raise* instead of *rise* for an increase in pay.

ROI Spell out *return on investment* in the first reference; use *ROI* afterward.

roll out, rollout Write as two words when used as a verb, as in *They plan to roll out the new software in April.* Write as one word when used as a noun. *The software rollout is scheduled for April.*

roll over, rollover Write as two words when used as a verb, as in *He plans to roll over his IRA when he changes jobs.* Write as one word when used as an adjective, as in *The seminar will cover rollover rules for IRAs.*

Rolodex This is often misspelled (not *Roladex*). Capitalize because it is a brand name, even though this term is used generically.

Roman numerals The numeral system uses seven letters: *I, V, X, L, C, D, M.* The equivalents are: *I* = *1*, *V* = *5*, *X* = *10*, *L* = *50*, *C* = *100*, *D* = *500*, *M* = *1,000.* Add when a letter follows one of equal or greater value, as in *XV* = *15.* Subtract when a smaller number precedes a larger one, as in *IV* = *4.* Do not put a comma before the Roman numeral when it appears in a name.

roman type Do not capitalize *roman* when referring to upright typefaces.

room names Capitalize the names of special rooms or numbered rooms: *Rainbow Room, Oval Office, Room 23.*

rostrum, podium, pulpit, lectern Pay attention to the prepositions (*on, in, behind*) for these terms. A speaker stands **on** a *rostrum* or *podium*, **in** a *pulpit* or **behind** a *lectern*.

roundup One word. *Each department head gave a roundup of major Q1 accomplishments.*

Route Capitalize *Route* when it appears in the names of roads, as in *Route 66.* In tabular material, use the abbreviation *Rte.* with the number, as in *Rte. 17.*

RSS Write with all caps; use *RSS* in all references. Stands for *Really Simple Syndication,* a format used by websites for distributing information to subscribers via *RSS* feeds.

RSVP Use *RSVP* in all references.

rulebook One word. *After the hurricane, the company realized its disaster-preparedness rulebook was inadequate.*

rulemaking Can be written as one word or with a hyphen. This stylebook favors one word. *Rulemaking under the new legislation is expected to continue into next year.*

· S ·

"Put yourself in the reader's place."
– Marc Rice, corporate communication account executive - environment
Southern Company

sacred writings Capitalize the names of sacred writings, as in *Upanishads, Old Testament, Gospels, Holy Bible, Koran.*

safe deposit box This phrase is not hyphenated. Avoid using this form: *safety box.*

salesperson Avoid a reference to gender by using *sales clerk, salesperson* (one word) or *sales representative.* If you need to express gender, *use saleswoman* instead of *salesgirl* or *salesman* instead of *salesboy.*

salutation If the gender of the addressee in correspondence is unknown, drop the *Mr.* or *Ms.* and use the full name in the salutation, as in *Dear Pat Wilson:.*

sanction It can mean either approve or penalty. Be clear in context. *The regulators sanctioned the heart medicine* or *The United Nations issued a report on the trade sanctions.*

Saturday Capitalize days of the week.

savings and loan association Spell out in the first reference; use *S&L* (with the *ampersand [&]* and without spaces) afterward. The plural is *S&Ls*. This is not interchangeable with *bank* or *thrift*.

scalable Note the spelling (no *e*).

school Lowercase unless it is part of a proper noun, as in *St. Luke's Grammar School, Public School 3, Richard E. Byrd School.* For colleges and universities, capitalize only when it is part of an official name, as in *the School of Teaching and Learning at The Ohio State University.*

scientific terms There are many style matters regarding scientific terms. It is best to double-check specific stylebooks (for instance, "American Medical Association Manual of Style").

scissors It takes a plural verb and pronoun, as in *The scissors are back in the drawer where they belong.*

screensaver, screenshot Each is one word.

sculpture Capitalize the titles of sculptures and use quotation marks, as in *Rodin's "The Thinker."* (The use of italics is to illustrate the example, not because the name of the sculpture should be italicized.)

seasons Lowercase all seasons: *winter, spring, summer, fall* or *autumn.*

second, secondly When enumerating, use *second,* not *secondly,* as in *First go to the home page; second click Careers.*

second-guess Write with a hyphen. It means to criticize or correct someone after an outcome is known. The person who does this is a *second-guesser.*

second hand, secondhand Write as two words when referring to the hands on a clock or when used as an adverb, as in *She heard about the layoffs second hand.*

Write as one word when used as an adjective. *She bought a secondhand car* or *The secondhand smoke bothered Mary Adele.*

Securities and Exchange Commission Spell out in the first reference; use *SEC* or *commission* (lowercased) afterward.

self(-) Many words with this prefix are hyphenated, as in *self-governing, self-addressed, self-service.* Check the dictionary if uncertain.

semi(-) Most words with this prefix are not hyphenated, as in *semicircle, semiconductor.* But use a hyphen to separate two consecutive *i*'s, as in *semi-informal.*

semiannual, semiyearly Both mean twice a year. These words can be confusing, so use *twice a year* instead.

semicolon A semicolon *(;)* adds more emphasis than the comma but is weaker than the colon *(:).* Follow these guidelines:

- Use a semicolon to join closely related statements: *Human resources deals with personnel issues; auditing deals with risk issues.*
- Use semicolons to mark off phrases or items in a series that would ordinarily be separated by commas except that the phrases or items already contain commas: *Sue Ciezcko, director of human resources, asks all new employees to read the Employee Manual; the Insurance Booklet, including the preface; the Employee Stylebook, even though it is more than 100 pages; and the Code of Ethics.* (Note the semicolon [not the comma] is used before the last phrase in the series.)
- The semicolon goes outside quotation marks or parentheses: *Mary Ellen read "Bartleby the Scrivener"; she then quit her job at the post office.*

Senate Capitalize references to the *Senate.*

senator Before a name, use the abbreviation *Sen.,* as in *Sen. Daniel Akaka of Hawaii wrote the article.* Lowercase in other references. *The senator from Hawaii wrote the article.*

senior, junior Use the capitalized abbreviations *Sr.* or *Jr.* with personal names. Use a comma before *Sr.* or *Jr.* For instance, *Anthony Forde, Sr.* In a listing by last name, the *Sr.* or *Jr.* comes last: *Forde, Anthony, Sr.*

Spell out and lowercase *senior* or *junior* to designate a member of the class.

SEO Short for *search-engine optimization* (note the hyphen). Unless your audience is familiar with this term, spell out in the first reference; use *SEO* after.

separate Often misspelled.

sergeant Often misspelled. Lowercase unless it precedes a name. Before a name, capitalize and abbreviate as *Sgt.*

serviceable Often misspelled.

service mark This refers to a name, brand, symbol or slogan that distinguishes a company or its products and is protected by law. Capitalize service marks in text. In some instances, companies follow service marks with the abbreviation ^{SM}, as in *App Store* ^{SM}. Use of registration symbols, such as ^{SM} or ^{TM}, depends on practice already established by individual companies.

services Write this with a singular verb when referring to an industry, as in *Health services is undergoing a major transformation.*

service sector Lowercase this term.

setup One word.

shall, will In American English, avoid *shall* for business communications, as it tends to sound overly formal or mannered.

shareholder, share owner The first is one word; the second is two.

she Do not refer to ships or countries as *she*. Use *it* instead.

s/he Some publications use *s/he* as a gender alternative to *he or she*. It takes a singular verb, as in *The person who wrote the letter did not include a name, although s/he expects a reply.* This stylebook does not recommend this construction.

shortfall One word. It is the amount by which something falls short of expectation, need or demand. *Analysts project a shortfall in demand for strategic minerals.*

short-lived Always write with a hyphen. *The economic recovery looks short-lived. It was a short-lived recovery.*

sign-in, sign in Write with a hyphen when used as a noun or adjective. *She didn't have time to complete the sign-in. The sign-in process is time-consuming.* Use two words when used as a verb. *I will sign in to the system from my home office.* Same for *sign-out, sign out; sign-up, sign up.*

signs When referring to *signs,* capitalize the first letter in each word, but don't use quotation marks. *There is a No Smoking sign in the lobby.*

silo, siloed Note the spelling of the past participle, which is used in business to mean separated, not integrated, even though it is not in some dictionaries. *The new COO thinks the technology team is too siloed.*

SIM card Use *SIM* in all references. It stands for *subscriber identity module.*

Sina Weibo Note the spelling of one of China's most popular social networks, which is a Twitter- and Facebook-like site. Use the full name in first reference and *Sina* afterward.

sitdown This is one word when it is used as a noun, as in *HR scheduled a sitdown with the new hires to explain office protocol.*

Six Sigma Capitalize this term, which refers to a corporate approach to quality management that is data-driven and aims to bring defects to near zero.

Skype Capitalize the name of this audio and video telephony company, which is also used as a verb, as in *I will Skype you over the weekend.*

slash It is a diagonal mark (/) used primarily to separate alternatives, as in *and/ or* or *his/her,* or to replace the word *per* as in *miles/hour.* The double-slash (//) is used for web addresses after the protocol, as in *http://.*

slowdown Write as one word when used as a noun. *Investors expect an economic slowdown in the third quarter.*

small-business man, small-business woman Use a hyphen. Note that in this usage, *businessman* and *businesswoman,* which are usually one word, become two-word forms. Write *small-business person* to avoid reference to gender.

smart card Two words.

smartphone One word.

SMS This term, which stands for *short message service,* is dated and may be unfamiliar to some people. Write *text(ing)* or *text message/messaging* instead. See **text** entry.

snail mail Coined to mean the alternative to *email,* this term is used for mail sent through the post office.

so-called Write with a hyphen. *We are going to Bali, the so-called Island of the Gods.* Be careful with this term, which can suggest that something is questionable or dubious, as in *His so-called list of achievements had little relation to reality.*

social media No need to hyphenate this term, whether used as a noun, as in *The company uses social media for recruiting,* or an adjective, as in *The company updates its social media policy twice a year.*

social network(ing) No need to hyphenate this term, whether used as a noun, as in *Luisa found her job through social networking,* or an adjective, as in *Mary's social networking experience is limited to LinkedIn.*

Social Security Capitalize this reference to the government insurance program, as in *Please include your Social Security number.* Write *SSN* for short.

software Capitalize the principal words in program names, as in *Microsoft Word.* There is no need to use quotation marks.

some time, sometime, sometimes *Some time* means a portion of time, as in *Robin will have some time to meet with you Tuesday. Sometime* means at an indefinite time in the future, as in *Robin will meet with you sometime next week. Sometimes* means occasionally. *Robin sometimes schedules meetings for 8 a.m.*

so-so Hyphenate in all usages. *The company reported so-so results for the third consecutive quarter. The company's results were so-so for the third consecutive quarter.*

spacebar One word.

spacing Use the tab key for a paragraph indent. Use a single space between sentences (not a double space).

spam Lowercase this term, which is another word for electronic junk mail.

Spanish names Many people from Spanish-speaking countries use both their mother and father's surnames, with the mother's surname last. For example, in the case of *Pablo Beltran Gabarra, Beltran* is the father's name and *Gabarra* is the mother's name. Shortened references use the father's last name: *Mr. Beltran* or *Beltran,* but never *Mr. Gabarra* or *Gabarra.* It is also correct to list both family names in shortened references, as in *Mr. Beltran Gabarra* or *Beltran Gabarra.*

When alphabetizing Spanish names in which both family names are used, always put the father's surname first, as in *Beltran Gabarra, Pablo* (not *Gabarra, Pablo Beltran).*

Note the difference from Portuguese, where the father's name comes second. See **Portuguese names** entry.

spec(s) Spell out *specification(s)* in the first reference; use *spec(s)* afterward. *The vendor emailed the specs for the new online version of the publication.* This stylebook favors using *spec* as a verb for informal communications. *Sue will spec the job before Friday.* In formal communications, avoid the verb form.

speeches Put the titles of speeches in quotation marks and capitalize the main words. *The keynote speech is entitled, "The Challenges of Leadership in Times of Change."*

spellcheck Write as one word, as in *Be sure to spellcheck the document before you print it.* This stylebook prefers *spellcheck* (rather than *spellchecker)* when used as a noun, as in *Please run the files through spellcheck before sending them to the client. Spellchecker* is also correct.

When you spellcheck a document or email, follow this guideline: Always use it; never trust it. The spellcheck only detects misspelled words. It will not detect the wrong form, as in *you* instead of *your.*

spinoff Write as one word when used as a noun, as in *The spinoff of the health-care division is scheduled for the third quarter.*

split infinitive See **infinitive** entry.

spokesman, spokesperson, spokeswoman Use *spokesperson* if you don't know or don't want to refer to the speaker's gender.

sports sponsorship Capitalize the name of the event, as in *AFF Suzuki Cup*.

spouse Use *spouse* instead of *wife* or *husband,* as in *The candidate invited executives and their spouses to the dinner.*

spreadsheet One word.

spring Lowercase seasons.

St. Use this abbreviation for *Saint,* as in *St. Anthony, St. Paul, Minn.*

stand-alone Write with a hyphen when used as an adjective. *The stand-alone service is available globally, but the suite of services is available only in China.*

Standard & Poor's Spell out in the first reference. Note the use of the *&* (spaces on either side) and the placement of the apostrophe. Afterward, use *S&P* (no periods or spaces).

When citing the index, write *Standard & Poor's 500-stock index* in the first reference; use *S&P 500* afterward.

standup meeting *Standup* is one word.

startup(s) Write as one word, whether used as a noun or an adjective. *Marc works in a startup* or *Marc works in a startup company.*

state There are 50 states in the U.S., but four are commonwealths (Kentucky, Virginia, Massachusetts and Pennsylvania). Lowercase all *state of* and *commonwealth of* constructions, as in *state of California.* Lowercase *state* when it precedes a level of jurisdiction, as in *state Rep. Thomas Feldman.* Apply the same style to phrases, such as *town of Warwick, city of Milwaukee.*

state abbreviations The Postal Service prefers the two-letter postal abbreviations when ZIP codes are included. Both letters are capitalized, no periods are used after the letters and no commas are used between the state and the ZIP code. Use these abbreviations only with full addresses.

In text, do not use the Postal Service abbreviations. Instead use the standard state abbreviations in conjunction with a city or town. Spell out the state name if no city or town is included. (Note that some cities do not require state names. See **cities** entry.) Many of the standard abbreviations are the same as those used by the Postal Service, but note the different use of capitalization and periods. In text a comma goes between the city and state and after the state abbreviation (unless it falls at the end of the sentence). *Margaret is moving to San Diego, Calif., next spring* or *Next spring Margaret is moving to San Diego, Calif.*

Note that eight states are never abbreviated in text: *Alaska, Hawaii, Idaho, Iowa, Maine, Ohio, Texas, Utah.*

Alabama: Ala. AL

Alaska: Alaska AK

Arizona: Ariz. AZ

Arkansas: Ark. AR

California: Calif. CA

Colorado: Colo. CO

Connecticut: Conn. CT

Delaware: Del. DE

Florida: Fla. FL

Georgia: Ga. GA

Hawaii: Hawaii HI

Indiana: Ind. IN

Idaho: Idaho ID

Iowa: Iowa IA

Illinois: Ill. IL

Kansas: Kans. KS

Kentucky: Ky. KY

Louisiana: La. LA

Maine: Maine ME

Maryland: Md. MD

Massachusetts: Mass. MA

Michigan: Mich. MI

Minnesota: Minn. MN

Mississippi: Miss. MS

Missouri: Mo. MO

Montana: Mont. MT

Nebraska: Nebr. NE

Nevada: Nev. NV

New Hampshire: N.H. NH

New Jersey: N.J. NJ

New Mexico: N. Mex. NM

New York: N.Y. NY

North Carolina: N.C. NC

North Dakota: N. Dak. ND

Ohio: Ohio OH

Oklahoma: Okla. OK

Oregon: Oreg. OR

Pennsylvania: Pa. PA

Rhode Island: R.I. RI
South Carolina: S.C. SC
South Dakota: S. Dak. SD
Tennessee: Tenn. TN
Texas: Texas TX
Utah: Utah UT

Vermont: Vt. VT
Virginia: Va. VA
Washington: Wash. WA
West Virginia: W. Va. WV
Wisconsin: Wis. WI
Wyoming: Wyo. WY

state of the art, state-of-the-art Write without hyphens when used as a noun, as in *The new teleconferencing technology is state of the art.* Hyphenate when used as an adjective. *The new offices have state-of-the-art teleconferencing technology.*

stationary, stationery Often confused. *Stationary* means standing still; *stationery* means paper for writing.

stellar Note the spelling (not *steller*). *The board rewarded the CEO for the company's stellar performance.*

straightforward One word.

stratum, strata The singular is *stratum;* the plural is *strata. The proportion of the population in the lowest stratum of society is growing.*

streaming media This refers to audio, video, newsfeeds and other media content that streams over the web.

street Spell out and capitalize in this construction: *Sue lives on Grove Street.* Use *St.* with figures in tabular material and with complete addresses. See **addresses** entry for more information. The style for two or more streets, as in *Grove and Burnette Streets,* is uppercase (not *Grove and Burnette streets).*

Street, the Capitalize *Street* when it refers to the Wall Street financial community. *The Street expects the Fed to lower interest rates.*

Student Loan Marketing Association Spell out in the first reference; use *Sallie Mae* afterward. Note the spelling of *Mae*.

subcontinent No hyphen; lowercase. *His new sales territory includes the entire Indian subcontinent.*

subjunctive Use this form of the verb for wishful thinking, as in *If I were a millionaire, I would buy the company* (not *If I was a millionaire*).

subpoena Often misspelled. When used as a verb, the past tense is *subpoenaed*, as in *The company's legal team subpoenaed court records.*

summer Lowercase all seasons.

Sunday Capitalize days of the week.

supersede Often misspelled. It means to take the place of.

supposed to Remember the *d* at the end of *suppose* in this construction: *He was supposed to leave the information with his assistant.*

Supreme Court Capitalize in all references. This is the highest court in the U.S., consisting of nine justices and having jurisdiction over all other courts in the nation. Also capitalize references to the state supreme courts, as in *Connecticut Supreme Court.*

suspensive hyphen Rather than repeat the words in a series of similar phrases that form adjectives, use the *suspensive hyphen,* as in *The facilities manager ordered one-, two- and three-inch nails for the project. The company released first- and second-quarter earnings results.*

sync, synced, syncing Use this abbreviated form of *synchronize/synchronization* in all references; no *h* is needed. *He synced his office and home computers. She is looking for a free syncing service for music.*

synchronicity Often misspelled. *Synchrony* is a form of *synchronicity.*

systemic This term denotes something that affects an entire system or multiple systems. *The financial reform legislation is designed to reduce systemic risk.*

· T ·

20/20 Write this with figures and a slash. *With 20/20 hindsight Sheila admitted that the other position would have been a better career move.*

24/7 Use figures and a slash.

10-K Use *10-K* in all references (note the hyphen and capital *K*). This refers to the Securities and Exchange Commission's *Form 10-K,* which is a financial statement that publicly held companies must file each year. (The *10-Q* is filed each quarter.)

For kilometers, write *10K* (without the hyphen), as in *Ayush finished the 10K race in record time.*

3D Use *3D* in all references, as in *The oceanographers used 3D imaging to map the ocean floor.* It stands for *three-dimensional.*

3G, 4G, 5G No hyphens needed for these cellphone networks.

360-degree review Include the word *degree,* using a hyphen, in the first reference. In subsequent references, this can be used interchangeably with *360* *review* or *360*, as in *Barbara received the results of her 360 last week.* This refers to performance reviews that include feedback from a person's supervisor, peers, direct reports and, in some cases, customers. It is also correct to use the degree symbol, as in *360° review,* though this takes longer to write on a keyboard.

tablespoon, tablespoonful(s) Spell out in text, but abbreviations are acceptable in tabular material. *Tablespoon* has three abbreviations: *T., tbs., tbsp.* Choose one and be consistent. A tablespoon is equal to 3 teaspoons.

tabular material Space is always a consideration in tabular material, so figures and abbreviations are preferred, regardless of spell-out and first-reference rules in text.

take-home pay Note the hyphen. This is the amount of salary after taxes and other deductions.

takeover It is one word when used in the sense of acquisition. *The proposed takeover will require Justice Department approval.*

task force Two words; no hyphen. *The task force will make its recommendations in Q2.*

taskmaster One word. This is someone who assigns tasks to others and is demanding about the outcomes.

tax-exempt Write with a hyphen.

taxpayer dollars No apostrophe needed.

tchotchke(s) Often misspelled. It means knickknacks.

teaspoon, teaspoonful(s) Spell out in text, but abbreviations are acceptable in tabular material. *Teaspoon* has two abbreviations: *t.* and *tsp.* Choose one and be consistent. It equals 1/3 of a tablespoon.

tech, technology When used as an adjective, *tech* is interchangeable with *technology,* as in *It was a tough week for tech stocks* or *It was a tough week for technology stocks.* But when *technology* is used as a noun, it is not interchangeable with *tech. The company spent more than $1 billion to upgrade its technology* (not to *upgrade its tech).*

technical vocabulary When writing about work, remember clarity is the priority. Every field has its own technical vocabulary, so explain terms that may be unfamiliar to readers. If a paragraph is weighed down with words like *port triggering, thread bump* and *disintermediation,* don't assume readers will understand. Offer simple explanations.

technology, media and telecom sector Spell out in the first reference; use *TMT sector* or *TMT* afterward.

teenage, teenager Do not use a hyphen.

telecom This is the shortened version of *telecommunication* (rather than *telecomm).* Spell out *telecommunication* in the first reference; use *telecom* afterward. *Telecom* and *telco* are shortened forms for *telecommunications companies.* Spell out the entire term in the first reference; use *telecom* or *telco* afterward.

teleconference One word.

telephone Use this interchangeably with *phone.*

telephone calls, telephone messages Return *calls;* answer *messages.*

telephone numbers Follow these guidelines:

- For the U.S. and Canada, start with *1* and use periods or hyphens to separate the numbers, as in *1 415.111.1111* or *1 415-111-1111.* This stylebook prefers periods; whichever style you choose, use it consistently.

- When a business uses a word instead of numbers, put a hyphen after the exchange and provide the numbers in parentheses, as in *1 614.000. ERGO (3746)*.

- If extensions are necessary, write *1 206.000.0000, ext. 5564*. Decide whether to lowercase *ext.* or capitalize it (*Ext.*). Choose one form and be consistent.

- If the telephone numbers are internal to an organization and all readers have the same area code and exchange, just write the extension, as in *Call Prajakta Shah, ext. 2781*. For informal communications, write *Call Prajakta, x2781*.

- If a number is toll-free, write *1 888.000.0000*. It is not necessary to specify toll-free with 888 or 800 numbers.

- If a number is pay-per-call, write the cost after the number, as in *1 900.000.0000, 90 cents per minute*.

- If writing international phone numbers for a U.S. audience, give the U.S. international access code (*011*), followed by the country and city codes, as in *011 44 171 000 0000*. Use spaces instead of punctuation (periods or hyphens) for international numbers. International numbers vary as far as punctuation goes and also in terms of how numbers are grouped. In addition, not all countries use seven numbers.

- If writing international numbers for an international audience, do not include *011* since this is the international access code from the U.S.

   Follow the same guidelines for fax numbers.

telepresence Do not capitalize unless referring to Cisco Systems' products (*TelePresence*). *The company is exploring options for telepresence videoconferencing. The company uses Cisco's TelePresence solutions.*

television, movie titles Use quotation marks for titles of television shows and movies (no need to italicize). Follow headline style and capitalize the first letter of the main words. (Lowercase articles [*the, a, an*], conjunctions [*and, or, for, nor*] and prepositions, unless they are more than four letters or they are the first or last words of the title or subtitle. Also lowercase the *to* in verb forms, as in *to Speak.*) For television shows and individual episodes, use quotation marks, as in "Blind Spot" on "Homeland." Movie examples: *"The Tree of Life," "Midnight in Paris," "Bagdad Cafe," "The Last Picture Show."* (Italics are used here only to illustrate examples.)

temperature To indicate temperature, use figures and the degree symbol for all numbers except zero: *It was 98° in Dallas yesterday* or *Do you think the temperature will rise above zero today?* Use a word, not a minus sign, for temperatures below zero, as in *The pipes froze because it was minus 10°.*

Fahrenheit is the temperature scale used in the U.S. If it is necessary to specify the temperature scale, write *32°F* (with a capital *F,* without a space before or after the degree symbol and without a period after the *F*).

Celsius is the temperature scale used in the metric system. If using this scale, specify *32°C* (with a capital *C,* without a space before or after the degree symbol and without a period after the *C*). To convert Celsius or centigrade temperature to Fahrenheit, refer to a converter on the internet. Note that both *Fahrenheit* and *Celsius* are capitalized.

Also note that everyone has a temperature, usually 98.6°, so do not write *Mark has a temperature.* Instead write *Mark has a high temperature* or *Mark has a fever.*

tense (verb tense) Try to minimize the unnecessary shifting of verb tenses. If the sentence begins in the past tense, the other verbs in the sentence should relate logically to that tense, as in *She said she was happy to see me.* When it is necessary to switch back and forth among past, present and future to express time, be sure the verb tenses are logical throughout. Shifting tenses indiscriminately gives the appearance of uncertainty. In addition, try to stick to the simple present or past tense when writing because it is more concise. For example, *The company plans to roll out the new product in March* is more concise than *The company is planning to roll out the new product in March.*

Texas Do not abbreviate in text, but use *TX* (capitals without periods) with full addresses, including ZIP code. *TX* is the two-letter Postal Service abbreviation. Seven other states are not abbreviated in text: *Alaska, Hawaii, Idaho, Iowa, Maine, Ohio, Utah.* See **state abbreviations** entry.

text Use this as a short version of *text message,* as in *Send me a text when you arrive at the airport.* It can also be used as a verb, as in *Text me when you arrive at the airport.* The past tense of the verb is *texted,* as in *She texted me when she arrived at the airport.*

texting This word is both a verb form, as in *She was texting throughout the meeting,* and a noun, as in *Email and texting have contributed to an evolution of writing style.* Another variation is *textism,* meaning the language used in text messages.

than, then Use *than* to introduce a second element in a comparison, as in *Karen is a better tennis player than John.* Use *than* when referring to amounts, as in *He earns more than $100,000 a year.*

Use *then* as an adverb in the sense of *at that time,* as in *I was still at the office then.* It is also used in *if/then* constructions. *If the meeting is in Singapore, then he will stop in the Tokyo office on the way home.* It is used as a noun, as in *By then the systems had crashed* or *The meeting is at 10 a.m.; until then, let's rehearse the presentation.* It can also be used as an adjective, as in *At the summit, then-Prime Minister Naoto Kan addressed his Asian counterparts.*

thank you, thank-you In most instances, write as two words. *Thank you for your assistance. The CEO sent a thank you message to all employees for their efforts during the year.* A hyphen works in this case: *As a thank-you for participating in the survey, we will send you a complimentary package of beauty products.*

Thank you in advance Avoid this phrase; just write *thank you* (no hyphen).

that is Follow with a comma if used in text. The Latin abbreviation for the equivalent of *that is* is *i.e.,* which stands for *id est*. In general, use this abbreviation for parenthetical material. It is lowercased, has two periods, is not italicized and is followed by a comma. *The design company developed the company's branded materials (i.e., letterhead, signage, business cards).* It is not interchangeable with *e.g.,* which means *for example* and stands for *exempli gratia*.

that, which To decide whether to use *that* or *which,* determine whether the information is essential (*that*) to the meaning of the sentence or merely helpful or nonessential (*which*).

Follow these examples: *I am looking for the presentation that has everyone's contact information in it. I am looking for the presentation on the new privacy policy, which reviews the reasons for the recent changes.* Use a comma before *which*. See **comma** entry for additional information.

that, who Use *that* when referring to things: *The software company that Ayush Trivedi cofounded has 10 employees.* Use *who* when referring to persons: *Ayush Trivedi, who is the keynote speaker, cofounded a software company.* For animals use *that,* as in *The owner of the dog that bit me apologized profusely.*

A common error is to refer to organizations as *who: For companies that haven't changed their policies, the court ruling was a wake-up call* (not *For companies who haven't changed*).

theater, theatre The first spelling is American English; the second is British English.

their, there, they're Occasionally these forms are confused. *Their* is a possessive pronoun: *their department, their cellphones, their domain. There* is an adverb indicating direction, as in *Don't go there. They're* is a contraction, meaning *they are,* as in *They're planning to expand the business in Africa.*

there is, there are Sentences beginning with *There is, There are* (and *It is*) can become monotonous. Rewrite and combine sentences to show a closer connection: *Relationships are everything is a deeply rooted business maxim* as opposed to *There is a maxim in business that relationships are everything. It is deeply rooted.*

When using *there is, there are,* be sure the verb agrees with the noun. *There are five programmers in the department,* not *There is five programmers in the department.* This mistake is especially common with the contraction *there's.* Do not write *There's five programmers in the department;* write *There are five programmers.*

theretofore This has a legal connotation. Use *until then* instead.

thinking outside the box The *of* isn't necessary (not *thinking outside **of** the box);* in general, avoid this cliched expression.

third generation Write the shortened *3G* (or *4G, 5G*) in references to wireless communications networks. For other uses of this term, spell out and write with a hyphen, as in *third-generation services.*

three Rs They are *reading, 'riting and 'rithmetic.* The National Commission for Writing for America's Families, Schools and Colleges issued a benchmark report in 2003, "The Neglected 'R': The Need for a Writing Revolution," that called for a writing agenda for the nation.

thumb drive Two words. Interchangeable with *USB drive.*

thumbs-up Use a hyphen; note the plural *thumbs. Our plan got a thumbs-up from senior management.*

Thursday Capitalize days of the week.

till It is interchangeable with *until.* Do not use the literary form *'til.*

time Use figures, as in *We will meet at 9 a.m. in the conference room* (not *nine a.m.*). It is better to specify *a.m.* or *p.m.* than to use the *o'clock* form. Note the space between the number and *a.m.* If the time is on the hour, it is not necessary to include a colon and two zeros. Just write *9 a.m.* Use the colon to separate minutes from hours, as in *9:15 a.m.* If the *o'clock* form is used, spell out numbers *one* through *nine,* as in *nine o'clock,* not *9 o'clock.*

timecard, timeframe, timeline, timetable Each is one word.

time zone Spell out and capitalize time zones in the first reference, as in *Pacific Standard Time, Central Standard Time, Eastern Standard Time.* But if a time accompanies the time zone, use abbreviations in the first reference, as in *11 a.m. CST.* Note that a comma is not needed after *a.m.* or *p.m.*

For *Eastern Standard Time,* the abbreviation *ET* is generally used in business; the alternative is *EST.* For *Pacific Standard Time, PT* and *PST* are the options. Whichever variations you choose, use them consistently.

titles Lowercase titles unless they precede a name, as in *Chief Executive Officer Bernard Arnault* or *Bernard Arnault, chief executive officer.* Unofficial titles (job descriptions) are lowercased even when they precede a name, as in *psychologist Mary Warwick, trustee Allen Burke.*

to, too Occasionally these words are confused. Use *too* to mean excessive, as in *too long, too much, too willing.* It also means in addition, as in *John Reilly will speak, too.* Note that a comma is necessary before *too* when it ends a sentence.

today Be specific. It is better to use the date in business writing, especially for correspondence between different time zones. Avoid using *today, this morning, tonight, yesterday, tomorrow.*

to-do Note the hyphen. *Nancy assured the staff that salary reviews were at the top of her to-do list.* Another meaning of this phrase is commotion: *Melinda Gates's appearance created a big to-do at the conference.*

toll-free Write with a hyphen.

tonight Not *tonite.*

toolbar One word.

toolkit One word.

topics Capitalize the names of topics, as in *Topics discussed at the conference included Belt-Tightening in Q3 and Diversity in the Workplace.*

tortuous, torturous These terms are often confused. *Tortuous* means winding or twisting, while *torturous* means anguishing.

totaled, totaling The preferred spelling in American English uses one *l.*

Total Quality Management Spell out in the first reference; use *TQM* afterward. This refers to programs used by corporations to improve quality.

touchpad, touchscreen, touchtone Each is one word.

toward This is preferred to *towards.*

To Whom It May Concern Capitalize all words in this greeting, which is followed by a colon (:).

trademark It is a name, symbol or slogan used by a manufacturing business and protected by law. In most textual material it is not necessary to use the registration symbols (®, ™, ℠), but this decision will vary at companies. The ® symbol and ™ or ℠ (capitalized without periods) are written as superscripts (in small type above the line). Advertising and marketing departments can contact the International Trademark Association for additional information.

When writing trademarked names, follow their spelling, punctuation and capitalization, as in *Yahoo!, iPad, LinkedIn.*

trans(-) Compounds formed with *trans-* are one word, as in *transoceanic, transshipment*. It is no longer necessary to capitalize proper names that follow *trans-*, as in *transatlantic, transpacific* (versus *trans-Atlantic, trans-Pacific*).

travel, traveled, traveling, traveler The preferred spelling in American English uses one *l*.

Treasury, Treasuries Capitalize when referring to Treasury securities issued by the U.S. Department of the Treasury. This stylebook prefers to write the plural as *Treasuries*, while some guides write *Treasurys*. Both are correct; just be consistent.

trickle-down theory Note the hyphen. This economic theory holds that financial benefits accorded to big-business enterprises will in turn trickle down to smaller businesses and consumers.

troll This noun also acts as a verb, as in *trolling*. A *troll* is someone who posts inflammatory or off-topic messages in an online community, chat room or blog. It also has the more generic meaning, as anyone who is intentionally provocative.

troubleshoot One word. *The technology team began to troubleshoot the problem as soon as the CIO became aware of the issue*. Although *troubleshot* is technically correct for the past tense (rather than *troubleshooted*), *troubleshot* sounds odd and is best avoided.

T-shirt Capitalize the *T*, even in the middle of a sentence, and use a hyphen.

Tuesday Capitalize days of the week.

Tumblr Note the spelling for this blog platform.

TV This is interchangeable with *television*, but use *TV* in all references to *cable TV*.

tweet, tweeted, tweeting, retweet Lowercase the verb forms for using Twitter. The word *tweet* is also the noun for these messages; a person who *tweets* is a *tweeter;* content can be *tweetable.*

Twitter Capitalize the name of this social networking service that allows users to post/read messages of up to 140 characters.

· U ·

"At least do a brief outline if you are writing a document of any length."
— Ann Collier, vice president, financial and public relations
Circuit City Stores, Inc.

U.K. It is acceptable to use *U.K.* as an adjective or noun in all references, as in *The U.K. office is headquarters for all Europe. The U.K. is headquarters for all Europe.* Use periods in *U.K.* for consistency with the abbreviation *U.S.* (even though the periods are not used in British English).

U.K. is not interchangeable with *Great Britain* or with *England* or *Britain.* The U.K. comprises Great Britain (England, Scotland and Wales) and Northern Ireland. (Northern Ireland is not part of Great Britain.)

uncharted waters Not *unchartered waters.*

Uncle Sam Capitalize personifications. *Mother Nature* and *John Barleycorn* are other examples of personifications.

underway Write as one word. *Work on a new compensation plan is well underway.*

unemployment rate Write this with a percentage figure: *The unemployment rate for August was 4%.* In the U.S., this statistic is compiled monthly by the Bureau of Labor Statistics.

uninterested This word has a different meaning from *disinterested*. *Uninterested* means not interested. *Disinterested* means neutral or impartial. *Employees seemed uninterested in the news that the board meeting would be held in Jordan. The companies signed an arbitration agreement to ensure that disinterested parties handle all disputes.*

union names In the first reference, give the full name of the union. Use a shortened form afterward. Shorten *United Brotherhood of Carpenters and Joiners of America* to *carpenters' union* or the *Brotherhood of Carpenters*.

unique Like *perfect*, it is or it isn't, so avoid *very unique, quite unique, rather unique*.

United Kingdom Use the abbreviation *U.K.* as an adjective or noun in all references, as in *The U.K. office is headquarters for all Europe. The U.K. is headquarters for all Europe.* Use periods in *U.K.* for consistency with the abbreviation *U.S.* (even though the periods are not used in British English).

    U.K. is not interchangeable with *Great Britain* or with *England*. The U.K. comprises Great Britain (England, Scotland and Wales) and Northern Ireland. (Northern Ireland is not part of Great Britain.)

United Nations Spell out when used as a noun, as in *Thord Palmlund works at the United Nations*. When used as an adjective, write *U.N.*, as in *Thord Palmlund works at U.N. headquarters.*

United States Use the abbreviation *U.S.*, when referring to the country, as in *The U.S. is increasing its investment in alternative energy*. Note the singular verb: *The U.S. is* (not *The U.S. are*). Also note the singular possessive: *The U.S. is increasing its investment in alternative energy* (not *their investment*).

    Write *U.S.* when used as an adjective, as in *U.S. investment in alternative energy is increasing*. When a distinction is necessary with the symbol for dollar, write *US$2.1 billion* (no periods in *US*; no space between *US* and *$*).

universities Verify the names and spellings of universities and colleges by checking their websites. Use the full name in the first reference, as in *Rutgers University.* Use the shortened version (*Rutgers*) afterward.

unprecedented It means for the first time.

uppercase It means capitalize and is a verb, noun and adjective. It is one word, no hyphen. The same goes for *lowercase.* Note the difference in how it is used. *Uppercase days of the week* or *Days of the week are uppercased* (with a *d*). To uppercase a word means to capitalize the first letter; it does not mean to use all capitals.

As long as comprehension is not jeopardized, the trend in business writing is to lowercase words. If a word has various meanings, as in *web,* context usually clarifies, so there's no need to make the distinction with an uppercase letter.

upside One word. *Downside* is also one word.

uptime One word. *The systems have two years of continuous uptime. Downtime* is also one word.

up to speed No hyphens needed. *Thomas brought the team up to speed on the new software.*

URL Use *URL* in all references. (It stands for *uniform resource locator.*) *Web address* and *URL* are interchangeable.

It is helpful to readers to include URLs as links when referencing a website or any online material. Write the sentence so that normal punctuation (such as a comma) does not cause confusion. It is not necessary to include the protocol *http://* as long as *www* is part of the address, as in *See www.nytimes.com for more information.* If *www* is not part of the address, then include *http://*.

When a URL has a protocol other than *http://* (e.g., *ftp, https*), then include that protocol.

U.S. It is acceptable to use the abbreviation *U.S.* when referring to the country, as in *The U.S. is increasing its investment in alternative energy.* Note the singular verb: *The U.S. is* (not *The U.S. are*). Also note the singular possessive: *The U.S. is increasing its investment in alternative energy* (not *their investment).*

Write *U.S.* when used as an adjective, as in *U.S. investment in alternative energy is increasing.* When a distinction is necessary with the symbol for dollar, write *US$2.1 billion* (no periods in *US;* no space between *US* and *$).*

USB drive, USB port Write *USB* in all references to this data storage device. It stands for *Universal Serial Bus.* Also called *jump drive* or *thumb drive.*

user-friendly Write with a hyphen. Write *more user-friendly,* instead of *user-friendlier,* which sounds awkward. Grammar checks may highlight *more user-friendly* to suggest a change to *user-friendlier* but ignore it. *Customers find the new interface more user-friendly than the earlier version.*

username One word; a username uniquely identifies someone on a computer. In an email account, the username is the part before the at sign @. When a username is paired with a password, this username/password combination is a *login* (one word).

Utah Do not abbreviate in text, but use *UT* (capitals without periods) with full addresses, including ZIP code. *UT* is the two-letter Postal Service abbreviation. Seven other states are not abbreviated in text: *Alaska, Hawaii, Idaho, Iowa, Maine, Ohio, Texas.* See **state abbreviations** entry.

utilize In most cases it is more concise to use *use.*

U-turn Use a hyphen and uppercase *U.*

· V ·

"Often I use search engines to resolve basic spelling issues, such as hors d'oeuvre. The word is usually spelled correctly before I have even typed half of it. When in doubt or when spellings may vary by use, I consult a dictionary."
– Jeff Cole, director of marketing communications
Dana Holding Corp.

v., vs. See **versus** entry.

value-added Use a hyphen.

venture capitalist Spell out in the first reference. Use *VC* afterward.

verb It is a word or group of words denoting action, occurrence or state of being. The verb, along with any words that modify its meaning, forms the predicate of a sentence: *am, worked, will retire, have worked, will have completed.*

verbal, oral *Verbal* refers to both spoken and written words. *Oral* refers to spoken communication only. Using *verbal* for just spoken communication is correct, but *oral* is more precise. *He needs to work on his oral skills.*

versus Spell out *versus* in text when not referring to court cases, as in *At the company softball game, it was the Titans versus the Spartans.* Use either *v.* or *vs.* for *versus* in court cases. (Whichever abbreviation you choose, use it consistently.)

The *v.* or *vs.* is set in a different font from the names, as in *Hirsch* v. *3Com* or Anderson *vs.* Reilly. If used in a headline, lowercase the abbreviation: Roe *v.* Wade Battle Continues.

very Use this word sparingly. It adds little meaning to a sentence.

Veterans Day No apostrophe is needed for this holiday. It is a U.S. federal holiday that takes place on November 11.

vice president Do not hyphenate. The title is lowercased when it comes after a name, as in *Sean Murray, vice president, will retire in June.* Capitalize when it precedes the name. *Vice President Sean Murray will retire in June.*

videoconference One word.

Vietnam War Capitalize the names of all wars. Write *Vietnam* as one word (not *Viet Nam*).

VIP Use *VIP* for *very important person* in all references. The plural is *VIPs.*

vis-a-vis Note the hyphens. No accent or italics are necessary. *Vis-a-vis* means in comparison with or in relation to.

vitamin Write *vitamin* in lowercase, but capitalize the letter for the *vitamin,* as in *vitamin A, vitamin B12.*

voicemail One word. Use the abbreviated form *vmail* only in informal correspondence.

VoIP Use *VoIP* in all references; note the lowercase *o.* Stands for *Voice over Internet Protocol.*

votes Use figures when they are paired, as in *The committee voted 10 to 6 in favor of launching the new service* (even though *six* is normally spelled out). When the number of votes stands alone, spell out numbers under 10, as in *The committee cast six votes against launching the new service.*

· W ·

wake-up call Note the hyphen.

Wall Street This is a name for the U.S. financial district in lower Manhattan. It also can be referred to as *the Street,* with a capital *S.*

WAN Use *WAN* in all references. It stands for *wide area network.*

war It is lowercased, unless it is part of the name of a specific conflict: *Gulf War, Iraq-Iran War, Six Day War, World War II.*

warrantee, warranty A *warrantee* is a person who gets a *warranty,* which is a guarantee.

Washington OK to use on first reference to *Washington, D.C.,* unless it would create confusion with the state of Washington.

weak-kneed Often misspelled.

web Use *web* (lowercased *w)* in all references. The term *World Wide Web* is dated.

web address Another way to write *web address* is *URL* (stands for *uniform resource locator).*

Include web addresses when referencing a website or online material that readers might want to consult. Write the sentence so that normal punctuation (such as a comma) does not cause confusion. It is not necessary to include the protocol *http://* as long as *www* is part of the address, as in *See www.nytimes. com for more information.* If *www* is not part of the address, then include *http://.*

When a web address has a protocol other than *http://* (e.g., *ftp, https),* then include that protocol.

webcam One word, lowercase. (If you capitalize *Web,* then capitalize *Webcam* for consistency.)

webinar Write in lowercase if you lowercase the word *web,* which is the style preferred by this book. (If you capitalize *Web,* then capitalize *Webinar* for consistency.)

webmaster One word. (If you capitalize *Web,* then capitalize *Webmaster* for consistency.) The role of *webmaster* varies by organization, but generally it's the person who manages a website.

Web 1.0, Web 2.0, Web 3.0 Capitalize these terms. Web 1.0 refers to the static stage of the web (i.e., personal websites), Web 2.0 refers to the participatory/ interactive stage (i.e., social networks), Web 3.0 refers to the "intelligent" stage of the web (i.e., mobile devices).

website One word, lowercased is the preference of this stylebook. Other variations (*web site, Website, Web site)* are correct; whichever you choose, use it consistently.

Wednesday Capitalize days of the week.

weekend, weeklong Each is one word.

weight Use figures and spell out the unit of weight, as in *The package weighed 7 pounds, 11 ounces.*

well-being Write with a hyphen.

West Capitalize when referring to a region, as in *The West is experiencing a dry spell. In the U.S.,* the term *West* encompasses 13 states broken into two divisions: Mountain (Arizona, Colorado, Idaho, Montana, Nevada, New Mexico, Utah, Wyoming) and Pacific (Alaska, California, Hawaii, Oregon, Washington).

If *west* is a direction and not a region, lowercase it, as in *I plan to drive west on Route 208.*

West Point Spell out *U.S. Military Academy* in the first reference; use *West Point* afterward.

what-if, what-ifs Use a hyphen in all references. *The contingency plan contains multiple what-if scenarios. The team reviewed all the what-ifs in the plan.*

whereabouts Most dictionaries allow either a singular or a plural verb. *His whereabouts is unknown* or *His whereabouts are unknown.* Choose one and be consistent.

white paper Lowercase this term, which refers to a position paper. *The Council of Economic Advisers issued a white paper on retirement income.*

who, whom Many style guides say to use *whom* only when it is preceded by a preposition (e.g., *to, with, for, from*) because otherwise it sounds overly formal even when used correctly.

If that suggestion for *who* and *whom* is unsatisfactory, follow this guideline: use *who* when pronouns serve as subjects, as in *Who finds this distinction unclear?* Use *whom* when pronouns serve as objects, as in *Whom did you ask?*

Sometimes it is difficult to figure out whether the word is functioning as a subject or an object. In that case, follow the advice of William Safire, the former language pundit from the New York Times: "When 'whom' is correct, recast the sentence."

wholesale price index Spell out in the first reference; use *WPI* afterward. This measures the prices that businesses pay for a basket of goods.

who's, whose The first is a contraction for *who is,* as in *Who's the point person for the press release? Whose* is the possessive for both people and things, as in *Karl Levitt, whose background is in journalism, edited the white paper* or *The Chinese company, whose head office is in Shanghai, announced it would acquire a Finnish company.*

why It is not necessary to put *why* in quotation marks or to use a question mark in constructions such as *Joe asked why it was necessary to meet twice a week.*

wide area network Use *WAN* in all references.

wifi Use *wifi* in all references. It is short for *wireless fidelity.* Also written *Wi-Fi* (a registered trademark), *WiFi* and *Wifi.*

wiki Lowercase when referring to a website that allows users to share and contribute information.

Wikipedia Capitalize the name of this online encyclopedia.

wildcard One word.

windfall One word.

Windows Capitalize when referring to the operating system.

winter Lowercase seasons.

win-win Write with a hyphen, as in *The internship program is a win-win for the company and for the students* or *It is a win-win program.*

with regard to Do not write *with regards to.*

words as words Use quotation marks with a word used in text as a word: *I looked up the word "verisimilitude" in the dictionary.*

word selection Try to use short instead of long words. Use "words that are short and strong; words that sedate are words of three, four and five syllables, mostly of Latin origin, many of them ending in 'ion' and embodying a vague concept," according to William Zinsser, author of "On Writing Well."

work Many compound *work* words are one word: *workplace, workforce, workstation, workday, workweek, workbook, workhorse, workload, workout.*

workers' compensation Note the apostrophe. This insurance system was formerly known as *workmen's compensation.*

works of literature When characters in plays or fiction are quoted, use the present tense, as in *Hamlet **says,** "To be or not to be" in the third act of the play.*

world-renowned Use a hyphen and don't forget to add the *ed.*

World Trade Organization Spell out in the first reference; write *WTO* afterward.

worldwide One word. *Nationwide* is also one word. Use a hyphen for *company-wide, enterprise-wide, firm-wide, industry-wide.*

World Wide Web This term is dated. Use *web* (lowercased) instead.

worst case, worst-case Write without a hyphen when *worst* by itself is the adjective, as in *That is the worst case of incompetence I have ever seen.* Write with a hyphen when the two words are used as an adjective, as in *worst-case scenario* (or *best-case scenario*).

worth Write an apostrophe in expressions using *worth,* as in *He did a day's worth of work in four hours* or *She got her money's worth when she bought the new computer.*

would-be Use a hyphen, as in *The IT department invited all would-be web designers to submit ideas for the new corporate website.*

wrongdoing This is one word, as in *The employee insisted he had engaged in no wrongdoing, despite the email evidence.*

· X ·

x-axis Use a hyphen. This refers to the horizontal line on a graph.

Xmas Do not use this form; write *Christmas* instead.

XML Use *XML* in all references. It stands for *Extensible Markup Language.*

x-ray Note the hyphen. The letter *x* can be lowercased or capitalized, as in *X-ray.* Whichever form you choose, use it consistently.

· Y ·

Y2K This reference to the year 2000 gained widespread usage at the turn of the century.

Yahoo! Inc. The name of this company includes an exclamation point (*!*), so include it in the first reference. Use *Yahoo* afterward.

Yammer Capitalize the name of this social networking platform for the workplace.

yard It is equal to 3 feet or 36 inches. Spell out *yard* in text, but abbreviate as *yd.* in tabular material.

y-axis Use a hyphen. This refers to the vertical line on a graph.

yearend, yearlong Each is one word.

years Follow these guidelines:

- Use figures for specific years, as in *1999, 2015.*
- When reducing a year to two digits, use an apostrophe if the year stands alone, as in *The project will be completed in early '14.* In charts, graphs and other tabular material, *14 is another option.*
- When referring to a span of years, write *2015–20,* dropping the century in the second year. The exception is when referring to a time span across two centuries: *1999–2015.* Note there are no spaces on either side of the dash or hyphen.
- When referring to the first two decades in the current century, write *2000s, 2010s* as the short versions don't work (writing *'00s* or *'10s* is confusing). When referring to decades in the previous century, use *1990s* or *'90s* (whichever is chosen, use it consistently).
- Do not use a comma between the month and year when they stand alone: *January 2016.*
- When the year follows a specific date, use a comma before and after the year, as in *Daniel was born Nov. 7, 2012, in Seattle.*
- If writing the entire date with numerals, use two digits each for the month, the day and the year: *03/10/16.* Note that in American English the month comes first, followed by the day, so that *03/10/16* refers to *March 10.* In many countries, *03/10/16* refers to *October 3.* If you are writing for an international audience and confusion could occur, spell out the month instead.
- Do not begin sentences with numbers, as in *2013 was a record year for the company.* Rather than spell out *2013,* revise the sentence: *The company had a record year in 2013.*
- In text, write out *year.* Use *yr.* for *year* in tabular material, slide shows, etc.

year to date In most cases it is best to spell this out in the first reference and use the abbreviation *YTD* afterward. *Year to date the company's sales in Taiwan are* *above forecast.* This term takes hyphens when used as an adjective, as in *Year-to-date sales in Taiwan are above forecast, but YTD sales in China are below forecast.*

Yelp Capitalize references to the company. *The employees of Yelp were yelping with joy when the stock surged 50%.*

yeses and noes This is the preferred form (not *nos).*

yesterday Be specific. It is better to use the date than the day in business writing, especially for international correspondence. Avoid using *yesterday, today, this morning, tonight, tomorrow.*

yet When you mean up to now, write *He hasn't started yet* (the present perfect verb tense) rather than *He didn't start yet* (the past tense).

yogurt Do not spell it *yoghurt.*

your, you're The word *your* indicates possession, as in *Your presentation was excellent. You're* is a contraction for *you are,* as in *You're going to receive a lot of feedback on your presentation.*

YouTube One word; capitalize the *Y* and the *T.*

yo-yo Use a hyphen. It can mean abrupt changes or reversals.

yr. Use *yr.* for *year* in tabular material, slide shows, etc. In text, write out *year.*

yuan Lowercase this word for China's currency. The word *yuan* is often used interchangeably with *renminbi,* although technically the terms differ. The *yuan* is the main unit of the currency and the *renminbi* is the currency. This style guide prefers *renminbi,* which is what the Bank of China uses. See **renminbi** entry.

· Z ·

*"Word processing makes revising and formatting easier,
but email encourages sloppy writing."*
– Glenn Wells, editorial consultant
Aflac

Zagat Note the spelling. When referring to any of the Zagat surveys, use an apostrophe, as in *Zagat's gave the Thai restaurant an excellent rating.*

zeitgeist In business writing, avoid this term, which is German for spirit of the age and may not be familiar to some readers.

zero(s) Note the spelling of the plural. Spell out *zero* in text and in references to temperature. Use the figure in tabular material, slide shows, etc.

zero hour The scheduled time for the start of an operation or action.

zero-sum game Note the hyphen.

zigzag One word.

ZIP code Capitalize *ZIP;* lowercase *code.* Do not use a comma between the state abbreviation and the ZIP code. When giving the nine-digit version, use a hyphen, as in *90022-5284.* The extra four digits in a ZIP code are called *plus fours.* The term *ZIP code* is a service mark and the ZIP stands for Zone Improvement Plan.

zodiac Lowercase.

SOURCES WE LIKE

WHILE THE BIBLIOGRAPHY at the end of the "The Business Style Handbook" is comprehensive, it doesn't give you a full assessment of the books we favor for style and guidance. The following books and websites are particularly helpful, clear and informative.

Stylebooks

"The Chicago Manual of Style" is one of the most comprehensive stylebooks. It is expensive but also an invaluable resource, especially for formal and academic writing. Its major drawbacks are that answers are sometimes difficult to find and it is geared for academic and scientific writing.

"The Associated Press Stylebook and Briefing on Media Law 2011" is one of the most accessible stylebooks on the market. This A-to-Z stylebook is used by the majority of Fortune 500 communication professionals. It is comprehensive, simple and inexpensive.

"The New York Times Manual of Style and Usage" is not as direct as AP, but style decisions are thoughtful. The book's editors are explicit about the degree of formality needed for the newspaper's "grammar-conscious readership." It does not have a business focus.

"The Yahoo! Style Guide" is another stylebook that includes useful information on the digital age. Yahoo! has an online edition that can be accessed at http://styleguide.yahoo.com/.

Strunk and White's "The Elements of Style" is a useful, brief and accessible book that offers invaluable advice on writing simple, clear prose. It's a classic. Business writers will need more specific answers, but it's good introductory material to jump-start the writing process.

Dictionaries

We prefer "The American Heritage Dictionary of the English Language" to "Merriam Webster's Collegiate Dictionary," even though most Fortune 500 participants use various editions of "Merriam-Webster's." (Note: The "Webster's" name is used by other publishers.) The "American Heritage Dictionary" is lively, and also has usage entries that give background as well as direction. As a supplement to the main dictionary, use "Microsoft Computer Dictionary" for technology terms.

Our online dictionary of choice is www.m w.com; some Fortune 500 participants referenced www.dictionary.com.

Writing books

"The Oxford Essential Guide to Writing" gets high marks for its clarity and approach. The focus is for the general writer, but people who write on the job could make significant strides in understanding language by reading this book.

"Plain Style: Techniques for Simple, Concise, Emphatic Business Writing" by Richard Lauchman is not a stylebook but is highly recommended for those who want to cut away the verbosity of their prose. Its focus is business writing, so it specifically tackles the issues that arise in this environment. The author has a lot to say about clarity, emphasis, brevity and simplicity.

"The Art of Clear Thinking" and all the other books we came across by Rudolf Flesch during our research were valuable. He was an early advocate of plain English in the workplace and everywhere else, and his work is as pertinent today as it was back in the '50s, '60s and '70s – perhaps even more so.

"On Writing Well" and, in fact, all William Zinsser's books are worth reading for those who want to deepen their knowledge of the writing process. His work is accessible, current, clear and simple.

"Words Fail Me" is a lively, brief book about some major stumbling blocks in the English language by Patricia O'Conner, a former Wall Street Journal editor. You won't have to read any of her paragraphs twice. They are concise, friendly and full of good sense.

"The Scott, Foresman Handbook for Writers" is a useful textbook on grammar, punctuation and writing. Anyone who wants to improve writing skills can benefit from a good grammar book that is simple yet comprehensive.

"Send: Why People Email So Badly and How to Do It Better," by David Shipley and Will Schwalbe, is a readable, informative book devoted to email.

NOTES

We conducted surveys of Fortune 500 communications professionals in 2001 for the first edition of "The Business Style Handbook" (McGraw-Hill, 2002) and again for the second edition in 2013 (McGraw-Hill, 2013). This stylebook incorporates their combined expertise. To find more information on the surveys and to see the names of the individuals who participated, see the Acknowledgments.

Introduction

William Zinsser, "On Writing Well," 6th ed. New York: HarperPerennial, 1998.

Adam Bryant, "He Wants Subjects, Verbs and Objects," New York Times, Apr. 25, 2009.

Lucy Kellaway, "Welcome Back, Semicolon; cu l8r, Sloppy Informality," Financial Times, Feb. 23, 2009, www.ft.com/intl/cms/s/0/97d8c6fe-0148-11de-8f6e-000077b07658.html#axzz1odn6jJO8.

Chapter 1

"The Business Style Handbook" is listed as the No. 1 "Top Resource[s] for Business Writing," Monster.com, http://career-advice.monster.com/in-the-office/workplace-issues/top-resources-for-business-writing/article.aspx.

Chapter 2

Sean Coughlan, "Spelling Mistakes 'Cost Millions' in Lost Online Sales," BBC, July 13, 2011, www.bbc.co.uk/news/education-14130854.

Jerry Useem, "Conquering Vertical Limits," Fortune, Feb. 9, 2001.

Adam Bryant, "He Wants Subjects, Verbs and Objects," New York Times, Apr. 25, 2009.

William Zinsser, "On Writing Well," 6th ed. New York: HarperPerennial, 1998.

Thomas S. Kane, "The Oxford Essential Guide to Writing." New York: Berkley Books, 2000.

The Global Language Monitor, based in Austin, Tex., is a "media analytics company that documents, analyzes and tracks cultural trends in language the world over, with a particular emphasis upon Global English." See www.languagemonitor.com/about/.

William Zinsser, "On Writing Well," 6th ed. New York: HarperPerennial, 1998.

Rosemary M. Magee, ed., "Conversations with Flannery O'Connor." Jackson, Miss.: University Press of Mississippi, 1987.

Sean Coughlan, "Spelling Mistakes 'Cost Millions' in Lost Online Sales," BBC, July 13, 2011, www.bbc.co.uk/news/education-14130854.

Graham Watson, "Victoria's Secret Fails with Cute Michigan State T-Shirt," Yahoo!, November 19, 2011, http://rivals.yahoo.com/ncaa/football/blog/dr_saturday/post/victoria-secret-fails-with-cute-michigan-state-t-shirt?urn=ncaaf,wp10226.

John Horton, "Eraser Needed for Misspelled Highway Sign in Strongsville: Road Rant," June 7, 2011, www.cleveland.com/roadrant/index.ssf/2011/06/eraser_needed_for_misspelled_h.html.

Sean Coughlan, "Spelling Mistakes 'Cost Millions' in Lost Online Sales," BBC, July 13, 2011, http://www.bbc.co.uk/news/education-14130854.

Erin Kelly, "A Shift in Style: J. Crew Finally Has a Business Plan to Match Its Classic Brand. But First the Finicky Family That Started the Company Had to Learn to Let Go," Fortune, Nov. 13, 2000.

Adam Bryant, "Thinking 'We' for Best Results," New York Times, Apr. 18, 2009, http://www.nytimes.com/2009/04/19/business/19corner.html?pagewanted=all.

Chapter 3

Joyce Russell, "Are Writing Skills Necessary Anymore?" Washington Post, May 22, 2011, www.washingtonpost.com/business/capitalbusiness/career-coach-are-writing-skills-necessary-anymore/2011/05/18/AFJLUF9G_story.html.

Stanley Fish, "What Should Colleges Teach?" New York Times, Aug. 24, 2009, http://opinionator.blogs.nytimes.com/2009/08/24/what-should-colleges-teach.

Diana Middleton, "Students Struggle for Words; Business Schools Put More Emphasis on Writing amid Employer Complaints," WSJ online, Mar. 3, 2011, http://online.wsj.com/article/SB10001424052748703409904576174651780110970.html.

"Write-Minded: New Report Identifies Top Writing Strategies," Vanderbilt Peabody College, spring 2007, http://peabody.vanderbilt.edu/write-minded_new_report_identifies_top_writing_strategies.xml.

Jeremy Rifkin, "Age of Access." New York: Putnam Publishing Group, 2001.

William Zinsser, "On Writing Well," 6th ed. New York: HarperPerennial, 1998.

Chapter 4

William Zinsser, "On Writing Well," 6th ed. New York: HarperPerennial, 1998.

Diana Middleton, "Students Struggle for Words; Business Schools Put More Emphasis on Writing amid Employer Complaints," WSJ online, March 3,

2011, http://online.wsj.com/article/SB1000142405274870340990457617465 1780110970.html.

Adam Bryant, "Thinking 'We' for Best Results," New York Times, Apr. 18, 2009, www.nytimes.com/2009/04/19/business/19corner.html?pagewanted=all.

Thomas S. Kane, "The Oxford Essential Guide to Writing." New York: Berkley Books, 2000.

Michael Shrage, "Need Innovation? Start by Locking Up the Tech Toys," Fortune, Dec. 18, 2000, http://money.cnn.com/magazines/fortune/ fortune_archive/2000/12/18/293102/index.htm.

Guy Kawasaki, "The Zen of Business Plans," HVACR Management magazine, Mar. 2007, www.hvacrbusiness.com/issue/article/369/the_zen_of_business_ plans.aspx.

Richard Lauchman, "In Plain Style: Techniques for Simple, Concise, Emphatic Business Writing." New York: AMACOM, American Management Association, 1993.

Chapter 5

Two interviews with Ida Lowe, an IT executive and instructor at City University of New York, were conducted: one in 2001 for the first edition and another in 2012 for the second edition.

Emails to Jeff Bezos of Amazon were sent for the first edition in 2001 and in 2012 for the second edition. Ryan Kipple responded to the 2001 email and Craig Berman, Amazon's vice president, global communications, responded to the 2012 email.

BIBLIOGRAPHY

Books

"American Heritage Dictionary." 5th ed. Boston/New York: Houghton Mifflin Company, 2011.

"American Management Association. The AMA Style Guide for Business Writing." New York: AMACOM, American Management Association, 1996.

Barr, Chris. "The Yahoo! Style Guide," New York: St. Martin's Griffin, 2010.

Booker, Dianna. "Would You Put That in Writing?" New York: Facts on File, 1983.

Bryant, Adam. "The Corner Office: Indispensable and Unexpected Lessons from CEOs on How to Lead and Succeed." New York: Times Books, Henry Holt and Company, 2011.

"Chicago Manual of Style." 16th ed. Chicago: University of Chicago Press, 2010.

Christian, Darrell, Sally Jacobsen and David Minthorn, eds. "Associated Press Stylebook on Briefing and Media Law." New York: Associated Press, 2011.

Flesch, Rudolf. "The Art of Clear Thinking." New York: Harper & Row, 1973.

Flesch, Rudolf. "Say What You Mean." New York: Harper & Row, 1972.

Geer, Sean. "Pocket Internet." 2nd ed. London: Profile Books, The Economist Newspaper, 2001.

Hairston, Maxine, and John J. Ruszkiewics, eds. "The Scott, Foresman Handbook for Writers." Glenview, Ill.: Scott, Foresman and Company, 1988.

Hale, Constance, ed. "Wired Style, Principles of English Usage in the Digital Age." San Francisco: HardWired, 1996.

Haslem, John A., ed. "Webster's New World Pocket Style Guide." New York: Macmillan General Reference, a Simon & Schuster Macmillan Co., 1997.

"The IFR Financial Glossary." 3rd ed. London: IFR Publishing, 1992.

Kane, Thomas S. "The Oxford Essential Guide to Writing." New York: Berkley Books, 2000.

Lauchman, Richard. "Plain Style: Techniques for Simple, Concise, Emphatic Business Writing." New York: AMACOM, American Management Association, 1993.

"Merriam-Webster's Collegiate Dictionary." 11th ed. Springfield, Mass.: Merriam-Webster, 2008.

"Microsoft Computer Dictionary." 5th ed. Redmond, Wash.: Microsoft Press, 2002.

O'Conner, Patricia. "Words Fail Me." New York: Harcourt Brace & Company, 1999.

Piotrowski, Maryann V. "Effective Business Writing." New York: HarperPerennial, 1996.

Rifkin, Jeremy. "The Age of Access." New York: The Putnam Publishing Group, 2001.

Siegal, Allan M., and William G. Connolly, eds. "The New York Times Manual of Style and Usage." New York: Times Books, 1999.

"Standard & Poor's Register of Corporations, Directors and Executives." 3 vols. Charlottesville, Va.: Standard & Poor's, 2000.

Strunk, William, Jr., and E.B. White. "The Elements of Style." 3rd ed. Needham Heights, Mass.: Allyn & Bacon, 1979.

Winokur, Jon, ed. and comp. "Advice to Writers." New York: Pantheon Books, 1999.

Zinsser, William. "On Writing Well." 6th ed., rev. and updated. New York: HarperPerennial, 1998.

Articles

Fortune 500 List for first edition. Fortune, June 14, 1999.

Fortune 500 List for second edition. Fortune, May 3, 2010.

Bryant, Adam. "He Wants Subjects, Verbs and Objects," New York Times, Apr. 25, 2009.

Bryant, Adam. "Thinking 'We' for Best Results," New York Times, Apr. 18, 2009.

Coughlan, Sean. "Spelling Mistakes 'Cost Millions' in Lost Online Sales," BBC, July 13, 2011.

Fish, Stanley. "What Should Colleges Teach?" New York Times, Aug. 24, 2009.

Horton, John. "Eraser Needed for Misspelled Highway Sign in Strongsville: Road Rant," June 7, 2011.

Kawasaki, Guy. "The Zen of Business Plans," HVACR Management magazine, Mar. 2007.

Kellaway, Lucy. "Welcome Back, Semicolon; cu l8r Sloppy Informality," The Financial Times, Feb. 23, 2009.

Kelly, Erin. "A Shift in Style," Fortune, Nov. 13, 2000.

Kirn, Walter. "Happy Families Are Not All Alike," New York Times Book Review, June 11, 2000.

Leonhardt, David. "In Language You Can Understand," New York Times, Dec. 8, 1999, sec. C: 1+.

Middleton, Diana. "Students Struggle for Words; Business Schools Put More Emphasis on Writing amid Employer Complaints," WSJ online, Mar. 3, 2011.

Ragan Report, The Weekly Survey of Ideas and Methods for Communications Executives, May 15, 2000.

Russell, Joyce. "Are Writing Skills Necessary Anymore?" Washington Post, May 22, 2011.

Shrage, Michael. "Need Innovation? Start by Locking Up the Tech Toys," Fortune, Dec. 8, 2001.

Shrage, Michael. "Take the Lazy Way Out? That's Far Too Much Trouble," Fortune, Feb. 5, 2001.

Useem, Jerry. "Conquering Vertical Limits," Fortune, Feb. 9, 2001.

Watson, Graham. "Victoria's Secret Fails with Cute Michigan State T-Shirt," Yahoo!, Nov. 19, 2011.

LIST OF FORTUNE 500 COMPANIES

ABOUT THE AUTHORS

Brenda Greene is the author of five books and a former editor at Working Woman magazine, Whitney Communications and North Jersey Herald & News. Greene wrote, with Coleen Byrne, "The Web 2.0 Job Finder" (Career Press, 2011). She is the author of both editions of "Get the Interview Every Time: Proven Resume and Cover Letter Strategies from Fortune 500 Hiring Professionals" (Kaplan, 2008) and "You've Got the Interview . . . Now What?" (Kaplan, 2006). She coauthored, with Tim Dahlberg and Mary Ederle Ward, "America's Girl: The Incredible Story of How Swimmer Gertrude Ederle Changed the Nation" (St. Martin's Press, 2009). "America's Girl" won the International Swimming Hall of Fame 2010 Buck Dawson award.

Helen Cunningham is director of corporate communications at a financial services company in New York. Previously, she worked at The Economist Group as editor of Business Latin America. At Philip Morris International, she was a business communications specialist in the international planning department. She worked in the media/communications and marketing departments of an international law firm and in Moscow on a joint venture. She teaches English as a foreign language.

Brenda Greene and Helen Cunningham have been friends since high school. They are still capable of having a lively discussion about the proper use of the semicolon.